The
AMERICAN DUCHESS
Guide to
18th Century Beauty

40 Projects for Period-Accurate Hairstyles, Makeup and Accessories

Lauren Stowell and Abby Cox

with Cheyney McKnight

PAGE STREET
PUBLISHING CO.

PAGE STREET
PUBLISHING CO.

Dedication

To our mothers; thank you for being the inspirational wild women that you are.

Contents

Part 2: Up, Up and Away! 54

Part 3: Let's Get Frizzical, Frizzical! 152

Epilogue 221

Introduction

Why We Wrote This Book

Dear Reader,

Welcome to *The American Duchess Guide to 18th Century Beauty*, wherein we take you on a journey of Georgian style as regards the head and shoulders. We realized, when we wrote *The American Duchess Guide to 18th Century Dressmaking*, we presented four of the most common styles of eighteenth-century gowns along with the millinery needed to complete each outfit for the 1740s, 1760s, 1780s and 1790s. While the hair and makeup in the first book were done using period-correct products and methods, we never discussed them in the book. We felt the absence of that information, as your hair and makeup are both essential to achieving that "stepped out of a portrait" appearance.

Georgian hairstyling, particularly in the last half of the eighteenth century, is of particular importance and interest to those re-creating this period. It is difficult to imagine Marie Antoinette without her famously tall hair, defying gravity. It has come to define the entire eighteenth century in pop culture today. So, with this book, we wanted to explore the wonderful world of eighteenth-century beauty and hair. On this journey, you will learn the historically accurate methods of dressing and beautifying the hair and face, the recipes and techniques to create the tools and products needed and a selection of millinery to top it all off.

There are a great many myths and mysteries surrounding makeup and hairstyling of this period. Our intent with this book is to present a correct picture of how women in the last half of the eighteenth century cared for their hair and complexions. Through myriad primary documents, close interpretation of imagery, inspection of original artifacts and ongoing experiments in re-creating the tools and techniques of the Georgian hairdresser, we can present to you here a much clearer, commonsense routine.

In this book, you will learn about eighteenth-century hair care and hygiene and how the methods and products used in the toilette made possible all of these sculptural coiffures. We then provide you with the recipes and step-by-step instructions to create these hairstyles yourself in the historically accurate method, along with fun millinery patterns to decorate your new style and finish your look perfectly.

We had a lot of fun writing this book, and we think that it shows in the pages to follow. While we strive to use period-correct terms and solid references throughout the projects, we were seldom able to find a definitive name for a hairstyle or cushion. They were either nameless or called many different things in fashion plates. So in the spirit of the French magazines, we have bestowed our own whimsical names on these creations. Be advised that the names are not historically specific or correct unless otherwise noted.

Now, with that, hold on to your comb, because your adventure in artifice starts now!

Abby   Lauren Stowell

Francis Wheatley, 1747–1801. Mrs. Barclay and Her Children. *1776–1777. Yale Center for British Art, Paul Mellon Collection. B1977.14.124.*

How to Use This Book

The American Duchess Guide to 18th Century Beauty is several books rolled into one. Here you will find a cookbook, a sewing guide and a hairstyling manual. Each of the sections works together to supply you with the tools, materials, skills and decorations needed to complete your Georgian-era ensemble beyond-the-dress.

In Part 1, you'll find recipes and instructions for making the tools of your toilette. These are original eighteenth-century recipes taken from *Toilet de Flora*, *Plocacosmos* and other primary sources. Each recipe yields a lot of product, so you may wish to halve or even quarter the weights and measures.

Part 2 deals with the hairstyles from 1750 to 1780 and focuses on sculpting hair on or around a cushion. If you're looking for a tall hairstyle to rock your best Marie Antoinette impression, this is the section for you.

Part 3 is all about the different types of curls and frizz worn in the 1780s and 90s. We demonstrate four different curling techniques: crape, papillote curls, heat-set with a small curling iron and a wet-set with pomatum. Experiment with the curling method that works best for your hair type.

Hair Length and Type

We have made every effort to address different hair lengths, types and textures. Please see page 13 for notes and advice on working with pomade, powder and your hair type. While the specific date of the style may not be what you need for your ensemble, the techniques for working with the hair are the same.

As always, there is variation and transition in styling. We may show a style done with long straight hair, but this does not mean the same style cannot be done accurately with curly hair, hairpieces or wigs. If we show a smooth chignon at the back, it does not mean you cannot choose a braided chignon instead. Study fashion plates and paintings to determine what was trendy in your chosen time frame.

No hair? Short hair? No problem. Georgian women made use of various hairpieces, blending their own hair into the carefully-matched additions, even if their natural hair was quite short. In the pages to follow, we include instructions on how to make your own toupee, chignon and curls or "buckles." All of these are incredibly useful for the modern woman!

Materials & Ingredients

We experimented with different stuffing options for our cushions, all of which would have been available in the period. Each stuffing material has benefits and drawbacks. Cork is a bit tricky to work with because it can spill everywhere and isn't as good at filling out the space in the cushions. Wool roving, while easy to find and use, is really difficult to pin through. Horsehair is the best to work with, easy to pin through but can be a bit itchy. [1] Experiment with the different options to decide what works best for you. [2]

All of our cushions are made from wool knit. In addition to being a historically accurate fabric, wool knit is easy to pin through, blends better with hair and helps hold hair in place while styling.

Eighteenth-century cosmetic recipes are interesting. We have elected to make some minor changes due to allergen issues and the availability of ingredients. All changes we made are noted in the recipes. We also strongly suggest that you do a spot test with any essential oils or ingredients to which you may be allergic.

Patterns

All of the gridded patterns in this book use a 1-inch (2.5-cm) grid scale. You can scale up the patterns on a computer, with a projector or by hand using 1-inch (2.5-cm) grid paper. None of the patterns include seam allowance, but in general we recommend adding ½ inch (1.2 cm) to turn and stitch for a ¼-inch (6-mm) finished hem.

Please note that the hair cushions, caps and other accessories are sized specifically for the hairstyle shown. It is important not to mix your time periods without altering the patterns for the accessories. For example, avoid pairing the very tall 1770s calash with the very short 1750s Coiffure Française. You may also wish to alter the patterns, particularly the cushions, for your head measurements.

Additionally, the social class of your character matters: would she be wearing her hair low and smooth or in a fashionably frizzed style? Alter the patterns to your liking and as relates to your persona's specific time period and social status.

We hope you enjoy using this book and learning about the second half of the eighteenth century from the shoulders up. Most importantly, explore, experiment and have fun!

Historic Stitches and How to Sew Them

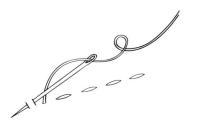

RUNNING STITCH

Working from right to left, weave the needle up and down through all the layers. When you're using running stitches for hemming or a seam, make sure that the visible stitch is very fine. Basting stitches should be long and even.

BACKSTITCH

Working right to left, anchor the knot on the wrong side of the fabric, bringing the needle up through all the layers. Travel a couple of threads to the right of where your needle came through, push the needle through all the layers and bring it back up equidistant from the first puncture. Bring the needle to that same thread entry point, pushing down through all the layers, traveling equidistant to the left, bring the needle up through and repeat. This is the strongest stitch, ideal for seams.

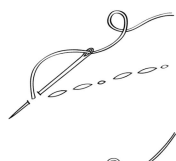

RUNNING BACKSTITCH

Using the instructions above, combine the running and backstitch. Stitch two or three running stitches and then a backstitch for strength.

PRICK STITCH

Working from right to left, anchor the knot on the wrong side of the fabric, and come straight up through all the layers. Bring your needle down 1 or 2 threads to the right, making sure the needle goes through all the layers. Bring the needle up equidistant from how far you spaced the stitches from the seam edge. For example, if you're sewing ¼ inch (6 mm) in from the folded edge, space your stitches ¼ inch (6 mm) apart. This careful and visible spaced backstitch is used most often on side seams.

Hem Stitch with Basting

Working left to right, turn up half of the seam allowance on the edge of your fabric and baste with long running stitches. Turn up the remaining seam allowance again to encase the raw edge. To hem stitch, bury your knot between the fold and fabric, bringing the needle out toward you. Travel a little bit to the left and pass the needle through the outer fabric, bringing it back in through the folded layers. The resulting stitch is visible on the outside of the garment, and should be small and fine.

Narrow Hem

Working left to right, turn up a narrow seam allowance (⅛ to ¼ inch [3 to 6 mm]) on the edge of your fabric and baste with long running stitches. Then fold this edge up again in half so the finished hem is between 1/16 and ⅛ inch (1 and 3 mm) wide. Hem stitch from right to left in the same technique explained above.

Edge Stitch / Edge Hem Stitch

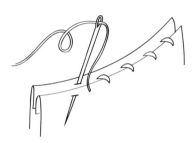

This stitch is commonly used to join the fashion fabric and the lining. Before stitching, turn in the seam allowances on both pieces and baste. With the two pieces placed wrong sides together, offset the fashion fabric to be slightly above the lining fabric and pin into place. With the lining side facing you, bury your knot between the two layers with the needle coming out toward you through the lining. Travel a small amount to the left and make a small stitch catching all the layers, and bring the needle back toward you. Repeat. This stitch is visible on the outside and should be small.

Milliner's Figure 8 Stitch

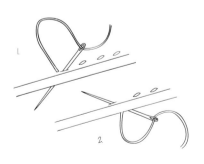

This technique is used in hat-making. It is a "traveling" stitch that creates a tiny, unobtrusive prick stitch on both sides of the fabric at once. Start on the underside of the fabric or brim. Pass the needle through to the other side, then back down behind the first point to create a teeny tiny backstitch. When you pass the needle through, do so at an angle in your direction of travel so that the needle comes out on the opposite side about ¼ inch (6 mm) away from the previous stitch. Repeat the motion with the tiny backstitch and angled needle to the top side, creating the hidden "figure 8."

BLANKET STITCH

In this book, the blanket stitch is used to securely attach millinery wire to the edge of a hat brim. Knot the thread and pass the needle through the underside of the hat brim. With the wire clipped in place right on the edge of the brim, pass the needle through the hat brim again from the underside to the topside, creating a loop of thread over the wire. With the loop still loose, pass the needle toward you through the thread loop and pull it all taught. Repeat the stitch again about ½ inch (1.2 cm) away from the first stitch.

APPLIQUE STITCH

This is performed just like the hem stitch except that the travel and catches are in reverse. The small stitch is the one you see, and you will travel on the underside. This is used when you're sewing from the right side of the fabric.

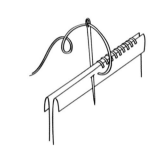

WHIPSTITCH

This stitch is commonly used over an edge, either raw or finished. Place the two pieces of fabric right sides together and pin. Working right to left, work with the needle pointing toward you, passing through all the layers. Bring the needle back around to the far layer, passing through the layers with the needle facing you. Repeat.

WHIP GATHER

Working right to left, whip over the edge of the fabric a determined distance. Then pull the thread, gathering up the fabric to the desired length, and knot the thread (but do not cut) before moving on to the next section.

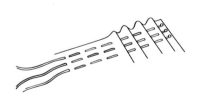

STROKED GATHERS

This technique is going to be used for your aprons and 1790s ensemble. It consists of three evenly spaced and stitched running stitches that are then gathered up to fit the desired space. The gathers are then carefully stitched with a hem or whipstitch, making sure that you catch every bump in the gathers.

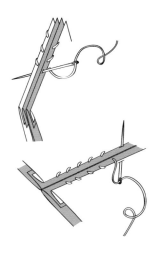

The English Stitch

Turn in the seam allowances on both fashion fabric pieces and both lining pieces and baste. Apply the lining pieces to the fashion fabric pieces, wrong sides together, with the lining edge placed just inside the fashion fabric edge. Baste the lining and fashion fabric together.

Next, place the two pieces with fashion fabric right sides together and pin. Working right to left, bury the knot of your thread between the lining and fashion fabric layer, then pass the needle through the three stacked layers—fashion fabric, fashion fabric and lining. Now turn the needle back, skip the lining layer and pass the needle again through the three stacked layers—fashion fabric, fashion fabric and lining. Keep your stitches very small and tight here, about 12 stitches per inch (2.5 cm).

Mantua Maker's Seam

The mantua maker's seam is an ingenious, efficient way to connect and encase raw edges. Though similar to a modern French seam or felled seam, the mantua maker's seam is fast, easy and period correct.

To work a mantua maker's seam, start with two layers of fabric, right sides together. Offset the bottom fabric by ⅛ to ¼ inch (3 to 6 mm), depending on how wide you need this seam to be. Fold the bottom fabric up and over the top fabric once and baste into place, sewing from right to left. Next, fold the baste edge up once more and hem stitch through all the layers. When you're finished, you will be able to open up this seam and have a clean finish on the outside and an encased raw edge on the interior.

Hair Textures and Types

Our goal with this project was to create an inclusive book for the modern costumer and reenactor. The eighteenth century, like the twenty-first century, was a diverse and complicated world. It would be a disservice to only present models of a single ethnic background. We have attempted to demonstrate historically correct eighteenth-century hair practices on a range of hair textures, length and color. We did this not only to reflect the diversity found in our costuming and reenacting community today, but to also ensure that techniques for your hair texture are represented.

Everyone's hair is different, with an endless variety of texture and characteristics regardless of one's race. You know your hair best, so experiment with the pomade, powder and styling techniques to find what works best for you.

On the following pages we provide a rough idea of what to expect with pomatum and powder based on the widely accepted Andre Walker Hair Typing System. [1]

Pompeo Batoni, 1708–1787. Portrait of a Woman, Traditionally Identified as Margaret Stuart, Lady Hippisley. *1785. Yale Center for British Art, Paul Mellon Collection. B1981.25.37.*

STRAIGHT HAIR

Type 1A & 1B – Straight and fine hair that is inclined to get oily. For most people with this hair texture small to moderate amount of pomatum with a lot of powder is needed [2] depending on dryness and chemical processing. The result is hair that is several times thicker in appearance and feel and lighter in color. This texture was the most common among our models and also very familiar to us, as we both also have Type 1A and 1B hair. Please see our 1750s and 1785 styles on pages 59 and 187 for this hair type.

Additionally, we found that working with Jenny, who is Chinese, we had to use less powder for her hairstyle because she was prone to a lot of breakage and flyaways. You will notice that we "puffed" on the powder with a modern-day bellows in this tutorial to avoid touching the hair with the powder brush. To see Jenny's 1776 hairstyle, turn to page 123.

Type 1C – Straight hair that is thick in texture. This texture can be found in multiple races and ethnicities, and it requires a lot of pomatum and powder. The physical feel is subtler than Type 1A & 1B, though the weight and thickness of the hair will definitely increase. You might find that pomading and powdering this hair texture will take hours versus minutes. For projects with models with this hair texture, please refer to our 1765 style with Cynthia and the 1774 tutorial with Laurie, pages 75 and 97.

WAVY HAIR

Type 2A – Fine texture but with some wave to it. We suggest the same pomatum and powder application as Type 1A and 1B, and you should expect the same results. Additionally, you'll have an easier time curling your hair with heat. Check out our 1782 tutorial with Nicole on page 165 for an example of this hair texture.

Type 2B & 2C – Wavy and thick (2C being much thicker and coarser than 2B). As with 1C, you'll need a lot more pomatum for your hair to get to that same "damp" appearance you need before applying the powder. You might also find that your hair doesn't hold powder as well because the pomade is absorbed into the hair follicle. Just keep adding pomade and powder as needed. For an example of this hair texture, see the 1790s chapter with Zyna on page 213, as her hair could go either 2C or 3A.

Curly Hair

Type 3A – Appears straight when wet but dries curly. Depending on how thick the follicle is and how dry the hair is, you might need a little or a lot of pomatum and powder. If you're inclined to oily hair, you'll need less pomatum and more powder, whereas dry hair needs a lot more pomatum. You also might find that your curls will straighten out a bit with the weight of the pomatum and powder. If you want to keep your curls in place, you might want to use less powder. If you have thick hair, look at our 1790s project on page 213. If you have fine or medium hair, most of the techniques found in the 1750s, 1782 and 1785 projects will still work for you.

Type 3B & 3C – Thickness of the hair varies, with tight to very tight curls or kinks. With this hair texture, we avoided backcombing as the curls gave us enough texture to work with. Pomatum and powder work fine with the hair. The amount used will depend on how fine the follicle is and how oily or dry your hair is. This is a very desirable texture for eighteenth-century hair, as most of the hairstyles focus on crape-ing and curling the hair to mimic this texture. Keep that in mind when comparing your hair to the projects—you might have less work to do! For an example of this hair type and the specific techniques we used, check out our 1780 style with Jasmine on page 141.

Very Curly to Kinky Hair

Type 4A – Very tight S-curl, and usually of a coarser texture. This hair type can be delicate and easily damaged. The amount of pomatum and powder you use will be dependent on if the hair is oily or dry and if the individual strands are thick or fine. Like with the 3C hair type, very tightly curled hair was considered quite beautiful and desirable. When you're re-creating the styles from the 1750s or 1782 chapter, you'll be able to use your natural texture. You also won't need to do any teasing or backcombing; you may need to straighten the hair a bit for the buckles and chignon, as seen on page 143.

Type 4B & 4C – Very tight and dense curls. This hair texture is great for creating eighteenth-century hairstyles depending on the length of the hair. The amount of pomatum and powder used is up to you. If you are of African descent with this hair texture, there is historical evidence of hair being worn with and without powder during this period. [3] The choice is yours. You may wish to use your false chignon and buckles hairpieces for ease of styling, or straighten your hair a little to achieve the chignon and buckles with your own locks. Teasing is not recommended for this hair type, and the use of cushions may also not be needed. To learn more, flip to pages 143 and 165.

While we hope that using this hair type system has covered the majority of hair textures and types, you might not identify with one particular project or type. We hope you will see the similarities in the different projects to piece together what works best for you. Hair is such a unique part of the human experience, and we cannot stress enough that your hair type and texture is truly unique to you. Have fun, experiment and find your best Georgian-hairstyling workflow.

PART I

Preparing your Toilette

Hey y'all! Abby here to share my experience living with eighteenth-century hair care and dressing every day for nearly a year. I'm going to bust all those falsehoods, myths and extreme rumors that surround eighteenth-century hair, its care and the people of the time period.

One of my favorite myths is that rattail combs were invented because women would leave their hair up in these elaborate hairstyles and rats would live in them. Seriously. Rats. Can you imagine having a rodent that weighs between 8 and 12 ounces (226 and 340 g) living on your head? [1] Now imagine Queen Charlotte of England living with rats on her head.

It just doesn't make sense. It's so illogical, it's funny. But for some reason, people have perpetuated this myth over and over again.

Good hygiene was an important part of eighteenth-century society, and it's important to address pomade and powder from this hygienic perspective. While the concept of germs, bacteria and viruses was not quite there, people of the eighteenth century understood that hygiene was closely associated with good health. Stench and foul odors of the body were linked to the transmission of disease. [2] Most people associate pomade and powder exclusively with the aristocratic elite, but these products were available to everyone. [3] This was hair care, as basic and simple as hopping in the shower for us today.

When looking through eighteenth-century hairdressing manuals and cosmetic books, you'll find that washing of the hair usually centered around dyeing the hair or an attempt to cure an ailment. [4] While it was understood that fresh water wouldn't damage the hair, hairdressers were against bathing in salt water unless it was recommended by physicians. [5]

It still seems weird, though. Can you have "clean" hair without water, shampoo and conditioner? I set out to answer that question, spending almost an entire year using pomade and powder made from eighteenth-century recipes as my main source of hair care, with only the occasional wash. Here's what I learned:

Gilles Edme Petit, 1694–1760. Le Matin. 1700s. The Metropolitan Museum of Art. 53.600.1042.

Toilet set in original leather case, *c. 1743–1745, The Metropolitan Museum of Art. 2005.364.1a-d-.48.*

Ravenet, S., Engraver, and William Hogarth. Marriage à la mode—the toilette scene / invented, painted & published by Wm. Hogarth ; engraved by S. Ravenet. *England, 1745. Photograph. Library of Congress. https:// www.loc.gov/item/95507453/.*

Combing your hair was encouraged in eighteenth-century hair care books for a reason. It moves the oils and powder away from the scalp and prevents buildup. On the other hand, brushing your hair is a terrible idea. Brushing makes the powder pile up and look like the worst case of dandruff of all time. It isn't a good look.

I had to do a fresh pomade and powder at minimum every two weeks, but it was best to do it every week. The fresh application of pomade and powder would clean and freshen my hair and make my scalp feel better. If I pushed it longer than two weeks, my hair would start to smell funky.

A day or so after applying fresh powder, it would start to disappear. While my hair wasn't as dark or glossy as it would be when freshly washed with shampoo and conditioner, it also didn't have that stereotypical powdered look. The powder would be absorbed, but I would still have the pliability and volume that I wanted while my hair was more natural in color.

I was able to dress my hair and take it down every day. The first day was always the trickiest, but by the following day the hair had been trained to assume the style. Throwing it over a cushion and redoing the buckles and chignon was really quick. At night I just had to pin up the pre-parted sections individually, so I didn't have to re-part my hair the next morning. I could dress my hair in just a few minutes. I didn't need to leave it up and sleep with my hair in full dress, another common modern myth that does not appear in original hairdressing manuals.

I never got lice, fleas, rats, bugs, unicorns, narwhals, boogeymen or unwanted vermin in my hair. I would find bits of thread and fuzz, though. I never got an infection, nor did I lose my hair. It was healthy and happy as long as I combed it.

I learned that eighteenth-century hair care and hygiene is completely viable and an incredibly intelligent way to care for my hair. I loved having hair that I could curl, mold and twist into beautiful designs on a whim. Rumors and myths have clouded logical judgment on this natural and healthy way to care for our hair. Women, men and their hairdressers were obsessed with keeping their hair healthy, nourished and in the best possible condition. It was incredibly important to those in the past, as every hairdressing manual and book reiterates over and over again.

CHAPTER I

What the Heck Is Pomatum?

Pomatum, or pomade, holds the honor of being one of the oldest, if not the oldest, hair care products in human history. Recipes can be found much earlier than the eighteenth century, and we still use variations of pomade today. Pomade helps us curl, alter and care for our hair. The main ingredient, though, can sometimes freak out modern people.

Animal fat. Specifically, pork lard and mutton tallow are the main fats used in pomatum. There are also recipes calling for chicken fat, bear's grease and other strange ingredients. [1] Today we're totally fine with putting dead dinosaurs in our hair (i.e., petroleum-based hair care products), but the idea of putting lard on your 'do usually elicits responses like:

"Ew! Doesn't that, like, totally stink?"

"I could never put bacon grease in my hair!"

"How can you get that stuff out?"

"Doesn't it attract bugs?!"

"That's just nasty."

Whew! There are myriad myths and rumors about pomatum that are simply not true. When you dress your hair with pomade and powder, be prepared for various reactions from others about the products you've used.

The animal fats used for pomade should not stink. Original recipes always stress the washing of the rendered fat to remove any bad smell. The pomade is then scented with essential oils or waters or infused with citrus or flowers. If your pomatum stinks, you're doing it wrong. [2]

Pomade Pot, *1735–40. The Metropolitan Museum of Art. 1993.58.1a-b.*

James Ward, *1769–1859. A Border Leicester Ewe. 1795–1800. Yale Center for British Art, Paul Mellon Collection. B2001.2.111.*

Pomade will not attract lice, bugs, rats or other vermin because of the scents used to prepare it. Clove oil, regularly featured in pomade recipes (including ours), is a natural pest deterrent, as is citrus oil. Both are often found in modern-day natural flea and tick repellents for your pets. Now you and your little ball of furry love have something in common. Neither of you will attract the wee beasties. [3]

Wearing pomade and powder will not cause you to get lice. While lice don't care if your hair is dirty or clean, they have a difficult time adhering to the hair strand if there is pomade and powder on it. So, wearing pomade and powder might actually prevent you from getting lice. [4]

Pomatum is incredibly healthy for your hair! The animal fats help nourish and condition your hair, so it's actually great, especially if you have dry hair. Every model in this book was thrilled with how her hair felt after being pom'd and pow'd.

If you're still worried that somehow you'll get a rat infestation in your hair by using pomatum, read about Abby's yearlong experiment on page 16. Remember, pomatum was simple to use and commonly used throughout most of modern history. It has only been in the past few decades that we've replaced natural products with cheap chemical imitations. Pomade is safe and natural and, as you'll see in the following recipes, very easy to make. However, if you don't want to make your own pomade, there are online retailers!

Common Pomatum Recipe

Common pomatum is the absolute first thing you need in your toilette. It is the first product used in dressing your hair, and it is also a great all-around deep conditioner. Our version is gently modified from its original recipe. [5] We cut the recipe in half (who needs that much pomatum?), wash the tallow for longer to get rid of the gamey smell and add more scent.

NOTE: Some people are sensitive to clove oil. Please check your sensitivity before going full hog (ha!) into this project. Instead of clove or lemon, try other essential oils such as lavender, rose, orange blossom, bergamot and rosemary.

- *2 lbs (1 kg) rendered mutton tallow*
- *1 lb (0.5 kg) rendered pig lard*
- *1½ tbsp (25 ml) lemon essential oil*
- *30+ drops clove oil*
- *Set of 12 "jelly" Mason jars (4 oz [113 g])*

1. In a very large bowl or bucket filled with water, break the rendered mutton tallow into chunks. Let the tallow soak in the water for 7 to 10 days, changing the water out every 2 to 3 days to remove all traces of the "gamey" scent. Do not skip this step—trust us. You don't want to smell like a sheep pen, do you?

2. After the tallow has been washed, drain the water, towel dry the tallow and allow it to air dry for a half to full day, allowing all the water to evaporate.

3. On your stove top, set up a double boiler. If you don't have a double boiler, you can use a large pot filled with water and set a heatproof bowl (such as Pyrex) on top of it, not touching the bottom. Add the mutton tallow and pig lard to the boiler, allowing it to slowly melt over the boiling water.

4. Once the tallow and lard are melted and mixed together, remove the fats from the heat. Using a mixer on a low setting, mix the liquid pomatum to hasten the cooling until it has a smooth, creamy consistency.

5. After about 30 to 40 minutes, once the pomatum has cooled off a bit, but before it turns opaque, add the lemon oil and 30+ drops of clove oil to scent. Mix well.

6. Now the pomatum is ready to be jarred. Make sure your jars are free of dust, dirt and debris. Pour the liquid pomatum into the jars. When the pomatum turns opaque, add the lids, and allow the mixture to harden overnight. You should have enough pomatum to fill twelve 4-ounce (113-g) jars.

7. Pomatum has a long shelf life (1+ years) if kept at room temperature. You can always put your jars in the fridge or freezer if you plan on having this batch for a long time.

Hard Pomatum Recipe

In many beauty or pharmaceutical books, hard pomatum immediately follows common pomatum. [6] This seems to reflect the prevalence and importance of hard pomatum in the hairdressing world and also how closely connected it is to common pomatum. Indeed, one is made from the other. Hard pomatum is great for hot climates and is also crucial when frizzing, crape-ing and curling your hair. The wax makes it harder and stickier than common pomatum, more of a tool in fixing your hair than a nourishing hair treatment. Hard pomatum was traditionally made and sold in rolls or sticks. [7] We've had some fun in our choice of shape. Whichever shape you choose, make sure the hard pomatum fits easily in your hand.

- *½ oz (14 g) Common Pomatum (page 20)*
- *2–3 oz (57–85 g) white beeswax pastilles*
- *Optional: essential oils for scent (clove, lemon, lavender, rose, jasmine, orange flower, etc.)*
- *1 creatively shaped silicone mold*

1. Over a double boiler, melt the common pomatum and beeswax, stirring to combine the ingredients together.

2. Once melted, remove from the heat and stir for about 10 minutes, until cool enough to accept the scent, but just before it turns opaque. The clove and lemon scent from the common pomatum has probably burned off from the heat, so you'll want to add more scent at this point. About 15 to 30 drops of oil should do it, but adjust according to your preferences.

3. Pour the hard pomatum into your molds and allow it to cool completely, about 2 to 4 hours in the fridge. The individual amount of hard pomatum bits you'll have depends on how large your molds are, so take this into consideration. All in all, you'll end up with about 2½ to 3½ ounces (71 to 99 g) of total product.

4. Pop your little hard pomatum shapes out of the molds, and store in a cool place.

Mareschal Pomatum Recipe

In addition to common and hard pomatums, there were loads of different types and scents available. We've seen advertisements from the period that read like a Yankee Candle Company store—every possible scent you can think of and mysteriously and romantically named scents like Pommade à la Du Berry. [8] One of our faves is mareschal pomatum, and, as always, the original recipes yield a bucket's worth of pomatum. [9] We've cut this recipe down considerably, but you might want to halve it again.

- *24 oz (710 ml) Common Pomatum (page 20)*
- *5 oz (142 g) white beeswax pastilles*
- *1½ oz (42.5 g) Mareschal Powder (page 30)*
- *Optional: essential oils to scent to your preference (lavender, clove, lemon, orange flower)*
- *Set of 4 "jelly" Mason jars (8 oz [227 g])*

1. Melt the pomatum and beeswax in a double boiler, and stir with a spatula until combined.

2. Remove from the heat and allow the mixture to cool a bit while being mixed with a stand or hand mixer, about 3 to 5 minutes. Mix in the Mareschal Powder (page 30), blending thoroughly for 10 to 12 minutes, and then add any additional scent (10 to 30 drops of each scent, adjusting to your preference).

1A 1B 1C

2A

2B 2C

2D

2E

3. Immediately after adding the scent (allowing it to mix for another minute) pour the pomatum into four 8-ounce (227-g) jars or tins, allowing it to cool completely before use.

4. This stuff cools off quite quickly, and the starch will create a film (ew) on the top. Be prepared to work swiftly, because once this pomatum begins to stick to the sides of the bowl, you have just a couple minutes before it's solidified and can't be poured into the jars.

NOTE: If the pomatum is not well blended just before pouring, the starch in the mareschal powder will separate from the pomatum. It looks weird and is not the desirable end result. Make sure it's all mixed quite well before pouring into the jars.

3

CHAPTER 2

Hair Powder—
The Original Dry Shampoo

In his book *A Treatise on the Hair* (1770), Peter Gilchrist writes that hair powder was first worn for full dress in France by Louis XIV's mistress, Madame de Montespan, sometime in the late seventeenth century. [1]

While the rest of France and other parts of Europe were quick to adopt this trend by the early eighteenth century, England was slow to adopt the use of powder until the last half of the century. [2] However, once the English adopted hair powder, it became a mainstay in British culture, outlasting France in its use. [3]

Oddly, hair powder has developed a poor historical reputation, which is particularly unfair. While most of us are aware that hair powder fell out of favor with the aristocracy during the French Revolution, the fall of hair powder is a bit more nuanced in the rest of the world. [4] Like France, Britain was experiencing a wheat crop issue that affected the cost and availability of bread, and instead of trying to solve the problem, the government decided to blame hair powder consumption and levied a tax via an annual license on hair product. [5] This, in addition to the propaganda being dealt out toward the use of hair powder, which led to assaults on hairdressers, barbers and individuals, essentially killed the use of hair powder. [6] While there was a slow growing movement toward less powder being used, the British government killed the fashion almost dead in its tracks. It wasn't until the early twenty-first century that hair powder returned as "dry shampoo."

However, there are some myths about hair powder that need to be addressed:

Flour was not the main ingredient for hair powder. It was starch, specifically wheat starch, that was created by soaking damaged kernels in water, draining, beating and repeating for a period of time. [7] If flour was used, it was only by the very poor, and even then on rare occasion. [8]

Quality was incredibly important for hair powder. The best powders were "as white as snow" and free of adulterations. [9]

Then, as now, you got what you paid for. Cheap hair powder could be tainted with lime dust, plaster, chalk and/or other impurities. These harmful substances were probably the cause of scalp damage. As William Moore

I.W. A Macaroni Dressing Room. June 26, 1772. *The Metropolitan Museum of Art. 1971.564.7.*

writes, "Cheap Powder is what you should be careful in buying, as many heads of Hair are burnt off, dried up, or turned Grey, by the Respiration stopt, through bad Powder." [10]

Hair powder could be colored and scented. Blue, rose, yellow, black and brown all existed in the eighteenth century. The scents were either delicate florals or fragrant spices. [11]

While the fashion for hair powder disappeared, it was still used in British culture throughout the nineteenth and twentieth centuries. You can even find recipes in pharmaceutical books up through the 1840s. [12]

While you may be tempted to buy some dry shampoo from the store, some additives and chemicals in our modern products don't lend themselves well to eighteenth-century hair dressing. Eighteenth-century hair powder is usually purer than our modern options, which are often filled with artificial scents and random additives. [13] Modern dry shampoos can also be incredibly expensive, a consideration when you need a lot to do just one style! [14]

Hair powder was integral to the incredible hairstyles that were achieved in the eighteenth century, and we're so excited to give it the credit it deserves today. It is the savior of every fine-haired girl out there. You'll love seeing what it can do!

White Hair Powder

For our hair powder, we adapted the most basic recipe from *Toilet de Flora*, #224, White Hair Powder, because of some twenty-first-century issues. [15] We swapped out wheat starch for cornstarch, because the quality of wheat starch today is questionable at best, just a high-quality flour at worse. We've also made the product usable for those with a gluten intolerance or wheat allergy. Lastly, cornstarch (or any starch—potato, rice and tapioca) looks and feels very similar to wheat starch and matches the descriptions of hair powder–appropriate starch in original hairdressing manuals. Other ingredients, such as cuttlefish, beef and sheep bone, lack modern equivalents fine enough for this use, so they have been omitted. [16]

- *½ lb (227 g) ground orris root*
- *4 lbs (1.8 kg) cornstarch*
- *Optional: essential oils for additional scent (lavender, orange flower, rose, jonquil, jessamine, lemon, etc.)*

I. In a large bowl or bucket, stir the ground orris root into the cornstarch.

IA   IB   IC

2. Sieve the ingredients together to wheedle out any larger bits. You want a fine powder to work with. Hairdressers would often describe it as "light as snow." [17]

3. If you are using scent, now is the time to add a few drops. Use 10 to 30 or more, at your preference, and stir/shift to combine.

4. Store the powder in an airtight container—a large Tupperware will do ya just fine—and scoop it out as needed. Plastic or paper lunch bags work for taking small amounts to events. You're going to go through quite a lot of hair powder when doing eighteenth-century hair regularly, so don't be intimidated by the volume. You may even try it as dry shampoo in your modern life!

Mareschal Powder Recipe

Original mareschal powder recipes are never identical, nor is the term "mareschal" always spelled the same way. We've found maréschal, mareschal, marschal, marchal, marechal and maréchale in eighteenth- and nineteenth-century documents. However you want to spell it, the result is a brown hair powder that has been scented and colored with ground clove, cinnamon and, occasionally, mace and/or ginger. [18] Some mareschal recipes have ingredients we don't recommend using, such as paint pigments. [19] I'm sure you can imagine the mess that would result in when mixing this with your pomatum. No, thank you! In lieu of literal paint on the head, we've pumped up the spice-to-powder ratio to get a pretty brown color that smells like cookies. Every perfumery had their own take on this recipe, so don't hesitate to change the ratios to best suit your olfactory preferences.

- *1 lb (454 g) White Hair Powder (page 28)*
- *4 oz (113 g) ground clove*
- *2½ oz (71 g) ground mace*
- *2½ oz (71 g) ground cinnamon*
- *Optional: additional essential oils (lavender, clove, orange, etc.)*

1. In a large bowl, add the white hair powder, clove, mace and cinnamon. Stir until blended.

2. Sieve the powder portion by portion into a large sealable container, adding any additional essential oils. Use 1 to 5 drops per sieve portion.

3. Voilà! You now have super fancy-schmancy mareschal powder. Add this as a finishing powder when your hairstyle is completely finished rather than in your regular pomading and powdering routine.

Papillote Papers

An essential tool of your eighteenth-century toilette is the humble papillote paper, a triangular piece of tissue paper used to hold in place and protect curls or crapes when they are heated with the iron. It takes a little practice to fold and twist the papers (page 211), but you'll get the hang of it in no time.

- *Tissue paper (enough to make a goodly stack of papillote papers)*
- *Ruler*
- *Scissors*

1. Fold your tissue paper evenly as many times as needed to achieve a measurement of approximately 8 x 6 inches (20 x 15 cm).

2. Using the ruler, draw a 5 x 5–inch (12.7 x 12.7–cm) square, then bisect it diagonally into two triangles.

3. Cut the triangles out. If you have any folds from step 1 remaining, cut those apart as well.

4. Now you have a stack of papillote papers, ready to get your curl on.

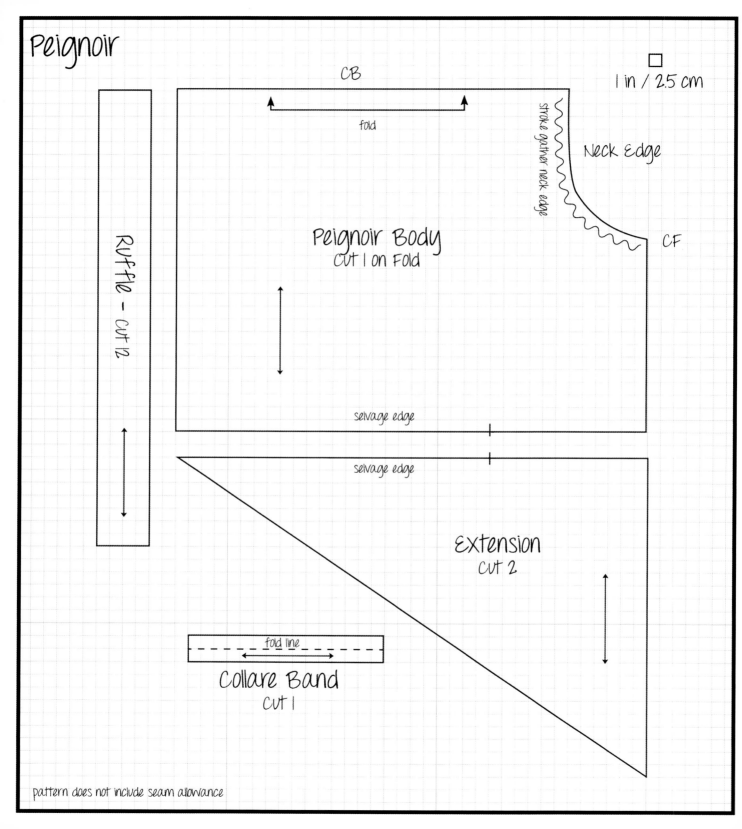

Peignoir

1 in / 2.5 cm

CB

fold

stroke gather neck edge

Neck Edge

Peignoir Body
Cut 1 on Fold

CF

Ruffle – Cut 12

selvage edge

selvage edge

Extension
Cut 2

fold line

Collare Band
Cut 1

pattern does not include seam allowance

Peignoir

Before you can get down and dirty (like . . . really dirty) with dressing your hair, you need something to protect your clothes, furniture, etc., from the hair powder blizzard. Sure, a towel or tablecloth would work fine for this situation, but Georgian women had more pizzazz than that! Long, full and covered in ruffles, the peignoir is the eighteenth-century equivalent of a hair salon cape, but much prettier. We drew inspiration from the large assortment of images depicting women at their toilettes. [20] The pattern is basic in its shape and easy to construct, and most of your time is taken up with hemming the ruffles, which are completely optional.

- 2½–3 yards (2.5–3 m) white cotton voile
- #50 thread
- ½ yard (0.5 m) ½-inch (1.2-cm)-wide ribbon

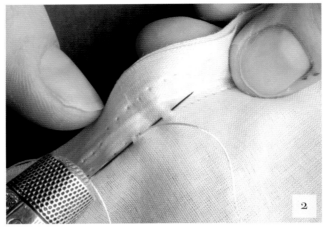

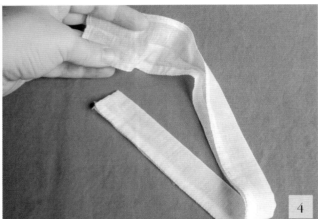

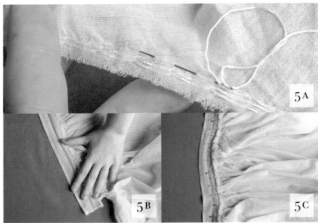

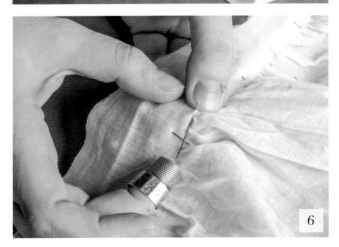

1. Cut out the peignoir according to the pattern (on page 32) and pin the triangular pieces to the main body as shown in the diagram.

2. Seam the peignoir together using a running backstitch (6 to 8 stitches per inch [2.5 cm]). If you're seaming raw edges together, use a mantua maker's seam (6 to 8 stitches per inch [2.5 cm]).

3. Fold the raw edge of the fabric up onto the fashion side of the fabric and running stitch into place. We're going to cover this raw edge with a ruffle, so it will not be visible. If you have omitted the ruffles, hem this edge to finish.

4. Baste up the edges of the collar, then fold the width of the collar in half and press.

5. Stitch stroke gathers (3 rows) at the neck edge of the peignoir. Gather up the neck to fit the collar, and pin the neck to the inside of the collar.

6. Applique stitch the neck to the collar, catching every bump of the gather.

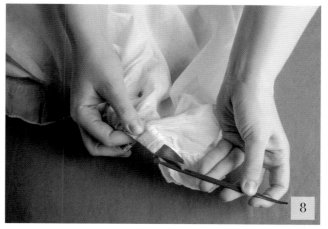

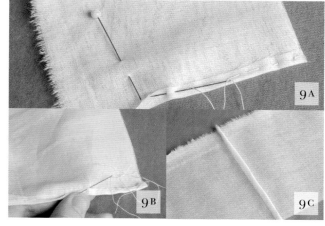

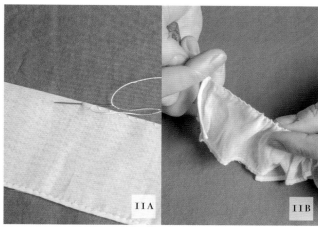

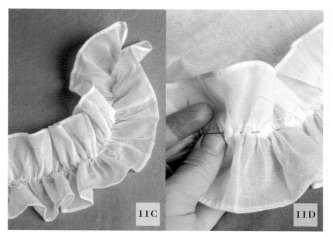

7. Fold the other half of the collar over the gathered neck, and repeat the applique stitches.

8. Run your ribbon through the collar so it can gather up around your neck when tied.

9. Join the many ruffle pieces together using a mantua maker's seam.

10. Hem 12 to 13 yards (11 to 12 m) of ruffles using a narrow hem. You'll want the finished hem to be between ⅛ to ¼ inch (3 to 6 mm) wide. This will take you many moons. Keep hemming. You're not done yet.

11. After your hands, fingers and eyes have recovered from all of that hemming, whip gather the ruffles to fit around the entire peignoir. The length of the ruffle is 1.5 times the edge of the peignoir. Gather the ruffle in pieces by sewing 12 inches (30 cm) and then drawing up the thread to 8 inches (20 cm). Tack stitch and move to the next section until the entire ruffle is complete.

12. Attach the ruffle to the peignoir using a prick stitch (4 to 5 stitches per inch [2.5 cm]) and you're done!

How to Pomade and Powder Your Hair

Before you can do any eighteenth-century hairstyle, you have to prep your hair with pomade and powder. Over the years, we've found that people often get confused about how much pomade and powder they should apply, and while there isn't a straight answer to that, because it totally depends on your hair type and texture, we want to show you an example of well pomaded and powdered hair.

- *Comb*
- *Hair clips*
- *Common Pomatum (page 20) or Mareschal Pomatum (page 24)*
- *Powder applicator (kabuki brush or swansdown puff)*
- *White Hair Powder (page 28)*

1. Comb the hair to free it of any knots or tangles, and then part the hair into easy-to-manage sections. Clip the sections to hold them out of the way.

2. Scrape the back of your thumb to get about a nickel- to quarter-size amount of pomatum on your hands. Rub your hands together to melt the pomade, and begin working it from roots to ends of your first section. You'll want the hair to look like it's been towel-dried from a shower, but not dripping wet.

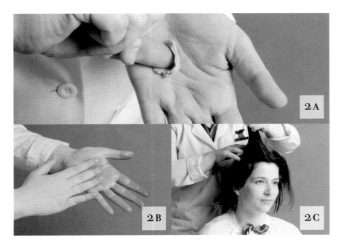

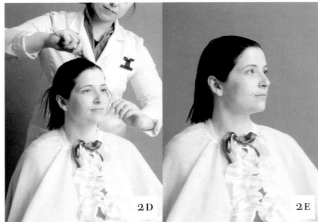

3. Take your powder applicator and dunk it into your hair powder, and as with the pomade, apply it from root to end of the hair section. Make sure that you've gotten everything covered in hair powder. Trust us, you don't want a 'damp' spot on the back of the head—it doesn't look cute. Keep applying powder until the section is powdered to your satisfaction.

4. Comb the section to make sure that everything is well blended, and add some more pomade and powder if you have any dry ends, missed spots, etc.

5. Continue steps 1 through 4 on the rest of the hair until you have a gorgeous lion's mane of pomaded and powdered hair. Run a wide-tooth comb through the hair one more time to make sure everything is blended and tangle-free.

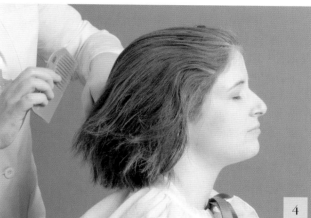

CHAPTER 3

Wigs, Hairpieces and Women

Contrary to popular modern belief, wigs were not the popular option for women in the eighteenth century. [1]

It's easy to assume that because men wore wigs, women obviously did as well, but think about the portraiture that exists. When men are depicted wearing wigs, it is extremely obvious, but women in portraiture almost never have the appearance of an unnatural hairline.[2] Hair was a representation of youth, beauty and health for a woman, and thus it was important to keep one's hair as well-nourished as possible. [3] When searching through the hairdressing manuals and advertisements from the period, the mention of full wigs being worn by women is minimal, at best, and is never the ideal. When you do find evidence of wigs, it's usually a satirical tool to mock women's vanity. Often the women depicted in these satirical prints are elderly, sick, poor or vapid—all unattractive traits in the eighteenth century. [4] For a woman, to be bald was to be ugly, and thus the target of mockery. [5] To put it bluntly, women wearing wigs were not as common as women dressing their hair. Did some women wear wigs in the eighteenth century? Absolutely! But did all women wear wigs? Absolutely not.

This isn't to say that women didn't use false hair to supplement their own. Some of the hairstyles you see in images cannot be achieved without fake hairpieces. Georgian hairstyling manuals are full of references to various types of falsies, and some books are even just thinly disguised advertisements for an array of bits and bobs sold by the authors. [6] William Moore, a hairdresser and perfumer in Bath, England, sold curls from 1 to 5 shillings a pair, long braids from 5 shillings to 2½ guineas, toupees from 3 to 14 shillings and cushions from 2 to 5 shillings. [7]

We recommend three very useful hairpiece types for your toilette—the chignon, the toupee and an assortment of buckles. Though most of the hairstyles in this book are demonstrated using the model's real hair, quite a few are supplemented with falsies, particularly for the chignons and buckles. The use of hairpieces in any combination will greatly reduce your styling time and make possible a great many of these coiffures regardless of your hair length.

When creating your hairpieces, we only recommend using real human hair. This is because real hair responds to the pomade, powder, heat and wet setting we demonstrate in this book. [8] Read on for tutorials on making your chignon, toupee and buckles. Then take a crack at your favorite style, and see how easy it is to achieve with these very Georgian hairstyling hacks.

Extensions–Chignon

You'll notice that every hairstyle tutorial in this book deals with the chignon, the hair at the back of the head. It was looped up, braided, left long and worked into buckles. If you already have hair down to your shoulder blades or longer, groovy—you can skip this part. For those of us deficient in the long and luscious department of hair, we recommend the good old-fashioned clip-in extensions to make it up in the back. [9]

- *1 package (22–24-inch [56–61-cm]) human hair extensions*
- *#30 silk thread in matching color*
- *4 or more wig clips*

1. Divide out enough wefts for your chignon to be nice and full. Remember that it will gain in volume when pom'd and pow'd, but it's better to err on the side of fullness.

2. Wefts often come in one long string. Don't cut the string, just fold it back on itself to form a stacked row about 6 to 7 inches (15 to 18 cm) wide. Stitch the two stacked wefts together.

3. Fold the weft back under to add to the stack and stitch. Continue until you have all of the hair wefts stacked and stitched.

4. Place four wig clips across the top of the chignon on the underside, teeth pointing down. Stitch each to the stack of wefts.

5. Pomade and powder the chignon before you clip it in, and then style as you like. To keep your chignon extension looking nice, store it in a loose hairnet inside a cloth bag.

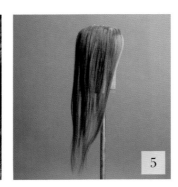

Extensions-Toupee

The toupee played an important role in eighteenth-century hairstyling, particularly in the 1750s and '60s, as well as the 1780s and '90s. Today we think of a toupee as a comical men's wig, but in the eighteenth century, the term referred to the hair at center-top of the head, whether it was one's own or an additional hairpiece. [10]

The toupee is a useful piece for everyone. If you have long hair, you can use the toupee to create the frizzed hairstyles of the 1780s without cutting your locks. If you have short hair, even a pixie cut, you can use this hairpiece to fill out the volume needed for many of the styles in this book and blend your own hair in at just the front.

- *¼ yard (0.25 m) millinery buckram*
- *¼ yard (0.25 m) wool or cotton knit fabric matching your hair color*
- *2 packages (8–10-inch [20–25-cm]) hair wefts*
- *#30 silk thread*
- *6 wig clips*
- *Common Pomatum (page 20)*
- *White Hair Powder (page 28)*
- *Large powder brush*

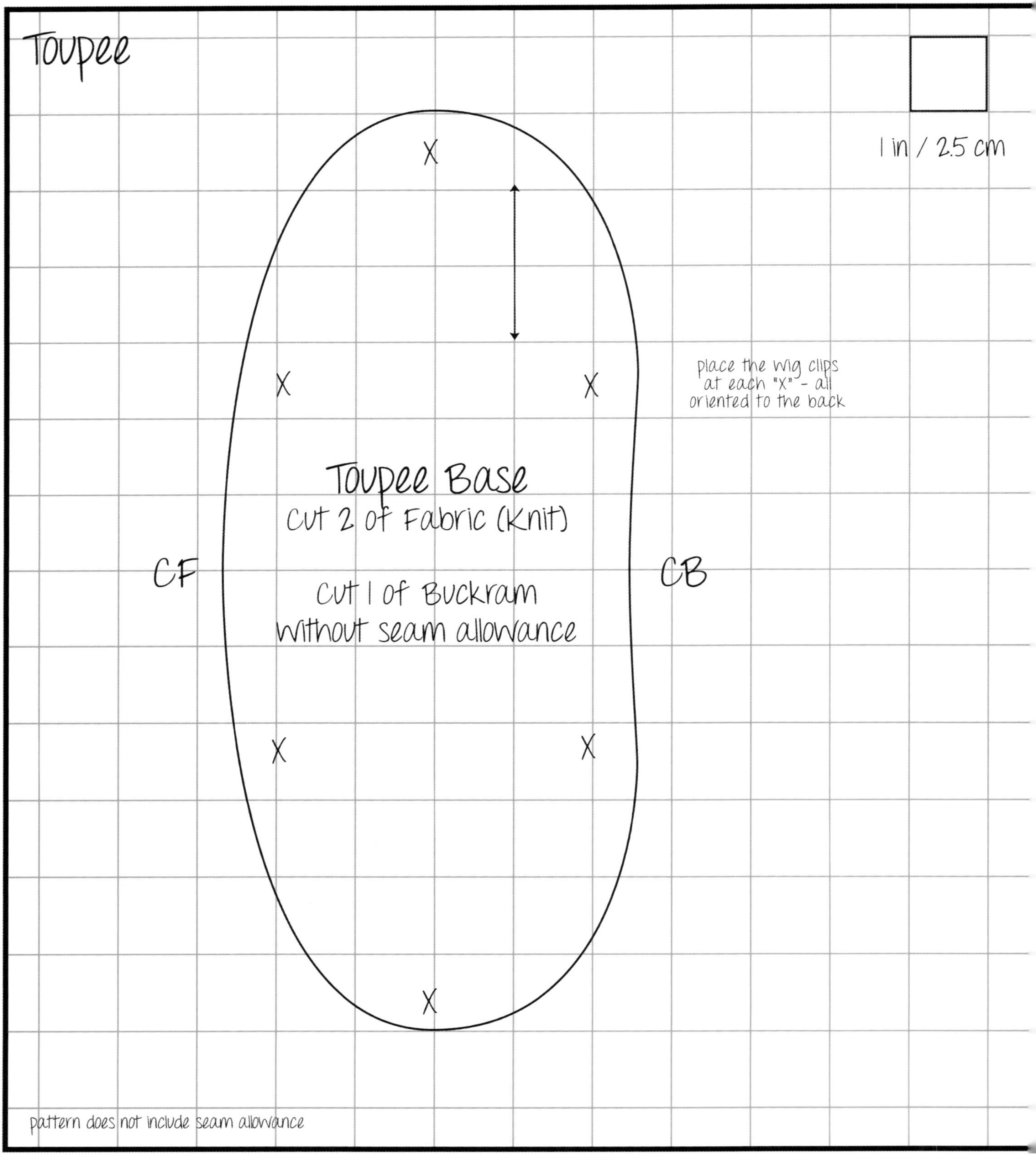

Toupee

1 in / 2.5 cm

X

X   X

Toupee Base
Cut 2 of Fabric (Knit)

place the wig clips
at each "X" – all
oriented to the back

CF   CB

Cut 1 of Buckram
without seam allowance

X   X

X

pattern does not include seam allowance

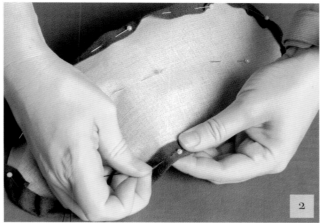

ASSEMBLE THE BASE

1. Measure your head from ear to ear and from 2 inches (5 cm) behind your hairline to where your skull begins to curve downward. Check your measurements against our pattern and adjust as necessary for your own dome.

2. Lay the buckram piece without the seam allowance in the center of one layer of the knit piece. Turn the edges of the knit over the raw edge of the buckram. Baste in place.

STITCH THE WEFTS

3. Divide out your stack of hair wefts into one long string. It's OK if you have more than one separate string of wefts—just end one and start the next in one line. Starting with one end of the wefts and at the front corner of your buckram base, stitch the wefts long-ways along the base. These stitches can be large and don't have to look nice.

4. Work the hair in a spiral pattern, starting from the outer edges and working to the center of the base. Space the wefts about ½ inch (1.2 cm) apart, and continue stitching until you've covered the entirety of your base.

5. Place the second piece of knit over the exposed buckram on the underside of your base. Turn in the raw edges of the knit, and applique stitch to the knit along the edges. This covers the stitches and the knit helps the pieces "stick" to the head and stay in place.

6. Now pull the hair on one side of the cushion in the opposite direction from how it is naturally laying, "flipping" the wefts so all the hair lays in one direction.

Clip It

7. On the underside of the base, place the wig clips at the two ends and two on either side of the center front and center back. All of the clips should be oriented to the back. Stitch each one in place.

8. Your toupee is now ready to use, but of course you need to style it! You may need to trim your toupee for the shape and fullness you like—we hacked several inches off ours. Any of the techniques for curling the hair can be used on your toupee, such as heat-set papillotes (page 210), wet-set pomade curls (page 187) or crape-ing (page 159). Your new toupee may also be used for the Coiffure Française (page 59).

Extensions-Buckles

Buckle rolls are one of the most iconic aspects of eighteenth-century hair, worn in various sizes, locations and quantities through the last quarter of the century. While you're welcome to try buckles with your own hair, creating an assortment of falsies will shorten your styling time and the potential swearing and crying that come with trying to style buckles on yourself. Eighteenth-century women also saw the value of these pin-in rolls and used them with abandon. [11]

- *1 package (15–20-inch [38–51-cm]) hair wefts*
- *#30 silk thread*
- *Hard Pomatum (page 22)*
- *White Hair Powder (page 28)*
- *Large powder brush*
- *Curling iron*
- *Size 15 (10-mm) knitting needle*
- *Comb*
- *Large U-shaped hairpins*

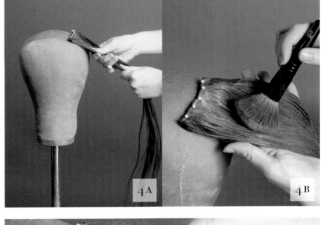

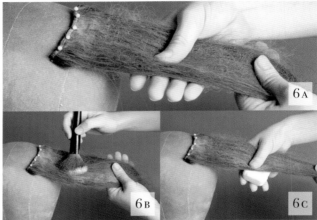

CONSTRUCT THE PIECE

1. Divide and cut out 12-inch (30-cm)-wide sections of hair wefts.

2. Beginning at one end, measure out 3 inches (8 cm), then fold the weft back on itself, just under the first length, and stitch the two together. Vary the width for longer and shorter buckles.

3. Continue folding the weft back and forth, stacking and stitching until the entirety is joined.

STYLE THE BUCKLE

4. With the top of the hairpiece secured to something sturdy, pomade and powder the hair thoroughly.

5. Next, tease the heck out of the hair. Tease it. Tease it more, add more pomade and hair powder, and keep teasing until the hair is all matted together.

6. Lightly smooth just the surface of the hair with the hard pomade and comb. Smooth out any snarls or curls.

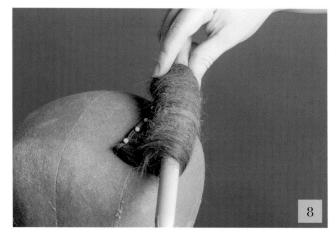

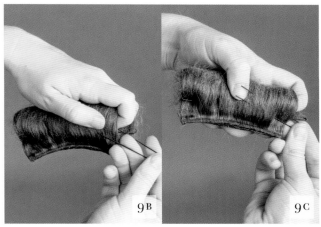

7. Rolling upwards, curl up the bottom few inches of the mess you just made with the curling iron, hold for about 10 to 20 seconds, then release.

8. Starting at the end, roll the hair upwards on the large knitting needle, smoothing the outside of the hair with the comb and your hands as you go.

9. At the top, slide the knitting needle out of the roll, then work one of the large U-shaped hairpins inside the roll. Hold the hairpin flat, aligned with the hair, and thread it in and out of the hair five or six times or until you reach the end. Repeat on the opposite end with another large U-shaped hairpin.

10. Your buckles are now ready to use. At minimum, wear one buckle behind each ear and play with the orientation—some were horizontal while others were nearly vertical. Stack an assortment of buckles upon one another, or pin them into various directions all over the back of your tall hairstyles.

11. Store your buckles carefully, each in its own silk bag, inside a box to prevent crushing.

CHAPTER 4

De-Clowning
Eighteenth-Century Makeup

Let's just get this out there, right now: The eighteenth century was not filled with people wearing bad clown makeup.

For some reason, people today are obsessed with the idea that everyone in the eighteenth century wore lead-based white face paint that caused their faces to fall off. Talk about a visual! This sounds like some sort of Marie Antoinette meets *Walking Dead* mash-up. No, thanks!

We're not saying that lead wasn't used in cosmetics at all. Eighteenth-century sources believed lead was used during the idealized Ancient Roman period, [1] and there is even a white face pomatum recipe in *Abdeker* (1756). However, even with the reference to white lead, *Abdeker* mentions that there were better options for white pigment. [2] Fast forward twenty years to the *Toilet de Flora* (1772) [3] and we find no references to the use of white lead in the recipes. By the 1780s, magazines are noting how dangerous lead-based makeup is to one's health.

> *"[...] it may be observed that the certain ruin of the complexion to say nothing of more serious maladies, must ever attend the constant application of this drug."* [4]

While white lead makeup did exist, we find it to be an avoidable extreme when pursuing eighteenth-century beauty. You'll notice we do not include any white paint/clown goop in our book. Why? Because eighteenth-century beauty was ultimately about improving what one already had. [5] Rouge, lip color and an eyebrow pencil are all a girl needs for that fashionable eighteenth-century appearance. Books like *Toilet de Flora* emphasize excellent skin care using creams, washes, waters and oils and a large selection of rouges, lip salves and ways to darken your eyebrows. [6] Portraits from the eighteenth century show women that look beautiful and natural. This is what we wanted to re-create with the following recipes.

Left: *François Hubert Drouais*. Madame Sophie de France (1734–1782). *1762. The Metropolitan Museum of Art. 64.159.1.*

Liquid Rouge

This easy-to-make, easy-to-use, lifetime supply of rouge comes from *Toilet de Flora*. [7] This recipe yields a lot of rouge! Rouge for every holiday and birthday for the next two years! You'll be the Oprah of rouge: everybody gets some rouge!

This rouge can be worn over modern foundation and produces a strong rosy flush on all skin tones. [8] A very little bit goes a long way, so start sparingly and layer the rouge for a stronger effect. Don't be afraid to wear this rouge quite boldly—eighteenth-century portraiture shows strongly-colored cheeks, particularly mid-century, an attractive counterpoint to the paleness of the powdered hair.

- 28-oz (794-g) Mason jar
- ½ oz (14 g) benzoin gum powder
- 1 oz (28 g) red sandalwood powder
- ½ oz (14 g) sappanwood powder
- ½ oz (14 g) alum
- 16 oz (473 ml) brandy
- 16 (1-oz [28-g]) vials

1. Wash and dry your Mason jar to remove any dust or debris. Then add your dry ingredients into the jar and give them a gentle shake to mix them around.

2. Pour the brandy into the jar and seal it tightly.

3. Shake it! Shake it! Shake it like a Polaroid picture, hey ya! [9]

4. Shake the jar once or twice a day, every day for 12 days. After that, your rouge is ready to use! Pour your rouge into sixteen 1-ounce (28-g) vials so it's easier to handle—and you have plenty ready to give as presents!

HEADS UP: The recipe never says to strain the solid powders from the liquid, so we do not suggest you do it here. Do not worry about the sediment in the rouge. It dries so fast on your cheeks that it's easy to dust the small bits of sediment off with your hands. Just keep rubbing your cheeks in small circular motions until the rouge is sufficiently blended in and the sediment dusts away.

Red Lip Salve

You can't be an eighteenth-century beauty without a little bit of lip color. This recipe from *Toilet de Flora* [10] is easy to follow and results in a pretty, moisturizing lip balm that works for any century. For this recipe, we exchanged the mutton tallow for cocoa butter—a less common, but still historically accurate, ingredient—to make this recipe vegan-friendly. If you have a nut allergy, you are welcome to exchange the sweet almond oil for jasmine oil. [11]

- ⅟₁₆ oz (1.8 g) cocoa butter
- 1 oz (28 ml) sweet almond oil
- Big pinch of alkanet root
- 1 (1-oz [28-ml]) tin or glass jar

1. In a double boiler, melt the cocoa butter with the almond oil over simmering water.

2. Once melted, add the alkanet root. Stir occasionally until you have the desired color.

3. Remove from the heat, and pour the mixture through some cheesecloth into the tin or glass jar. Allow the product to cool overnight before use.

TIP: The alkanet root can be left for quite a long time to give a deeper color. The resulting color on the lips will be considerably lighter than how it appears in liquid form. If the final color is just not strong enough, the mixture may be melted down again in the double boiler, making sure to add more alkanet root, and allowing it to sit longer. Additionally, a dab of Liquid Rouge (page 50) on the lips followed by this lip salve will create an even deeper, rosier tint.

PART 2

Up, Up and Away!

We begin our hairstyling adventure in 1750, a time when low, un-cushioned hairstyles were en vogue in both England and France. Though these hairstyles greatly differed between the two cultures, hairstyling had not significantly changed for decades. We've chosen this mid-century date as our origin point, illustrating throughout this section the transition from low styles to hair of great enormity in a thirty-year span.

Entering the 1760s, coiffure begins to rise. Hair as an art form emerges in France, driven by Legros de Rumigny, hairdresser to the court of Louis XV and particularly Madame de Pompadour. Legros's signature style was highly powdered, complex and sculptural, adorning the heads of aristocratic women with buckles, shell curls, frizzes, latticework chignons and an array of headdresses. [1]

Legros's influence was widespread, particularly after the publication of his book *L'Art de la Coëffure des Dames Françoises* in 1768, which gave detailed descriptions of tools, products, methods and haircuts, along with twenty-eight color illustrations of his coiffures with descriptions. [2]

As the 1770s open, a significant change occurs in hairdressing. Hair had already been ascending gradually but would take on new heights with the appointment of Léonard Autié as hairdresser to Marie Antoinette in 1772. Léonard came from the theatrical world and first gained notoriety for his fanciful headdress at the Théâtre de Nicolet. [3] His flair for the dramatic perfectly aligned with Marie Antoinette's desire to make her mark through fashion, and together they introduced the vogue for what we think of today as iconic eighteenth-century hair.

As the Queen always needed to be the trendsetter, Léonard obliged with ever more invention and skill. Here is where we first see enormous cushions such as the donut (page 95) and ski slope (page 119) in use, topped with feathers, flowers and the pouf, yet another Léonard creation. All of Europe and the Colonies responded to these impressive headdresses, and the fashions even trickled down to the lower classes, [4] driven by the widespread distribution of fashion magazines, one of which, *Journal des Dames*, was managed by Léonard himself with the blessing and financial backing of Marie Antoinette. [5]

The growing extravagance and skill in French hairdressing made its way to England, with evidence in fashion plates and descriptions of hairstyles [6] showing and describing a correlation between Legros's and Léonard's work and the wider world. Powder becomes more popular and regularly worn in England, creating the texture and pliability needed for the fashionably high hairstyles. [7] However, through the beginning of the 1770s many English-women still preferred a simpler "English" style with little to no powder used. This difference is important when deciding how to style yourself for your 1750s–1770 look—do you want to look more French or English? [8]

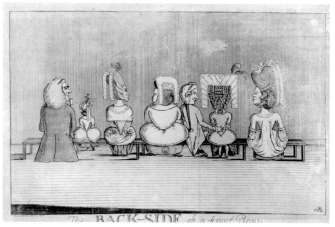

Matthew Darly. The Back-Side of a Front Row. 1777. Jan. 1. Photograph. Library of Congress. https://www.loc.gov/item/2006681194/.

Rapilly. Headdress Engraving. 18th Century. The Los Angeles County Museum of Art. www.lacma.org. M.83.194.6.

Benjamin West, 1738–1820. Queen Charlotte. 1777. Yale Center for British Art, Paul Mellon Collection. B1977.14.115.

It was around the late 1760s and early 1770s that hair cushions came into fashion. As James Stewart recalls in 1782, "It is not above 12–13 years since cushions were first wore, then they appeared like an exceeding small women's pin-cushion; but from this cushion, the plan of the hair has ever since depended on. The hair has been wore higher since, wider, narrower, lower, heavier, lighter, more transparent, more craped, smoother, &c. &c. With one curl, two curls, three curls, four curls, five curls, and no curls at all, but all from the same foundation." [9]

In this section, we take you from the 1750s through Legros's influence in late '60s styling, all the way through the 1770s high hair. We provide instructions for dressing the hair as well as appropriate hair decorations, including one heck of a pouf. This is a fun and frivolous period of hairstyling, so don't be afraid to go all out. An extravagant coiffure is just the thing to top off your beautiful ensemble and impress the heck out of everyone, just as Marie Antoinette intended.

CHAPTER 5

1750s–1770

Coiffure Française

The 1750s to the turn of the 1770s present a period where there appears to be a distinct difference between French and English taste in hairdressing, with the former choosing a well-powdered, tightly curled updo and the latter opting for more natural styles with little or no powder. [1] For this chapter, we have chosen to emulate the French and so define the origin point of the high and mighty hairstyles to evolve later, on both sides of the English Channel.

The style we are demonstrating was much beloved of the French court, particularly of Madame de Pompadour, [2] and featured sculpted curls which could be worn all over the head [3] or on the crown only, paired with a smooth or braided chignon in back. The style persisted in fashion for quite some time, gaining in height, and is seen well into the early 1770s. Various versions are illustrated in *L'Art de la Coëffure des Dames Françoises* by Legros de Rumigny (1768), and appear in portraits of the young Marie Antoinette around 1770. [4]

You may be thinking, "Isn't this style called a *tête de mouton*?" Some describe the tête de mouton (sheep's head) as the frizzed front of the head only while others describe it as curls covering the back of the head, while still others write that it is the entire head dressing. [5] For our purposes, we aren't getting in the middle of that history squabble, so we have opted to call it simply the Coiffure Française, or the French Hairstyle.

As with all of the Georgian hairstyles in this book, a lady's hair would have been cut for this particular style—that is, business in the front and party in the back. [6] Simple face-framing layers or short bangs make for a wonderfully fluffy front, plenty of *mouton* for your *tête*. The style can be also done *sans frisé*, without frizz, sculpting longer hair into the structured rolls that are so iconic of this period.

While this hairstyle can be worn on its own, more fluff was a welcome addition in eighteenth-century headdress. We've provided a very simple pattern and tutorial for a cap ("lace head") [7] trimmed in lace, as well as a set of lace lappets that can be recycled again and again for later styles.

The Coiffure Française is an easy style with a lot of room for creativity. It can be simplified or made more complex, decorated with the cap or a few flowers, heavily powdered or left more natural. Experiment with this versatile style.

Coiffure Française Hairstyle

DIFFICULTY: EASY TO INTERMEDIATE

RECOMMENDED HAIR LENGTH: SHOULDER-LENGTH OR LONGER WITH BANGS OR FACE-FRAMING LAYERS

To help you put your best Madame de Pompadour foot forward, we present this very French take on a mid-eighteenth-century hairstyle. This hairstyle, while not a *tête de mouton*, [8] was worn from the 1750s up through the very early 1770s. This is an easy hairstyle to achieve whether your hair is long or short. If your hair is long, use your natural hair for the chignon and your false toupee (page 41) for the front; if your hair is short, this style may be done with your own hair while your false chignon (page 40) will easily fill in the back; and if your hair is a pixie cut, the use of both the false toupee and the chignon will create the style with your own short hair blended in at the front, a perfectly period-accurate method [9] with excellent results. Abby has type 1A hair that is shoulder-length with blunt-cut bangs, but bangs are not required to successfully pull off this look. Try crape-ing your small wispy hair or some short layers around your face, or skip the crape-ing steps altogether and just work your hair into the sculpted curls.

- Common Pomatum (page 20)
- White Hair Powder (page 28)
- Large powder brush
- Rattail comb
- Alligator hair clips
- Flat iron
- Papillote Papers (page 31)
- Hard Pomatum (page 22)
- Teasing comb
- ½-inch (1.2-cm) curling iron
- Size 15 (10-mm) knitting needle
- Hairpins large and small

CRAPE-ING THE FRONT

1. Start with the model's hair already pomaded, powdered and combed through (pages 36).

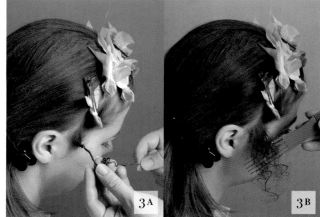

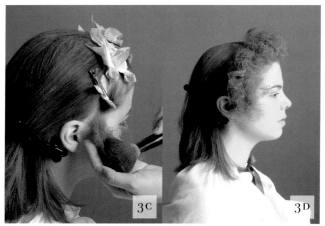

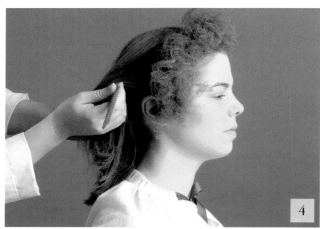

2.　Part the hair from ear to ear, separating the front from the back.
Hold the back portion out of the way with clips.

3.　Using the flat iron, crape the front of the hair following the
instructions on page 159. Comb through, powder, fluff and back comb
the curls to create the frizz. The frizz will be worked into the rolls
behind it.

ROLLING THE TOUPEE

4.　Next, part the hair across the upper back of the head for the middle
section with the sculptured curls.

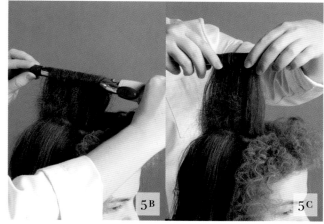

5. Working in rows running from the front to the back of this section, divide out a 1-inch (2.5-cm)-wide hank of hair. Backcomb the base of this hair thoroughly, then curl the ends downward with the ½-inch (1.2-cm) curling iron. Remove the curling iron, then starting at the ends again, roll the hair around that huge knitting needle we made you buy all the way down to the scalp.

6. Slide the knitting needle out of the curl, holding the curl in place with your fingers. Pin inside the curl from the front, catching some of the crape'd hair in the pin as you work it into the curl. Also pin inside the curl from the back, wiggling the pin up and down through the hair at the scalp to secure it.

7. Repeat steps 4 and 5 from ear to ear. The hair should curl upwards from the ears. At the center-top of the head, the two curls will curl toward each other. Remember to pull the crape-ing back and work it into the rolls to blend these two sections together.

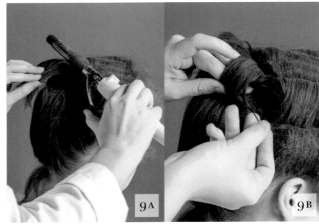

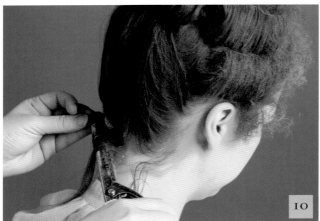

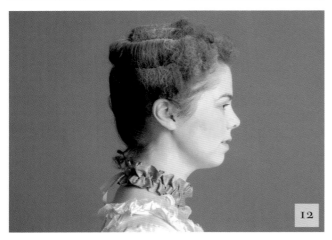

Finishing the Chignon

8. To treat the hair at the back of the head, comb the chignon smoothly upwards, bobby pinning securely at the top. If you don't have quite enough hair of your own to accomplish this look, experiment with your false chignon from page 40.

9. At the top of the chignon, divide the ends into three sections and curl under with the curling iron. Pin each curl in place.

10. If you have baby hairs floating out at the base of your neck, curl these with a ¼-inch (6-mm) small barrel curling iron, or be very eighteenth-century and just cut them off! [10]

11. For an extra-French look, add more powder! Really lay it on there, friends!

12. Ta-da! Your impressive mid-century French hairstyle is complete. Add the 1750s cap (page 63) and lappets (page 67) to top it all off, or try a few flowers tucked into the top of the chignon.

Coëffure de Dentelles Cap

This incredibly pretty and simple cap [11], lovingly dubbed the "head doily," is based on portraits from the 1750s and the examples that survive in the Museum of Fine Arts Boston, the Metropolitan Museum of Art and the Victoria and Albert Museum. [12] The lace and lappets create an elegant look, and—bonus—the lappets can, and will, be removed for different looks throughout the eighteenth century.

The biggest challenge with this project is sourcing the lace. Because it is really difficult to find so many widths of passable eighteenth century–style lace, we opted to use silk organza for the caul instead.

- ¼ yard (25 cm) silk organza
- #30 and #50 silk thread
- 18 inches (46 cm) narrow cording or ⅛-inch (3-mm) cotton tape
- 30 inches (76 cm) 2-inch (5-cm)-wide lace

1. Cut out the pieces according to the pattern on page 64. For the lappets see page 67.

2. Baste the caul around all edges ⅛ inch (3 mm).

3. At the bottom of the caul, right above the folded edge and at the center, poke a hole for the eyelet.

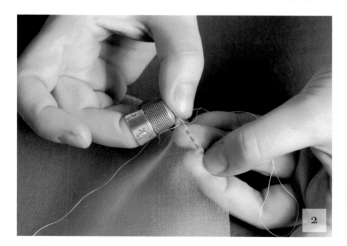

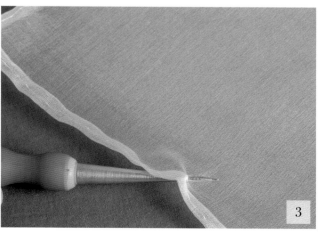

1750s - 1770 Coëffure de Dentelles

A lace with one straight edge and one scalloped edge is recommended for this project. You may also use a hemmed strip of matching fabric instead.

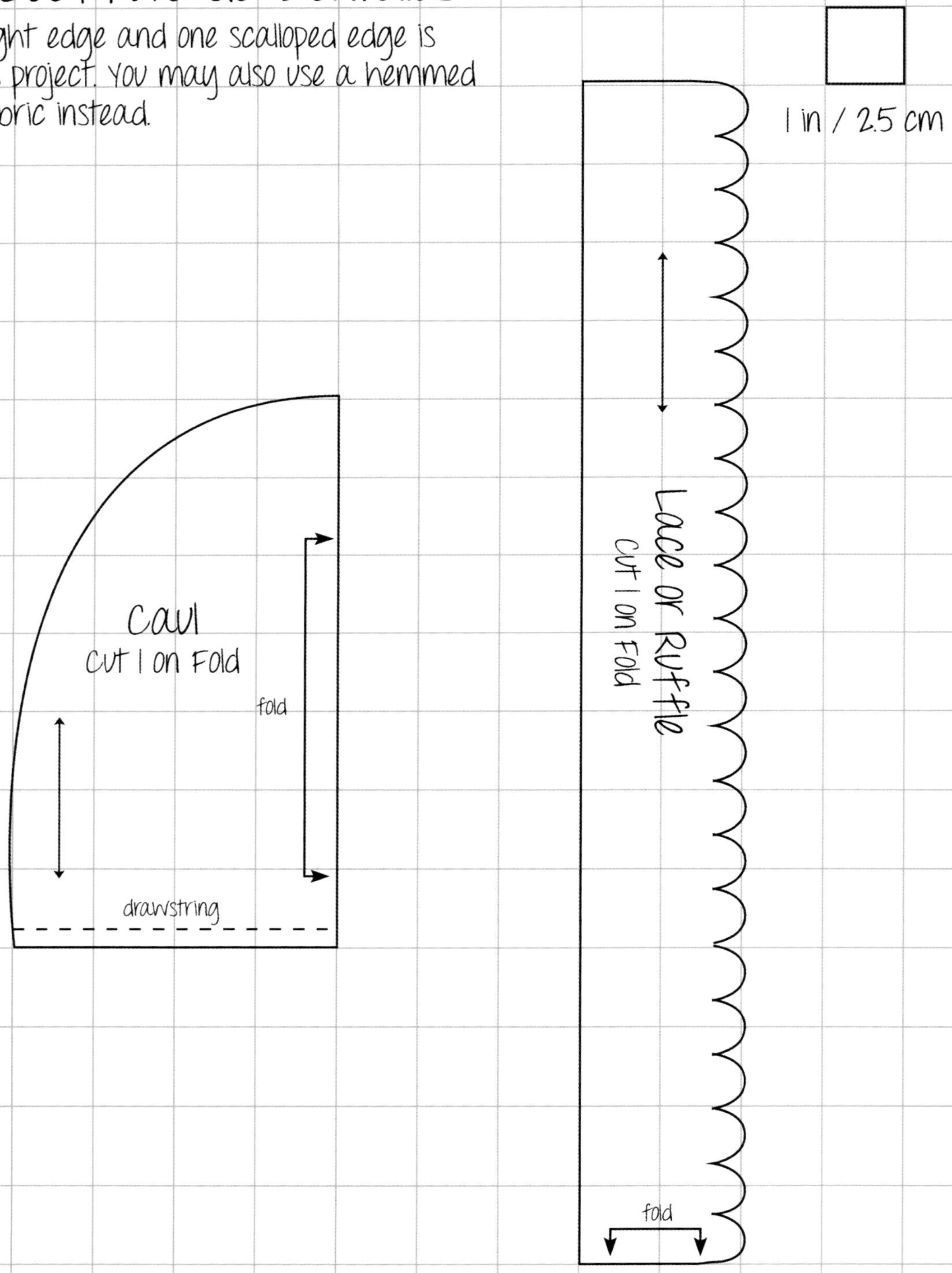

1 in / 2.5 cm

Caul
Cut 1 on Fold

fold

drawstring

Lace or Ruffle
Cut 1 on Fold

fold

pattern does not include seam allowance

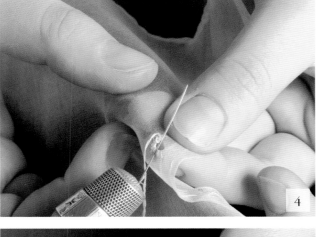

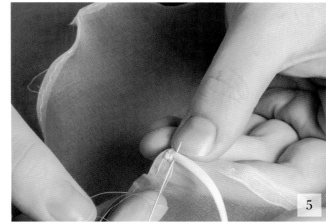

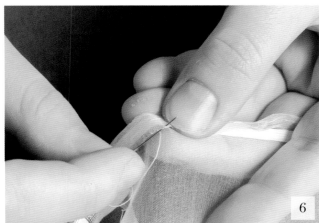

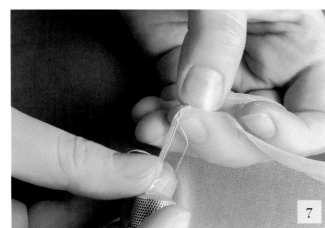

4. Whip open the eyelet using doubled #30 silk thread.

5. Attach the cording or tape on either edge at the bottom of the caul and stitch into place. Push the excess cording through the eyelet.

6. Fold the bottom of the caul up and over the tape, and hem stitch into place (8 to 10 stitches per inch [2.5 cm]).

7. Stitch a fine hem around the rest of the caul.

8. Next, for the ruffle you will need 2-inch (5-cm)-wide lace. If you cannot find lace this wide, you can make your own by stitching together an edge lace and an insertion lace. We stitched ours together with a small running stitch.

9. Roll hem the raw edges of the lace as best as you can—because lace is an absolute beast to hem.

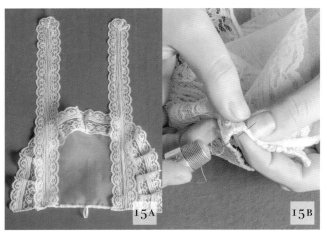

10. Fold the lace in half, and pin mark the center. Next, do a small box pleat toward the center of the pin (⅛ to ¼ inch [3 to 6 mm] deep) and pin into place.

11. Pleat the rest of the lace to fit the caul. Follow the pleat direction dictated by the center box pleat. The pleats need to be between ⅛ and ¼ inch (3 and 6 mm) deep, and pin them into place.

12. Fold the caul in half, and pin mark the center. Match up the center of the lace to the caul, and right sides together, pin together. Pin the rest of the ruffle around the edges of the caul.

13. Whipstitch the lace ruffle to the caul, making sure that you catch all of the pleats.

14. Press the ruffle and the caul, and use a bit of spray starch if needed to create nice crisp pleats.

15. For the lappets (page 67), you can have them attached to the caul or to the ruffles; We chose to attach ours to the caul. With right sides together, whipstitch the lappets to the caul, making sure you don't accidentally stitch the drawstring. Press the lappets open.

Make-Your-Own Lace Lappets

Eighteenth-century lappets came in a variety of shapes, sizes, lengths and styles. This popular bit of head decor was worn in one way or another through the entire century. Lappets could be passed down through the generations, especially if they were made from very fine lace.

It can be difficult and expensive to lay hands on lace lappets from any period today. This tutorial will show you how to create your own by cleverly combining historically plausible lace. Though this lace is narrow, the straight edge allows an attractive join that doubles the width and gives a pleasing finished appearance.

Choosing historically plausible lace can be tricky. Carefully study paintings and surviving lace examples to "train your eye" for that lucky estate sale or thrift store find.

- 2.2 yards (2 m) 1–1½-inch (2.5–4-cm)-wide lace with at least one straight edge
- #50 silk thread

1750s - 1770 Make-Your-Own Lace Lappets

A lace with one straight edge and one scalloped edge is recommended for this project.

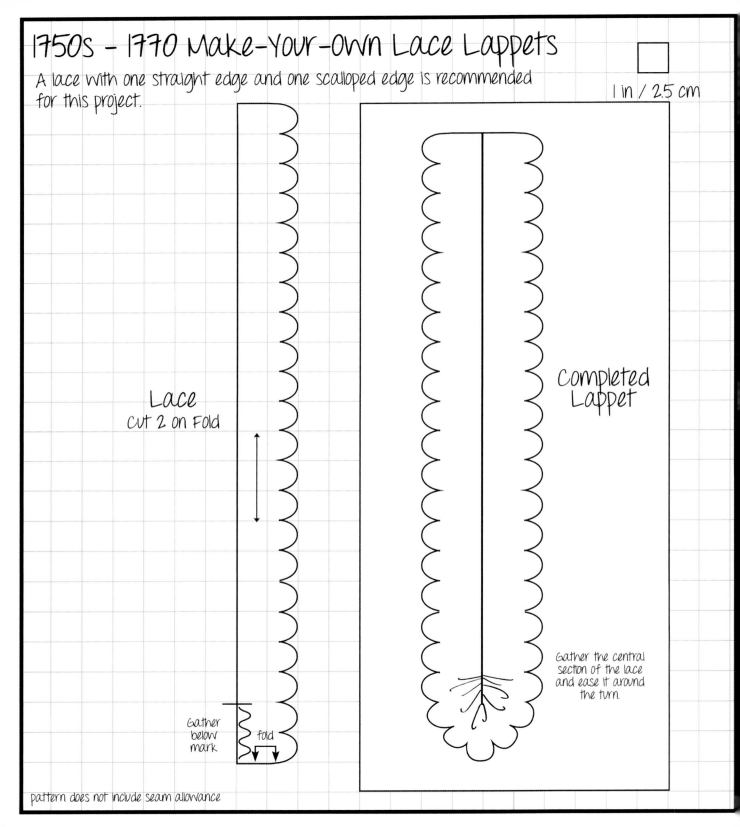

1 in / 2.5 cm

Lace
Cut 2 on Fold

Gather below mark

fold

Completed Lappet

Gather the central section of the lace and ease it around the turn.

pattern does not include seam allowance

1. Cut your lace into two pieces each 38 inches (96.5 cm) long, then find the center point of each piece and mark with a pin. On either side of the center point pin, mark where the gathering stitches will start.

2. Run a fine gathering stitch between these points. We will gather this portion up later on to make the turn at the end of the lappet.

3. Fold the lace in half, matching the straight edges. Pin, then finely whipstitch from the end all the way to the start of the gathering stitch.

4. Pull up the gathering thread nice and tight, then with the lace still folded, align the gathered edges and continue to whipstitch the edges together, catching each bump of the gathered portion.

5. Open the lappet out flat and gently tug the lace apart to "pop" the whipstitches open. Press, particularly the gathered "turn" at the end of the lappet.

6. Turn over the top edge of the lace by ¼ inch (6 mm) and baste, then turn again and finely hem stitch to finish the end.

7. Repeat steps 1 to 6 for the second lappet.

You can now use these lappets throughout your eighteenth-century costuming adventure, across many decades and as decoration in your hairstyles and on various cap designs.

CHAPTER 6

1765–1772

Coiffure Banane

The mid-1760s into the early 1770s brings a great deal of change to women's heads. While pomatum and powder were ubiquitous in France, they still weren't quite the thing in Britain and the Colonies until the early 1770s. This is a time of powdery divides: to powder or not to powder? In *A Treatise on the Hair* (1770), David Ritchie describes each hairstyle worn either with or without powder, and discusses how finicky some of his English customers are with these products:

> *"There are many ladies who complain that pomatum is disagreeable to them, and are very desirous their hair may be dress'd without it when powder'd; but is found by experience that the hair cannot be dress'd near so well; for without a sufficiency of pomatum, the hair will become too dry, and will not retrain the powder […] and occasion many loose hairs appearing, which will disfigure the dress."* [1]

Just as Ritchie describes, we find working with pomatum and powder makes dressing the hair much easier and we choose to use it in our tutorial, but opt for a very light powder application at the end to look more English or American versus French.

It's in these transitional years that we see the beginnings of the great vertical follicle explosion that peaked in the late 1770s. While it is tempting to make your hair as tall as possible, we suggest practicing caution. Does your ensemble and target time period really warrant super-tall hair?

Additionally, in this chapter we have created two millinery projects perfectly suited to the late 1760s. The popular bergere hat is a great piece to wear across multiple decades, but our favorite project from this chapter is the "Proto-Pouf" (page 81). [2] It's a unique piece of trendy headgear seen in Europe, England and America for this relatively short time, and we think you'll love it!

We hope you enjoy experimenting with this transitional period in hairdressing; read on for our step-by-step tutorial.

1765 - 1772 Banana Hair Cushion

1 in / 2.5 cm

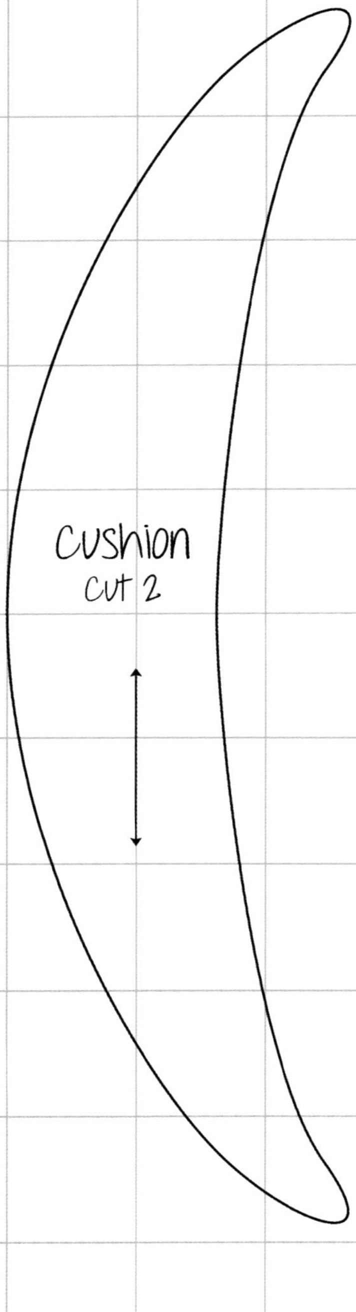

Cushion
Cut 2

Adjust the length of this cushion
to match the measurement of your
head from ear to ear.

You may also adjust the width of
the cushion to achieve different
heights for your
hair.

pattern does not include seam allowance

Banana Hair Cushion

Probably the most ubiquitous and obvious hair cushion from the 1700s—and heck, even today—is what we lovingly refer to as the "rotten banana," because, well . . . just look at it . . . now imagine it in dark brown wool knit. We start seeing them in use in the mid-1760s when hair begins to rise, and they continue into the 1770s, growing in size to produce even higher hair. Easy-to-use, variable sizes make this piece of head fruit a staple in your eighteenth-century toilette. We styled Cynthia's hair to be fashionable from the late '60s and early '70s, so our hair cushion is on the smaller side. Don't be afraid to make yours a bit bigger if you want!

- ¼ yard (25 cm) wool knit
- #30 thread
- Granulated cork, horsehair or wool roving

1. Cut out the pattern as shown.

2. With right sides together, backstitch the fabric pieces together, leaving a 1-inch (2.5-cm) gap at the center of the banana's bottom seam.

3. Fill the cushion with your stuffing material, making sure to work it into the ends of the cushion.

4. Once it's filled to your satisfaction, whipstitch the hole closed.

5. Dang. That was easy. Read on to enjoy the fruits of your labor . . . .

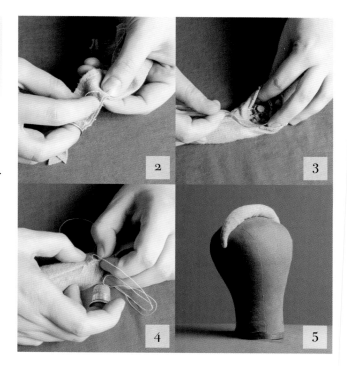

Coiffure Banane Hairstyle

For this hairstyle, we referenced late 1760s and early 1770s portraits and prints to develop a style with a bit of volume in the front, rows of curls and buckles and three small braids up the back to finish. With this hairstyle, you can add accents of pearls and flowers or sport the proto-pouf or a fancy cap. We also used only Cynthia's own shoulder-length hair. As a redhead, Cynthia has a lot of very thick hair, giving us a lot to work with. Those with longer hair will easily achieve this style; those with shorter hair will want to experiment with the false toupee, chignon and buckles to achieve this look.

- Common Pomatum (page 20)
- Large powder brush
- White Hair Powder (page 28)
- Rattail comb
- Alligator hair clips
- Teasing comb with wire pick
- Banana Hair Cushion (page 73)
- Hairpins (short & long)
- ½-inch (1.2-cm) curling iron
- Size 11 (8-mm) and size 15 (10-mm) knitting needles
- Bobby pins
- Small rubber hair ties or leather thongs
- Flowers, cap or other decoration

DRESSING THE FRONT

I. Follow the instructions on page 36 to pomade and powder the hair.

1 A   1 B

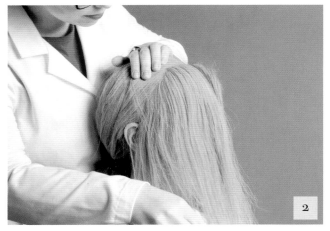

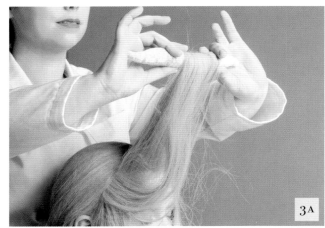

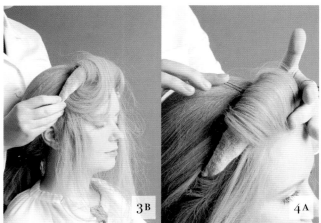

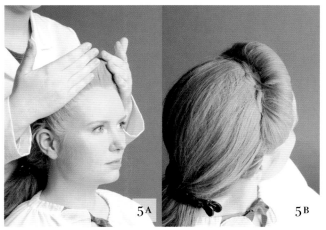

2.   Once satisfied, part the front of the hair from ear to ear. Clip the back of the hair out of the way.

3.   Tease the back side of the hair at the crown. Then wrap the ends of the hair around the banana cushion, rolling it away from the face. Continue rolling the hair over the cushion until you reach the head. Secure the roller on either end with short hairpins, pushing the pins through the cushion, rotating the ends around to catch hair on the scalp, and back up into the cushion to secure it into place.

4.   Using the pick, carefully spread the hair out to either side of the cushion to completely cover it. Pin the hair from behind to secure it into place. Ideally, you'll have a really clean finish for this part of your hair.

5.   If some of the hair falls out of the roller, it's OK, just tease it a bit and shape it over the hair cushion and pin into place. Once the hair is smoothed over the cushion, gently smooth the front of the hair with a small bit of common pomatum warmed up in your hands.

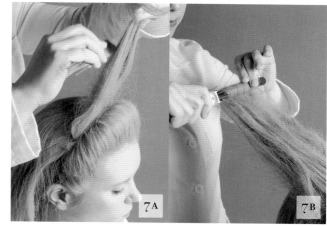

Buckles, So Many Buckles

6.   Now we move on to the row of curls that will sit immediately behind the front cushion. Part the hair so you have a chunk of hair that goes to about 2 inches (5 cm) from the end of the front of the hair, and is about 1 inch (2.5 cm) thick. The leftover hair on either side, above the ear will be used to make vertical buckles later on.

7.   Tease the hair, then curl the end of the hair around the ½-inch (1.2-cm) curling iron in the direction you're going to roll the hair.

8.   Release the curling iron, then roll the ends of the hair around the size 11 knitting needle. Roll the hair down to the head, then carefully remove the knitting needle. Using long hairpins, weave them up and down inside the curl to secure it to the head. Take some small hairpins and gently slide them between the front of the hair and the buckle so they're connected and smooth. Use your wire pick to smooth the curl and make sure there are no gaps. Pin as necessary.

9.   If you have a lot of hair, repeat steps 6 through 8 for a second row, making it ever so slightly shorter than the first.

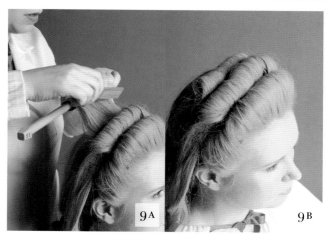

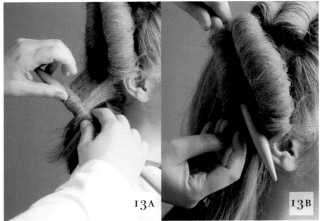

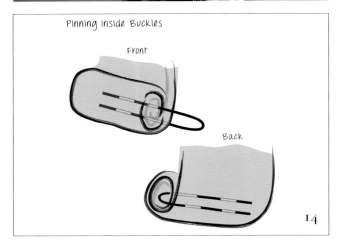

Pinning Inside Buckles

Front

Back

14

10. Now for the vertical buckles. Part the hair down the back of the head into three sections. Note: the ones next to the ears must have the same amount of hair! Clip the middle section of hair out of the way.

11. The easiest way to achieve long, vertical buckles is to work two separate buckles and then work the hair together at the "join." Start with the top buckle first. As always, tease that hair until it stands awkwardly out on its own, the moment that you let it go, you laugh, and want to take a picture—that's the amount of teasing we're looking for here.

12. Curl the hair with the ½-inch (1.2-cm) curling iron in the direction you're going to roll it. In general, buckles curl upwards or forward. Release the curling iron once you feel heat through the layers of hair.

13. Using the size 11 knitting needle, roll the hair toward the scalp, paying particular attention to the angle of the finished roll.

14. Once the curl is where you want it, carefully remove the knitting needle and secure the buckle with large hairpins on either side, weaving them up and down inside the curl toward the scalp to secure the hair to the head.

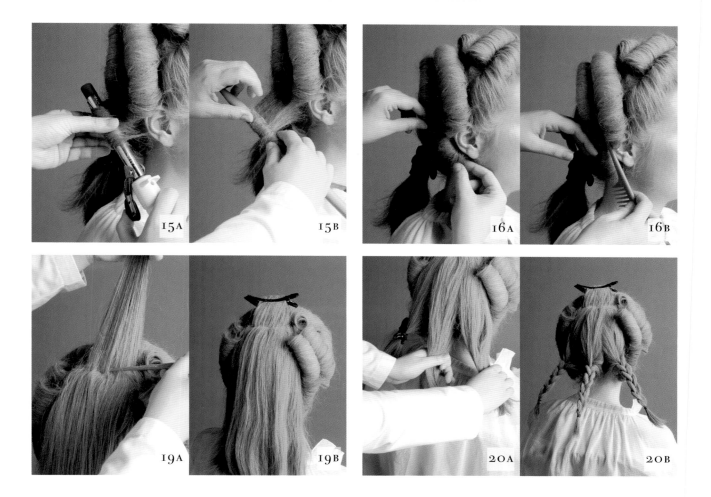

15. Repeat steps 11 through 14 for the lower buckle, making sure that when you're rolling the hair on the knitting needle that the opening of the curl matches the top one, and the angle looks pretty on the face.

16. Gently work the curls together where they meet using a pick. Though this step is optional, it creates a very cool über-buckle look popular in the early 1770s.

17. Pinning the bottom of the lower buckle is a bit tricky; you might want to do a little cheaty-poo and sneak a bobby pin in there for extra hold. If you're feeling saucy you can allow the bottom curl to eventually work its way out and hang ever so elegantly down the neck, but try to avoid that "Prom Night 2001" look.

18. Now the hard part—repeat steps 11 through 17 for the opposite side, making sure that the angle and the size of the curls are as identical as possible. Symmetry is so dang difficult, but it looks so good!

BRAIDED CHIGNON

19. While there are many different ways to do the back of the hair, we chose three small braids for Cynthia's style. This is a great way to easily work short hairs at the neck into the hairstyle. Part off a small bit of hair horizontally at the top of the back and clip out of the way. It should take up the width of the leftover hair and be about 1 inch (2.5 cm) thick. This is going to be a small buckle that will cover up the ends of the braids to create a clean and pretty finish.

20. Divide the remaining hair into three even sections. Braid all three sections as shown, tying off the ends with small hair elastics or leather thongs, for the purists.

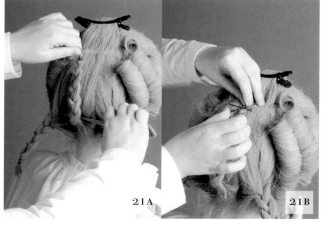

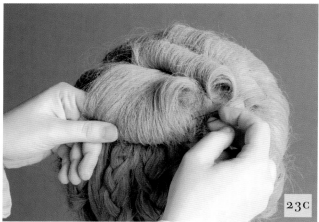

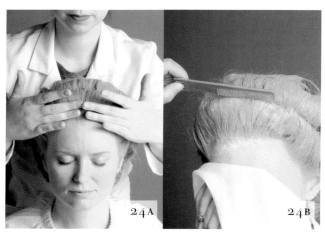

21. Using your rattail comb to help with a clean fold, pull up the end of the braid toward the top of the head, and pin into place with hairpins and/or bobby pins. Repeat for the remaining two braids.

22. Using small hairpins, secure parts of the braid to the scalp to keep a neat, tidy and secure appearance. Warm up some common pomatum in your hands and smooth any flyaways that might have escaped.

23. Going back to that last bit of undressed hair at top of the head, tease the hair and follow steps 11 through 14, making sure that the direction of the curl is toward the back of the head so it will cover up the ends of the hair and the modern hair elastics.

24. To finish, smooth any flyways on the front of the hair with pomatum warmed up in your hands, and apply a final dusting of powder. If you're feeling particularly French, this can be quite a heavy application, but English and American women weren't very keen on the powder quite yet, so your application can be much, much lighter. It's up to you.

Your late 1760s/early 1770s hairstyle is now complete! Add the flowers, feathers or other decoration as you like. Even though they're "just" decorations, these bits and pieces are amazing at hiding any little imperfections that you might see. A fashionable cap or proto-pouf will also top this coiffure wonderfully.

"Proto-Pouf"

This little bit of frilly joy seems to have been popular from the mid-1760s to the very early 1770s. Evidence of this headdress can be found in French and English fashion magazines, [3] many French and English portraits, and also appears in portraits of wealthy and fashionable women of America. [4] We call this little frippery the "proto-pouf," a precursor to the fashionable madness that would top the tall coiffures of the 1770s. There is no right or wrong way to decorate this cap. The idea is to add different textures to the triangle. Don't be afraid to really pile them on! We have used organza puffs, gathered lace and satin ribbon.

- ¼ yard (25 cm) stiff taffeta
- #50 silk thread
- 1 yard (1 m) 18-gauge millinery wire
- 1 yard (1 m) silk organza
- 3 yards (3 m) 1-inch (2.5-cm)-wide lace
- 1 yard (1 m) 2-inch (5-cm)-wide silk ribbon
- #30 silk thread

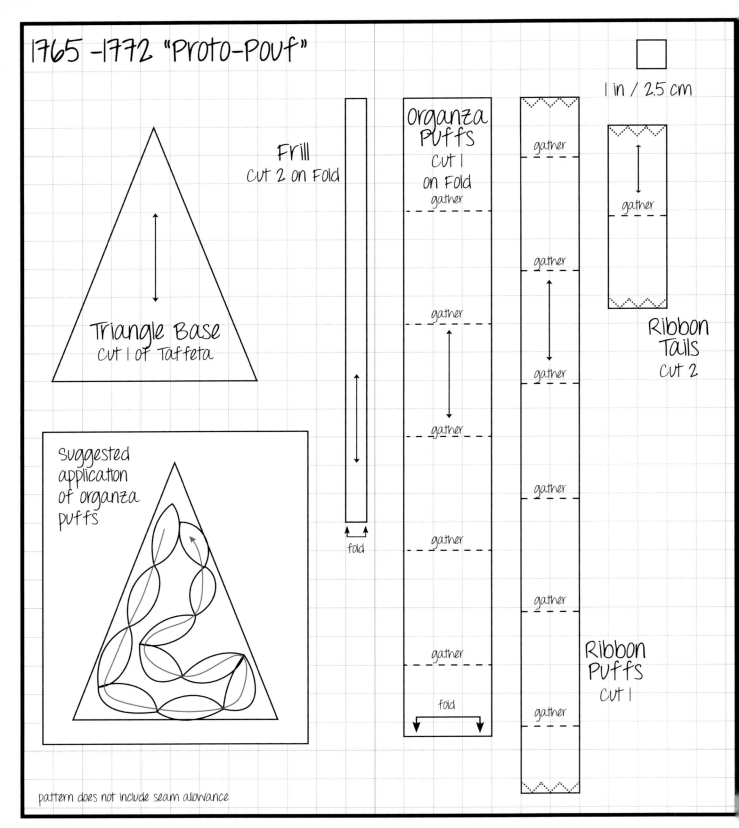

1765 -1772 "Proto-Pouf"

Triangle Base
Cut 1 of Taffeta

Suggested application of organza puffs

Frill
Cut 2 on Fold

fold

fold

Organza Puffs
Cut 1 on Fold
gather
gather
gather
gather
gather
gather

gather
gather
gather
gather
gather
gather
gather

Ribbon Puffs
Cut 1

1 in / 2.5 cm

gather

Ribbon Tails
Cut 2

pattern does not include seam allowance

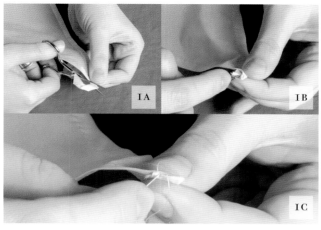

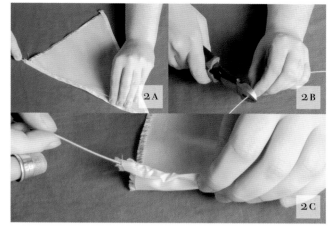

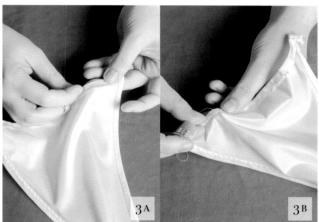

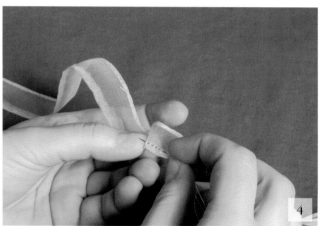

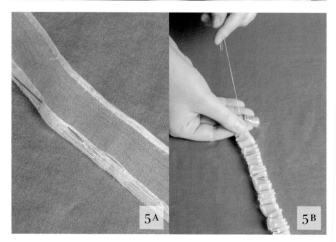

Triangle Base

1. Cut out the triangle base with a ½-inch (1.2-cm) seam allowance, then turn up ¼ inch (6 mm) on each long edge and baste. Turn up these edges again and hem stitch, working the ends at the sharp point.

2. Cut the millinery wire to match the length of the long edges of the triangle, then insert into the casings.

3. Fold up the short side of the triangle ¼ inch (6 mm) and baste, then fold up again ¼ inch (6 mm) and hem stitch, leaving one end open. Cut the wire to length and insert it into the channel, then stitch the end closed to secure.

4. Cut and finely hem both sides of the frills. Then mark one long side of your organza frills at ½-inch (1.2-cm) intervals. These are the marks for your running stitches.

5. Run three lines of running stitches according to the ½-inch (1.2-cm) marks. These running stitches should be very close together, only ⅟₁₆ inch (1 mm) apart or so. Pull all three ends up together to gather the ruffle.

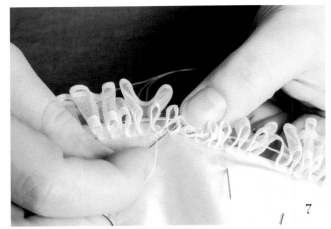

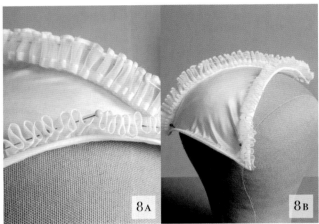

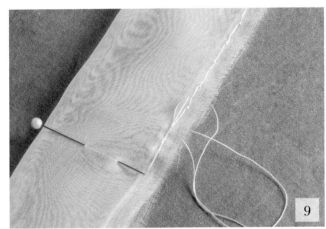

6. This next part is the trickiest. Arrange the gathered organza ruffle along one wired long edge of the triangle. Arrange the pleats evenly using small scissors or a similar tool to space the pleats. Pin as needed to hold it all in place.

7. Roll down the wire and ruffle together, exposing the base of the pleats where they touch the taffeta. Whipstitch the bottom "U" shape of the pleats to the taffeta using one to two stitches per each "U," then fold the wired edge with the ruffle back up.

8. If you'd like to work your ruffle into figure eights, lightly pin through the middle of the pleats, arranging in even sets and shoot a little steam onto them with your iron. Futz until you've got them how you like, then gently pull the pins out.

FLUFF

9. To create the organza puffs, seam a long strip of organza right sides together with a running backstitch. Turn right side out. Do not press.

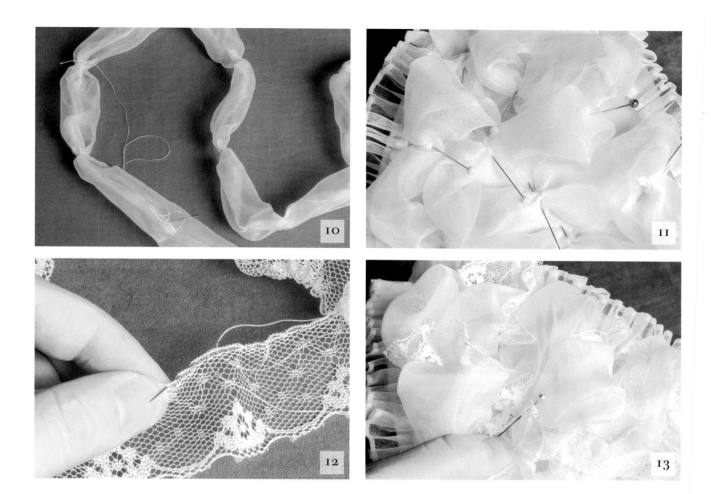

10. Mark the gathering points, then gather across the width with a running stitch. Pull up the thread and knot at each point. Cut the thread and move to the next gathering point.

11. Once your puffs are complete, arrange in a pleasing way on the bare part of your triangle. There is no particular way to arrange—in a spiral or zigzag way is just fine. Pin at the gathering points, then stitch each of the points to the triangle.

12. Next, gather up one long edge of your lace at roughly 2.5x the length. We gathered 2¼ yards (2 m) down to about 2½ feet (76 cm).

13. Pin one end of your gathered lace at the front of the triangle point, then weave it over and under the organza puffs, pinning where needed to hold it in place. Futz and arrange to your taste. Stitch at these pinned points.

RIBBONS

14. For the top floof ribbon pile, cut a 24½-inch (62-cm) length of 2-inch (5-cm)-wide ribbon, and cut the ends of your ribbon into a zigzag to finish the edges in a fun, easy and period-correct way.

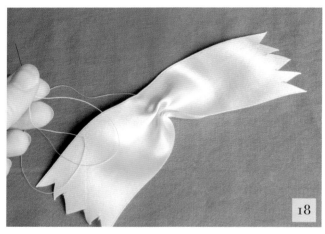

15. Next, mark the gathering points along the ribbons according to the pattern—every 4 inches (10 cm).

16. Gather across the width with a running stitch, pulling up the thread and knotting at each point.

17. Arrange the ribbon on the top of the cap close to the point, with the zigzag tails positioned at the back. The gathering points will be placed quite close to each other. Stitch through the gathering points to secure the bow to the taffeta triangle. If the puffs are a little unruly, pop them with a little steam from your iron and gently press with the palm of your hand.

18. For the short tails, cut 6½-inch (16.5-cm) lengths. Gather across the middle with a running stitch, pull and secure into place.

19. Fold over at the gathering points and place these Vs at the back corners of the triangle. Tack in place with a few stitches.

Your proto-pouf is now ready to wear, but if you feel you need even more decoration, add more ribbons, flowers, puffs and lace. This is also an excellent project with which to wear your lace lappets (page 67).

Trimmed Bergere Straw Hat

In our first book, we showed you two extremes with what could be done with a straw hat, very plain and incredibly ornate (and a bit brainy). For this book, we give you the middle ground, a 1760s and '70s straw hat lined in silk and trimmed in silk satin ribbon to give a pretty and sophisticated finish. We took our inspiration from a surviving hat in the Metropolitan Museum of Art's collection. [5] As for your hat, follow the tutorial precisely or look for prints and paintings that inspire you and adapt our instructions to suit your taste.

- *½ yard (0.5 m) silk taffeta for the under brim in a color of your choice*
- *#30 silk thread, white*
- *1 (14-inch [35.5-cm] diameter) shallow-crowned straw hat blank*
- *3 yards (3 m) 2-inch (5-cm)-wide silk ribbon in a color of your choice*
- *1½ yards (1.5 m) 1-inch (2.5-cm)-wide silk ribbon in a color of your choice*
- *#30 silk thread, matching the color of your silk*

NOTE: Depending on the depth and diameter of the crown of your hat, the pattern will need to be adjusted. Check the diameter of the top of your hat's crown and the width of the band. Also, measure the circumference of the brim of your hat and adjust the pattern/length for the edge binding ribbon.

1765 - 1772 Trimmed Bergere Hat

This pattern uses a 14 inch [35.5 cm] diameter shallow-crowned hat blank with a 4.5 inch [11.4 cm] diameter crown. Measure and adjust the pattern as needed for any other size hat brim and crown.

1 in / 2.5 cm

Do not add seam allowance on the outer edge of the brim

Brim Lining
Cut 1

stitch ties here X

Add 5/8 in [1.6 cm] seam allowance inside here

stitch ties here X

Ribbon Ties
Cut 2

Ribbon Puffs
Cut 1

gather

gather

Total length is approx. 56 in [142 cm]

Add 1/4 in [6 mm] seam allowance to outer edge of crown

Crown Lining
Cut 1

Add 1/4 in [6 mm] to all edges of the crown band

Crown Lining Band
Cut 1

pattern does not include seam allowance

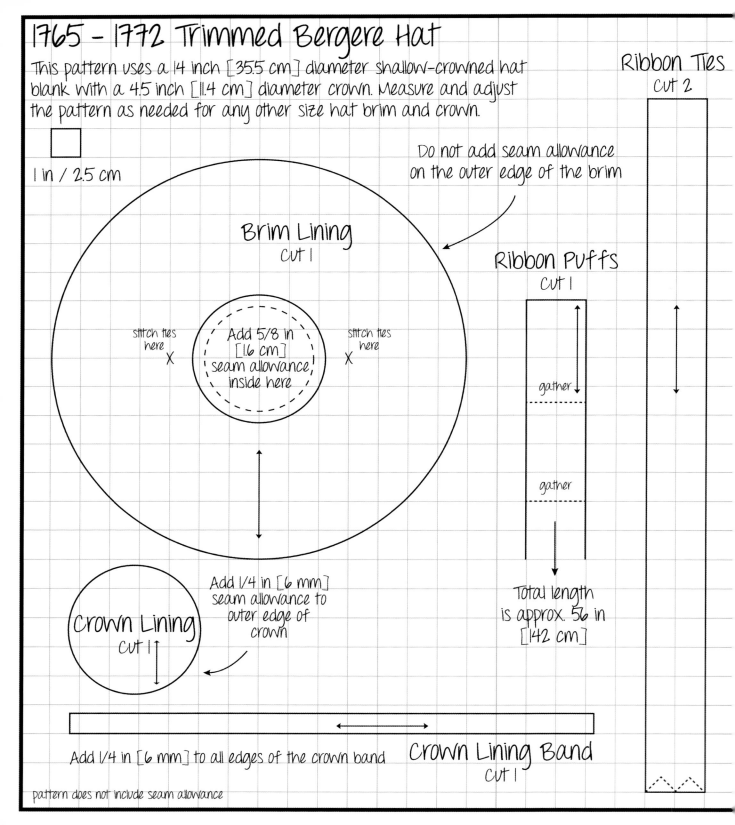

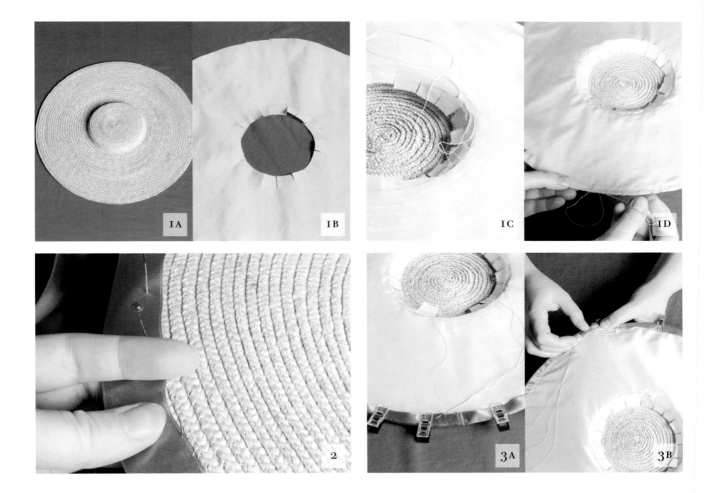

IA   IB   IC   ID
2   3A   3B

Brim Lining

1. Placing the silk lining onto the underside of the brim, match up the outer edges and hold in place with clips or pins. Clip into the seam allowance on the inner circle of the brim, then fold these pieces down into the crown. Baste the silk in place close to the base of the crown, then smooth any wrinkles out of the silk, working from the inner to the outer edge, and baste around the outer edge to hold everything in place.

2. Starting from the top side of the brim, place your edge binding against the brim with half of the ribbon on the brim and half to be folded over later. Example: if your ribbon is 1 inch (2.5 cm) wide, place ½ inch (1.2 cm) onto the brim. Applique stitch through the edge of the ribbon and the hat straw, easing the ribbon around the curve as you go with small tucks or gathers. If you're new to sewing, go nice and slow here, this is the hardest part, and it's trickier than it looks.

3. Once the top edge binding is completed, fold the second half of the ribbon over the edge of the brim and applique stitch around the edge on the underside, again easing the ribbon around the curves. If desired, give this edge binding a little press with the iron to flatten out any gathers that may have decided to show up for the hat party.

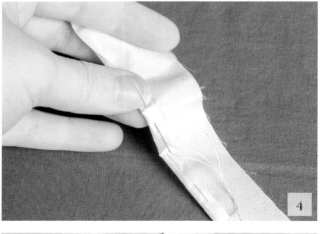

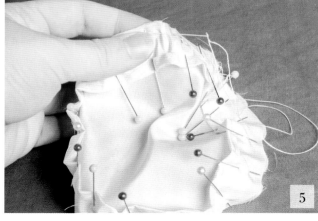

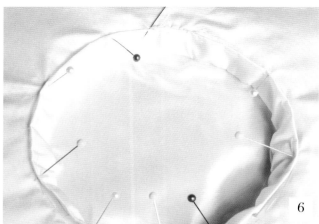

CROWN LINING

4. Turn up and baste ¼-inch (6-mm) seam allowance on the bottom edge of the crown lining band.

5. With right sides together and matching raw edges, stitch the crown lining band to the crown lining circle with a fine running stitch. Clip the curved seam allowance, then fold out and press.

6. Join the ends of the crown lining band to create the three-dimensional form, then place this inside the hat crown with the finished edges visible and the raw edges hidden.

7. Applique stitch the turned edge of the crown lining band over the brim silk lining at the base of the crown. It's OK to sew through all layers at this point—any stitches on top will be hidden by the ribbon decoration later on.

8. Take a few very small tacking stitches on the sides of the crown, just to hold the lining in place.

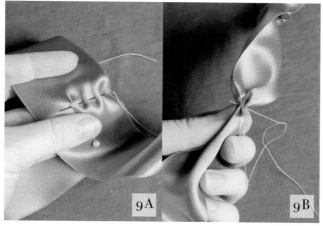

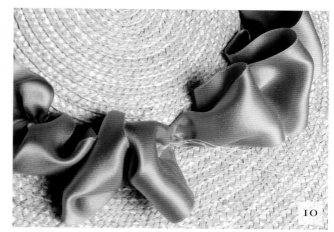

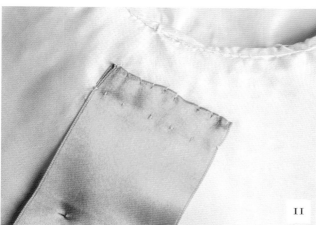

Ribbon Puffs & Ties

9. Using pins, mark the gathering lines for your ribbon puffs according to the pattern. Then at each point, running stitch across the width, pulling up the thread to gather the ribbon. Tie off the thread and cut before moving to the next point.

10. Pin one end of the puffs to the crown of the hat, then work around the hat, placing the gathering points of the puffs about 1 inch (2.5 cm) from each other. Arrange the puffs evenly around the crown, then stitch each puff in place at the gathering points, moving from point to point with one continuous thread.

11. The last step is to stitch the ribbon ties to the hat. The ties should be about 2 feet (61 cm) long each and placed at opposite sides of the underside of the hat, close to the base of the crown. Turn under the raw edge of the end of the ribbon, applique stitch the ends of the ties securely, then take small prick stitches about ½ inch (1.2 cm) from the applique stitched edge, catching just the silk lining underneath.

12. Your fluffy bergere can now be worn as-is, or decorated even more with feathers, ribbons and flowers. To see how to create ostrich plumes for your hat, see page 132.

CHAPTER 7

1772–1775

Coiffure Beignet

The early- to mid-1770s hairstyles have become so iconic that it seems everyone can visualize some sort of variation of the Marie Antoinette–style "tall, white, powdered hair/wig" cliché. Don't even get us started on those heinous white plastic Halloween wigs. In reality, the vertical hair of the 1770s was only fashionable for a relatively short time.

When examining portraiture from the beginning of 1772, we see hair starting to rise in the front, but it isn't really that tall yet, maybe only an additional 1 to 2 inches (2.5 to 5 cm). It's not until about 1773–1775 that hair goes zooming up quite high and is very cylindrical and vertical in silhouette. Even then there is a delicate balance of proportion: too high isn't even attractive—it's just silly.

The next question inevitably is "how" it was done. When examining images of women with or having their hair dressed, you'll notice shadowing that indicates the hair is being wrapped over and into something. [1] The portrait of Madame de Saint-Maurice by Joseph Siffred Duplessis is a great example of the shape the donut hair cushion gives. [2] This visual information, in addition to hairdressers exclusively referring to cushions (and not cages) for women's hairdressing, helped us develop the beloved "donut" hair cushion. [3]

The 1770s are really the only time in the last half of the eighteenth century when the "mullet" haircut does not make sense. With the extreme—and trust us, anything over 4 inches [10 cm] is way up there—height of the front hair in this decade, the shorter shag cuts seen before and after the 1770s just don't work. Long hair was in.

With this tall hair comes some incredible headgear. For this chapter we've created a ginormous calash to protect your 'do when going outside. We've also added a French Night Cap [4] style cap (page 103) that will cover all that tall hair for a more simple "day" look. As you'll see in the following pages, this hairstyle is huge. As a result, the accessories are just as big. We strongly suggest you scale these patterns down when planning to use a smaller cushion or lower hairstyle for shorter hair or a different look.

1772 - 1775 Giant Donut Hair Cushion

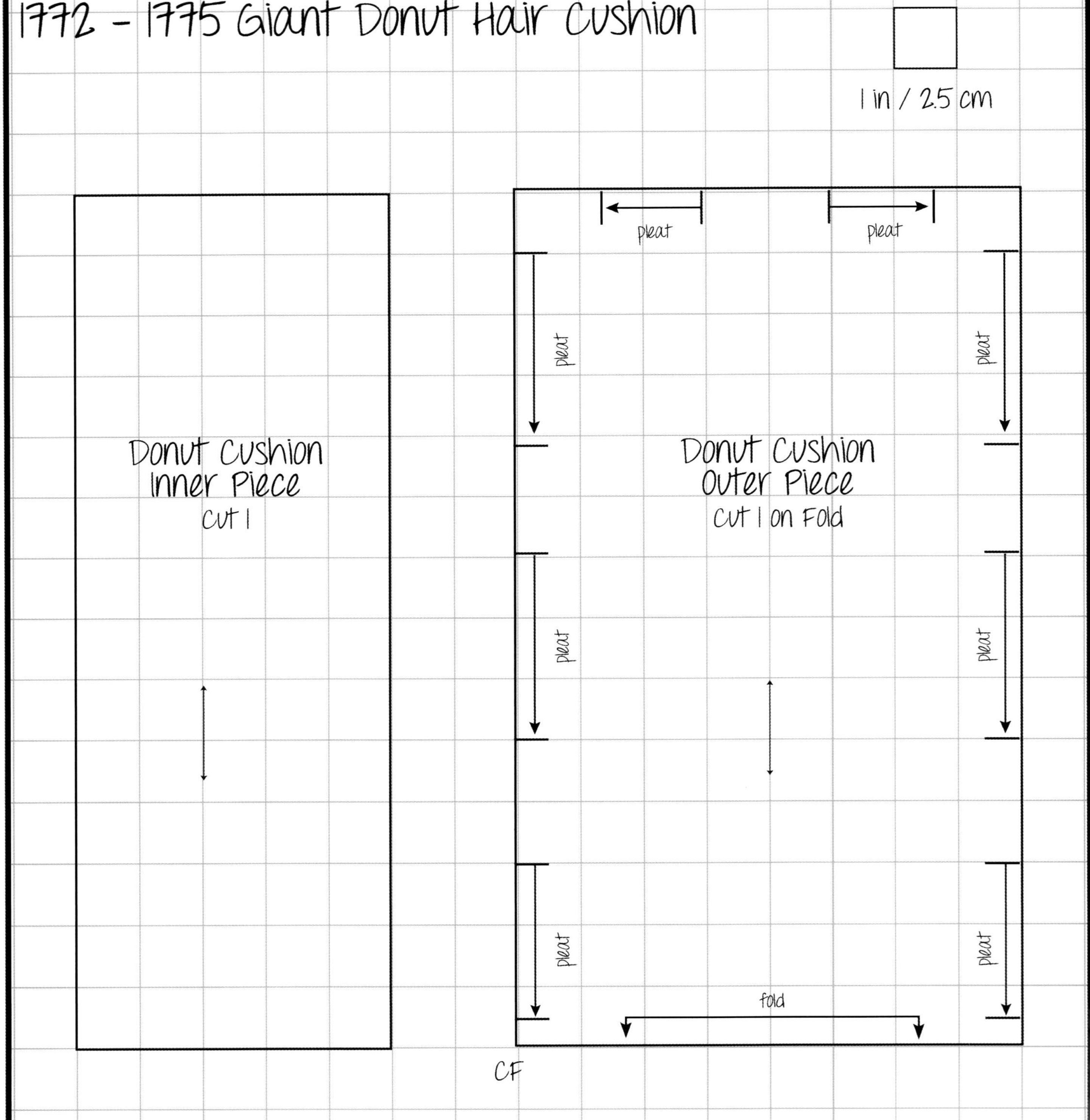

1 in / 2.5 cm

Donut Cushion
Inner Piece
Cut 1

Donut Cushion
Outer Piece
Cut 1 on Fold

pleat

pleat

pleat

pleat

pleat

pleat

pleat

pleat

fold

CF

pattern does not include seam allowance

Giant Donut Hair Cushion

As the trend for high hair ascends at the turn of the 1770s, the need for bigger and bigger cushions arises. This tutorial will create the grandaddy of hair cushions, what we call the "donut"—a round pad with an ingenious hole in the middle that allows the hair to be formed, supported and controlled over this utterly huge form.

The size of your donut should relate to the length of your hair. Big donuts need very long hair, like Laurie has in this chapter, whereas ladies with shorter hair will use a smaller donut. The hair must be able to wrap up and over the sides and back down into the donut hole.

It is important to note that the French Night Cap (page 103) and Calash Bonnet (page 109) in this chapter are also very large and are meant to be worn with this huge donut. If you need or want to reduce the size of your pastry, you will also want to reduce the scale of the cap and calash as well.

- *1 yard (1 m) wool knit*
- *#30 thread*
- *Horsehair, wool roving or granulated cork stuffing*

1.   Choose a wool knit that is close in color to your hair when powdered. Cut out the pattern and mark the pleats on the outer piece.

2.   Pleat the outer piece, working each side toward the center point. Also pleat the short ends according to the pattern. Pin, then test your pleating against the small inner piece to make sure the long and short edges match up. Baste through all of the pleats.

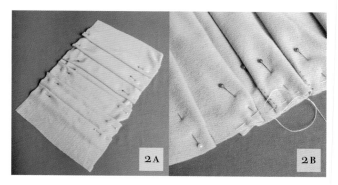

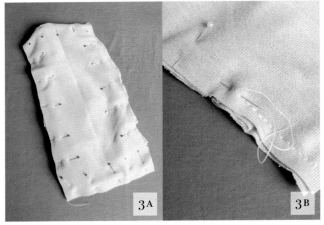

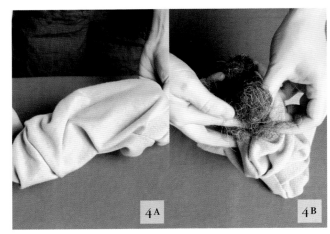

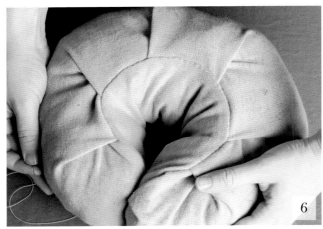

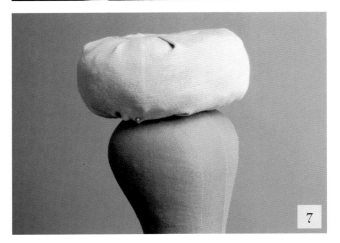

3. With right sides together, match all edges of the outer and inner piece. Pin, then backstitch with strong thread, leaving about a 3-inch (8-cm) opening on one short end between the small pleats.

4. Turn right side out, then cram this sucker full of horsehair stuffing. We've chosen horsehair for this cushion because it is very lightweight with tons of body.

5. Once you've got what now looks like a giant larva stuffed full, turn in the open edges on the end and whipstitch the opening closed.

6. The larva will naturally wish to curl into its final donut shape, which makes it easy to match up the short ends and roughly whipstitch them together from the outside. This doesn't have to be pretty, just secure.

7. Congratulations! You've completed your enormous donut hair cushion! Now remember, this is a very easy pattern to reduce in size. If your hair isn't quite long enough or you just want something a little less gigantic, play with the dimensions of the donut cushion for different effects.

Coiffure Beignet Hairstyle

Here it is, the donut you've all been waiting for. This iconic hairstyle is baked into the very definition of eighteenth-century hair today. It is the smooth, tall, powdered coiffure of your dreams, but did you know that this is also one of the easiest hairstyles in the book? The donut style is achievable for anyone with hair about shoulder-length or longer, but in this case the longer the hair the better. Read on to learn how to quickly and easily do this classic eighteenth-century 'do.

- Common Pomatum (page 20)
- Large powder brush
- White Hair Powder (page 28)
- Rattail comb
- Alligator hair clips
- Elastic hair bands (if needed)
- U-shaped hairpins (short & long)
- Donut Hair Cushion (page 95)
- Teasing comb with pick
- ½-inch (1.2-cm) curling iron
- Size 50 (25-mm) knitting needle
- Bobby pins
- Flowers, cap or other decoration

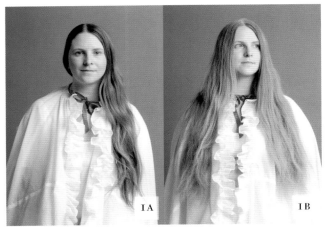

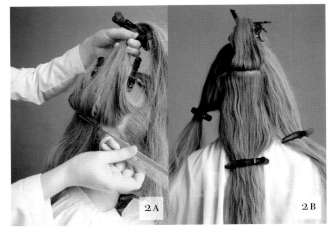

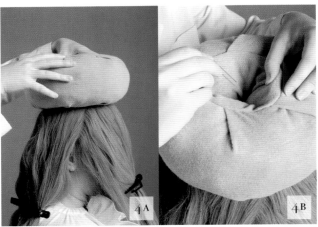

DRESSING THE DONUT

1. Follow the instructions on page 36 to pomade and powder the hair.

2. Start by carefully parting the hair with the rattail comb, working around the head in sections in a "circular" fashion from ear to ear. Divide the hair into multiple sections: two chunks on each side, a top back chunk, and a top bottom chunk.

3. For those with very long and thick hair, [5] we're going to anchor the donut by making a hair nub. To do this, section out a small hank of hair on the very top of the head and tightly braid it. Tie off the end with an elastic hairband, then twist the braid up to make a nub on top of the head. Pin in place with a couple hairpins.

4. Now place the donut atop the head and centered over the braided nub. Using long hairpins, secure the donut to the nub down in the hole. This is a little tricky, but just make sure the donut is properly fastened to the head.

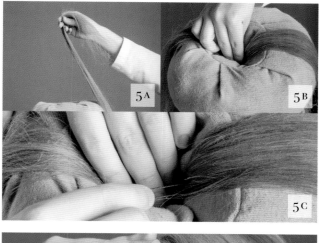

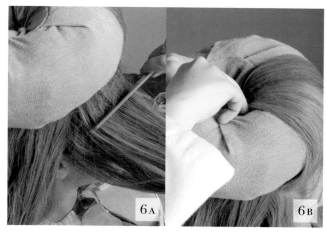

5. It's time to start frosting this pastry. Starting from the front and working in 2- to 3-inch (5- to 8-cm) sections, tease the roots of the hair a little, then smooth the hair up and over the donut and back down into the hole in the center. Using the U-shaped hairpins, secure each section of hair inside the donut hole, stabbing the ends of the hairpins into the cushion. You can tuck all the loose ends of the hair down into the donut hole and later top your style with a cap or pouf, but for this tutorial we are going to finish the ends of the hair later on, so we have left them loose and free of the hole.

6. Continue around the head teasing and smoothing the hair up and into the hole and pinning to secure. Use your pick and comb to very lightly smooth the sections of hair together for a uniform look.

7. Since we've left the ends of Laurie's very long hair free, we're going to finish the top of the hair by curling these ends in small sections. This was a popular way to "decorate" the top of these tall hairstyles and is also—thankfully— very easy to do! Section the hair into 1- to 2-inch (2.5- to 5-cm) pieces and wrap around the ½-inch (1.2-cm) curling iron. Slip the curling iron out and use a couple small hairpins to hold the curls in place.

8. Curl and pin the ends of the hair all around the top of the donut until it all looks balanced and pleasing.

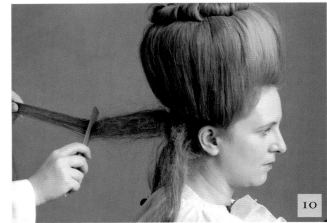

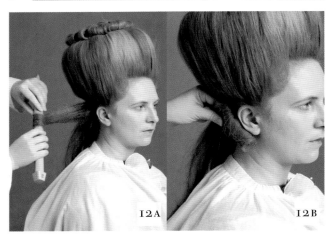

Big Ol' Buckles

9. Start by sectioning the hair into three parts.

10. The large buckles are created with the hair behind each ear. Due to their size we recommend working the hair in two sections and then joining them with the comb later on for a cohesive look. Section the hair behind the ears into two pieces—a top and a bottom—and then tease the heck out of both pieces independently.

11. When your buckle hair is sufficiently standing out on its own, roll up the ends with your ½-inch (1.2-cm) curling iron to help guide the curl. Release.

12. Starting with the lower buckle, roll the hair onto the knitting needle starting from the ends of the hair and working toward the scalp. These buckles are fairly vertical and at a slight angle toward the back, so be sure to angle your roller to match as you go along. Once you've rolled the hair up nice and tight, carefully slip the knitting needle out, spread the hair out with your fingers, and secure the buckle by weaving a large hairpin on the inside of the buckle roll, working the hairpin so it points downward.

13. Repeat the teasing, curling, rolling up, spreading and pinning for the upper buckle, then very carefully work the hair together to join both buckles visually and create one big honkin' piece. This is a little tricky so take your time—it doesn't have to be perfect, just cohesive. Buckles are definitely an area where "practice makes perfect."

14. Repeat steps 10 through 13 for the other side of the head. You can also use these techniques to make as many buckles as you like and position them all over the back of the head, whatever floats your big hair boat.

LOOPED CHIGNON

15. Using the tail of the comb to guide the loop, determine how long you'd like the chignon loop to be, then tie off the hair with an elastic band at the end where it will meet the base of the donut. Because Laurie has such long hair, this elastic band is pretty high up the section, but the placement of this band will vary based on your hair length and how you'd like to treat the chignon.

16. Loop the chignon up again and place the hair band at the base of the donut, securing with two crossed bobby pins.

17. We're now left with a long hank of hair. For this tutorial, we're going to smooth this up and over the donut, blending it seamlessly with the vertical hair from the first part of this tutorial. Use your pick and comb to blend the hair in, and pin at the top with hairpins.

18. Curl the loose end of the hair with the ½-inch (1.2-cm) curling iron, then roll this curl under and secure with hairpins.

19. Finally, hide the hair band and pins from step 16. You can use any number of decorations here such as feathers, fake flowers or ribbons. We tied a simple bow with silk ribbon and used straight pins to secure it to the style.

20. To finish everything off, warm up some pomade in your hands and very gently smooth the hair in the front and around the sides of the donut, moving your hands in the direction the hair is going. This tames any flyaways.

21. At this point, your coiffure of great proportion is complete. Although for this tutorial we did not apply more powder, you may wish to powder the style even more, particularly if the hair is looking greasy or "wet" in any section. Very lightly apply powder with the large blush brush or swansdown puff. Brush away any powder residue from the forehead and pass a fine-toothed comb very gently over the hair to break up any powder clumps.

You did it! You have achieved the high hair of the early 1770s! Now that you know the basic construction, feel free to play around with this style. Try curling your hair beforehand for a textured coiffure, or adding more buckles at the back. There is scope for creativity and personal expression, so have fun!

French Night Cap

This cap is based on several early 1770s prints and portraits [6] and reflects the very high hair fashionable in the early 1770s. We've made our version in cotton voile and trimmed the band with silk ribbon, but this cap may also be made in silk organza, cotton organdy or a fine linen for different looks.

The proportions of this cap are particularly important, with a very large caul and deep ruffles that cover the tops of the ears. It has been sized to work with the Giant Donut Hair Cushion (page 95). If you have elected to reduce the size of your donut hair cushion, we recommend shrinking the proportions of this cap as well. This cap made as-is will not work with low hair—it will swallow your head—so be sure to shrink it if you intend to use it for less voluminous styles!

- ½–1 yard (0.5–1 m) cotton voile
- #30 and #50 silk thread
- 18 inch (46 cm) cording or candlewicking
- 1–2 yards (1–2 m) 1–2-inch (2.5–5-cm)-wide silk ribbon

1772 - 1775 French Night Cap

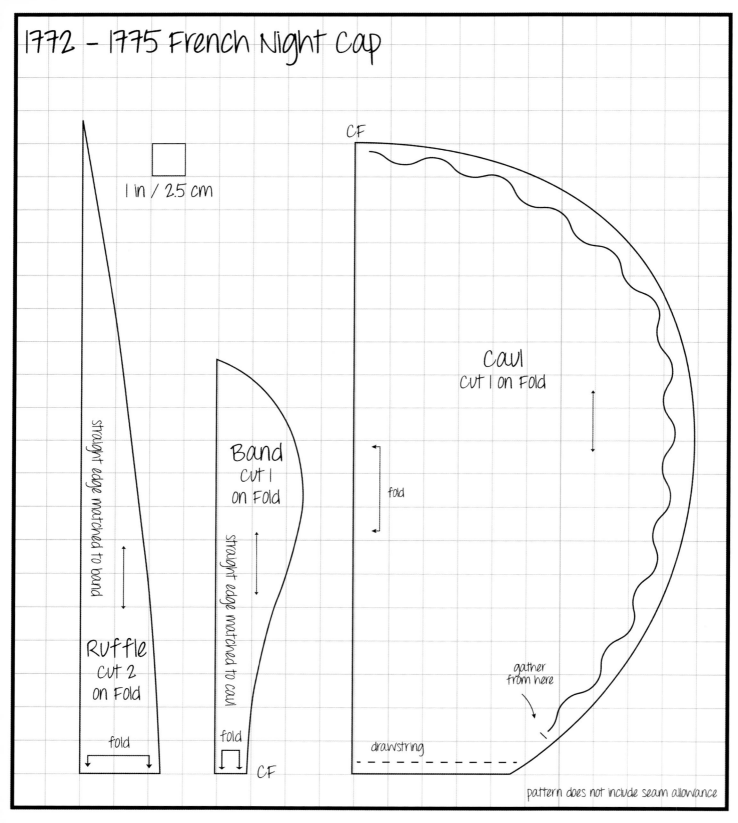

1 in / 2.5 cm

Ruffle
Cut 2
on Fold

straight edge matched to band

fold

Band
Cut 1
on Fold

straight edge matched to caul

fold

CF

CF

Caul
Cut 1 on Fold

fold

gather from here

drawstring

pattern does not include seam allowance

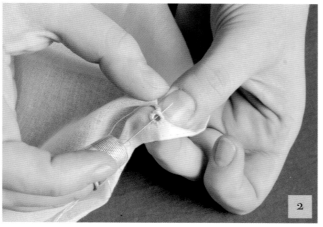

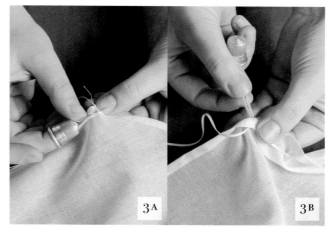

Preparing the Pieces

1. Baste the caul edges all the way around ⅛ to ¼ inch (3 to 6 mm), then baste up the bottom of the caul ¼ inch (6 mm).

2. Fold the caul in half, and, using an awl, poke a hole just above the basted edge. With heavy silk thread, whip the eyelet open, and poke the hole with the awl again to open it back up.

3. Backstitch the cord or candlewicking to each side of the bottom edges of the caul, and pull the tails through the hole.

4. Turn up the bottom edge of the caul over the cord and finely hem, making sure to not catch the cord.

5. Turn the remaining basted edges up again and finely hem.

6. On the band piece, baste ⅛ to ¼ inch (3 to 6 mm) and finely hem using running stitches on all sides.

7. For the ruffles, baste up ⅛ to ¼ inch (3 to 6 mm), then turn up again and finely hem all sides.

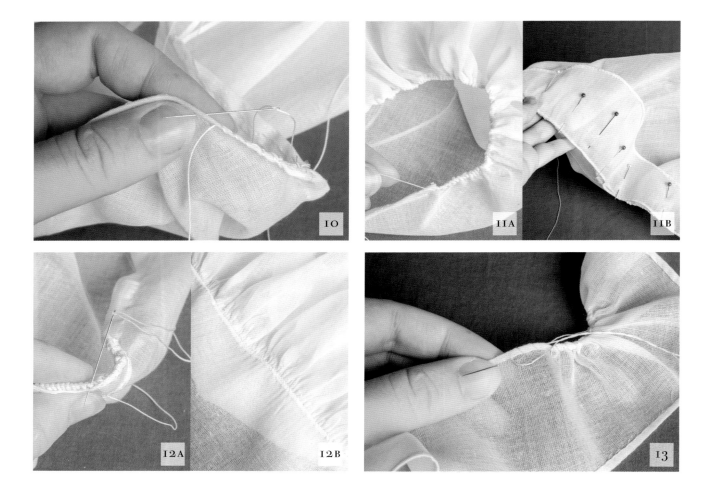

ATTACHING THE CAUL TO THE BAND

8. Mark the straight sides of the caul just where the sides begin to curve into the top of the caul. Reference the pattern for these points.

9. Fold the caul in half and pin to mark the halfway point at the top.

10. Whip gather over the hemmed edge of the caul from one side up to the center point at the top. Repeat with a new thread on the other side.

11. Working one side at a time, pull the thread to tightly gather up the caul, then match the tightly gathered edge to the straight edge of one half of the band. Arrange the gathers evenly and pin. Repeat for the other side of the caul and band.

12. Starting from one end, tightly whipstitch the gathered caul and straight edge of the band together, catching every tiny little bump. This is super tedious, but the result will be splendid. When done, open the two pieces out and gently tug to "pop" the stitches into place. Press it all flat if needed.

JOINING THE RUFFLES TO THE BAND

13. Run a whip-gathering stitch over the straight edge of each ruffle piece, spacing your stitches about ¼ inch (6 mm) apart.

14. Pull up the thread to gather the ruffles tightly. It will help to lightly press the ruffles with the iron to help them behave.

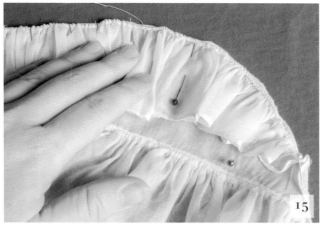

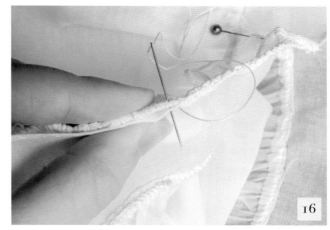

15. Working each side separately, pin the gathered edge of the ruffle to the curved edge of the band, right sides together.

16. Whipstitch the ruffle to the band, catching each bump of the gathers.

17. Open the ruffle and band out flat and gently tug the pieces apart to "pop" the stitches into place. Press the open pieces.

TRIMMING THE CAP

18. The last step, and possibly the most fun, is to trim your new gigantic early 1770s cap in ribbons to match your gown. We found it easiest to add the ribbon once the cap was already on the head. We used a simple 1-inch (2.5-cm)-wide silk ribbon and discreetly pinned it in place at the base of the cap in back.

19. Construct a simple 4-Loop Bow (page 198) in the same ribbon, and pin it at the center front of your cap.

Woo! You've now completed one heck of a cap to adorn your gigantic hair. Remember, this cap is intentionally huge, but you can play around with the sizes and proportions of the caul, band and ruffles for different looks and uses.

Calash Bonnet

One of the most bizarre headwear fashions of the late eighteenth century is the calash bonnet. Named after a popular convertible carriage, [7] a lady's calash bonnet telescoped up and over the elaborate coiffures of the 1770s, 1780s and 1790s, continuing well into the first half of the nineteenth century. The size and shape of these bonnets changes over time with the hairstyles. Early calashes were cut on the straight and used simple rectangles in construction, [8] making the most of the fabric and taking the least time in labor. Calash bonnets were commonly made in green, black, brown or purple silk, and lined in pink or ivory to reflect light onto and flatter the face. [9] Many calash bonnets feature ruffles around the face, other decorations such as bows at the back and variations in the design of the holding strings. This is the hardest project in this book. Don't worry—stick to it, and you'll have an amazing calash at the end.

- 2½ yards (2.5 m) green, brown, black or lilac silk taffeta
- 1½ yards (1.5 m) pink or ivory silk taffeta
- #30 heavy silk thread in matching color of outer fabric
- 15 feet (4.5 m) 4.5-mm round reed
- #1 reed —45 inches (114 cm)
- #2/#3 reed —47 inches (119 cm)
- #4 reed—40 inches (102 cm)
- Drill
- 1 yard (1 m) ½-inch (1.2-cm)-wide ribbon

PREP THE CALASH BODY

1. Turn in ½-inch (1.2-cm) seam allowances on the outer and lining fabric on the front edge of the calash body. Baste the outer fabric, then fold in the lining to sit just inside the edge of the outer fabric. Pin, then edge stitch the outer and lining fabrics together.

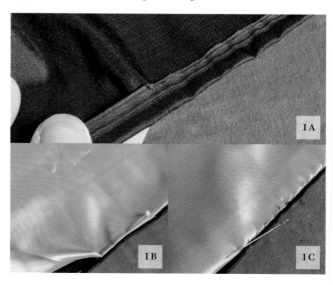

1770s Calash Bonnet

Calash Strings - 36 in [91.4 cm]

1 in / 2.5 cm

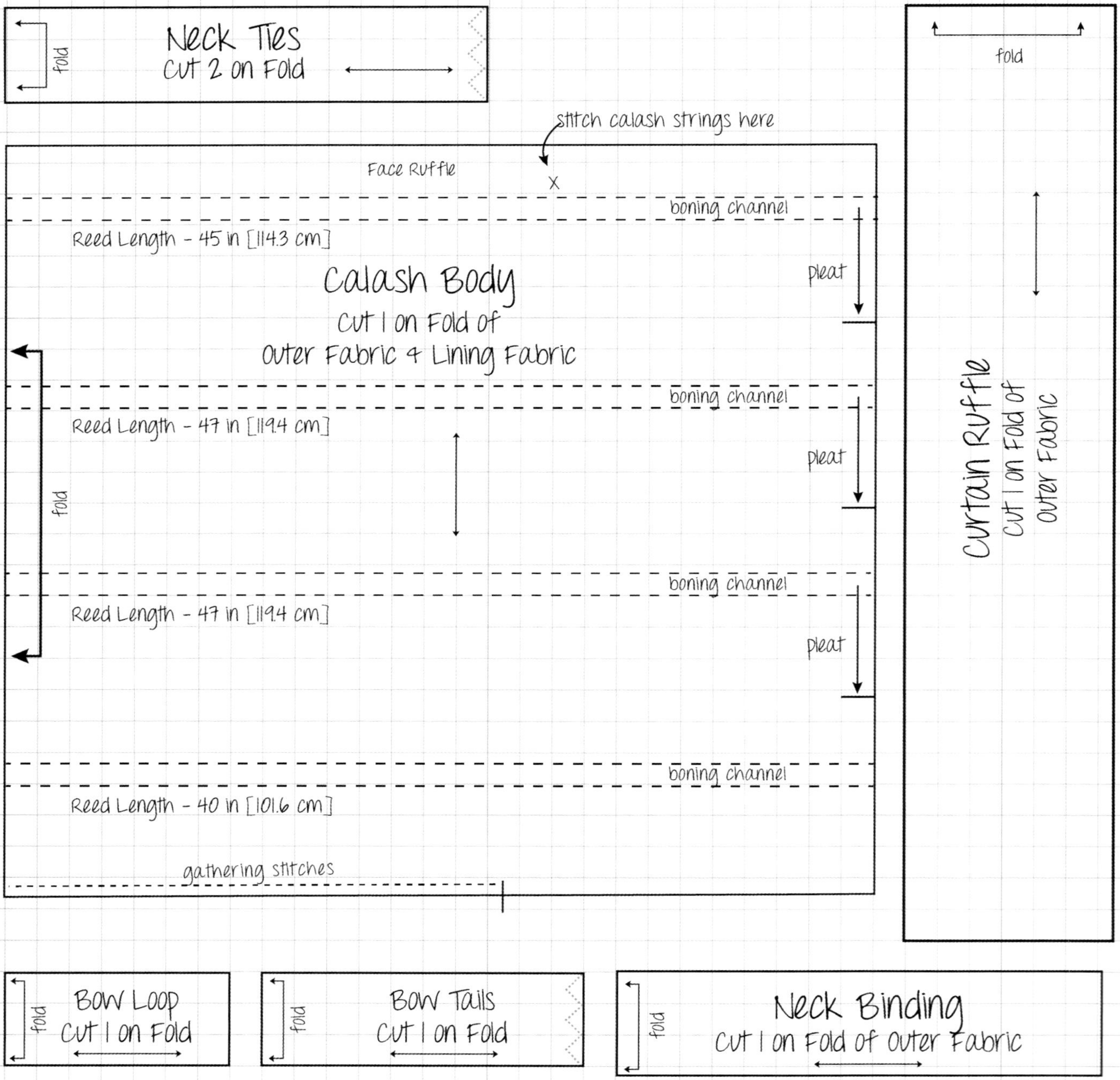

Neck Ties
Cut 2 on Fold

fold

stitch calash strings here

Face Ruffle

X

boning channel

Reed Length - 45 in [114.3 cm]

Calash Body
Cut 1 on Fold of
Outer Fabric & Lining Fabric

pleat

boning channel

Reed Length - 47 in [119.4 cm]

pleat

fold

boning channel

Reed Length - 47 in [119.4 cm]

pleat

boning channel

Reed Length - 40 in [101.6 cm]

gathering stitches

fold

Curtain Ruffle
Cut 1 on Fold of
Outer Fabric

Bow Loop
Cut 1 on Fold

fold

Bow Tails
Cut 1 on Fold

fold

Neck Binding
Cut 1 on Fold of Outer Fabric

fold

pattern does not include seam allowance

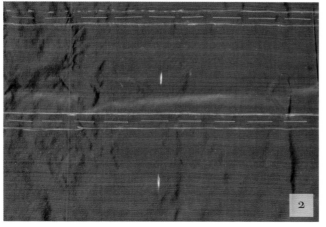

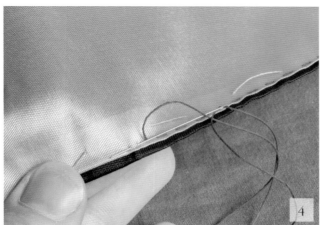

2. Mark the five boning channel fold lines on the outside of the calash body piece. Lay the outer and lining fabrics wrong sides together, then baste through both layers along the fold lines in the center of the boning channel marks.

3. Turn up and baste the seam allowance on both the outer and lining fabric on the back edge of the calash body. Baste the two turned edges together as well. The sides are still left open.

4. Finely running stitch the outer and lining fabrics of the back edge of the calash body together between the two marks on either side of the center back. Run a gathering stitch between the marks on the back edge.

5. Fold the fabric along the first boning channel center basting, wrong sides together. Backstitch along the marked line, approximately ⅜ inch (1 cm) from the folded edge. Repeat for all five of the basted boning channel lines. This creates the bone casing for each reed on the outside of the calash body.

6. While the calash body is still flat, pleat the sides and baste, making sure not to catch the boning channels in your basting stitches.

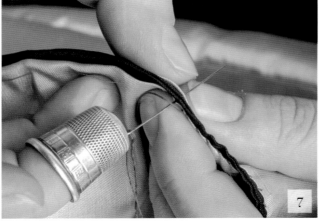

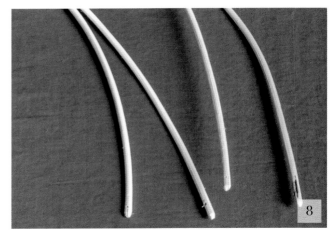

7. Fold the calash body in half, right sides together, matching the center back seam. Pin below the mark for the gathering stitches. English stitch this seam from the base to the marks.

8. Cut the reeds to length—follow the length guide on the pattern. The front and back reeds will be shorter than the reeds in the mid-section of the calash body. Mark the ends of the reeds with colored markers to keep them organized.

9. If your reeds are too curly, you'll need to soak them in water for about 15 minutes, then straighten them out a bit into a gentler curve. Hold them in position—we used jaunty rubber traffic cones—and allow the reeds to dry in the new shape. The reeds do not need to be straight but rather arced more or less in the shape and curve that the finished calash will be.

10. Using a tiny drill bit, carefully drill a hole at both ends of each reed. You can also use a very small nail to press a hole through the reeds. Be very careful not to split the reeds on the ends. Sand and smooth any rough burrs or bits on the ends of the reeds.

11. Feed the reeds into the boning channels until the end lines up with the raw edge of the opening.

12. Now carefully stitch through the holes in each reed, taking a few strong tacking stitches and carrying on to the next reed. This is a little tricky to find the holes but do NOT skip this step. It's vital that the reeds be anchored in place. It's going to be a total mess on those raw bottom edges but don't worry—all these sins will be covered later on.

13. Gather the excess fabric up along the reeds. Once the reed ends and the raw edge of the fabric are aligned, once again stitch through the holes in the reeds to secure them into place, folding the channel toward the back and stitching it down too. Arrange the gathers evenly.

14. On the inside, pull up the gathering stitches nice and tight around the hole at the center back seam. Arrange the resulting "bumps" in a fairly symmetrical way and then whipstitch it all together as best you can. This doesn't have to be perfect, but be sure to pull the stitches nice and tight. Catch all of the bumps, then flip the calash to the outside and whip the bumps together on the outside as well. This will be covered by a bow later on, so it doesn't have to be perfect.

15. On the neck binding piece, fold in ½ inch (1.2 cm) on all sides and baste. With the calash body laid out as flat as possible, apply the neck binding to the outside of the calash body, aligning the raw bottom edge halfway, along the centerline of the binding. Applique stitch the top edge of the binding in place.

16. Turn the calash body over and fold the neck binding to the inside, encasing the bottom edge cleanly. Pin to hold, then hem stitch the top edge of the neck binding in place. Finish the ends by stitching them shut, and press the bottom edge of the neck lightly. Now you're on to the home stretch!

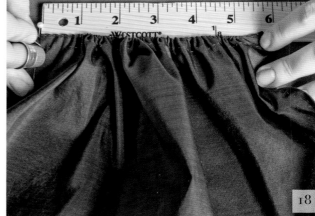

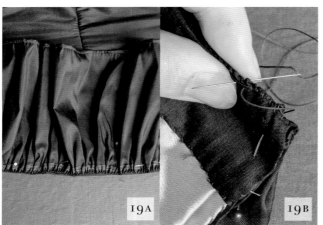

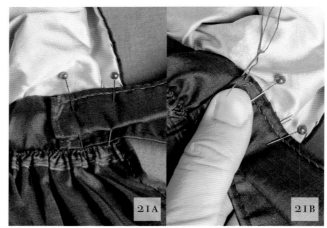

NECK CURTAIN

17. Hem all four edges of the neck ruffle, leaving the top edge un-hemmed.

18. Mark the center and 15 inches (38 cm) on either side to divide the curtain into four sections for gathering. Now whip gather over the finished top edge of the curtain. Every 15 inches (38 cm), gather the volume down to 5¾ inches (15 cm), tack stitch, then carry on with this method until the entire length of the curtain is gathered down to 23 inches (58 cm), the length of the bottom edge of the calash body.

19. With the calash laid out as flat as possible, align the top boned edge of the neck curtain with the bottom edge of the calash body, right sides together. Pin, then tightly whipstitch the pieces together. When complete, fold down the neck curtain ruffle and gently pull to "pop" the seam into place.

NECKTIES AND FINISHING THE INTERIOR

20. The neckties play a vital role in holding your calash in position. You can use premade ribbon or the same fabric as the calash, hemming the edges. The neck ties should be about 3 inches (8 cm) wide and 30 inches (76 cm) long, able to be comfortably tied in a bow around the neck.

21. Turn in ½ inch (1.2 cm) allowance on the ends of the neck ties and baste. Pin into place at the base of the neck of the calash, placing the edges about 1 inch (2.5 cm) inside, along the neck binding. Take a pleat to narrow the width of the neck ties to match the width of the neck binding, then securely hem stitch around the end, both sides and at the front edges. There is a lot of stress on these stitches, so make them strong.

STRINGS AND BOWS

22. The additional strings on the sides of the calash are to hold while wearing the bonnet and to keep it up and in position. You can use narrow ribbon in a matching or similar color or self-fabric narrow hemmed. We used 36 inches (91 cm) of ½-inch (1.2-cm)-wide black silk ribbon. Stitch these strings on the interior near the first bone, about 10 inches (25 cm) up the sides of the calash.

23. Lastly, and for extra floof, construct a bow in self-fabric. Start by hemming two pieces of silk fabric on each long edge—the first should be 14 inches (35.5 cm) by 3 inches (8 cm) and the second should be about 20 inches (51 cm) by 3 inches (8 cm).

24. On the shorter piece, match the raw short edges right sides together and running stitch. Turn the loop right side out and arrange the seam at the center back, then running stitch through both layers in the center. Pull up the thread to gather the center of the bow and tie off.

25. Fold the longer piece into a triangle at top so that both right sides of the ribbon show. Tuck down the point at the top, then place this top behind the bow loops. Stitch the tails to the bow through the center point with a few strong stitches. Cut the ends of the tails into zigzags or at angles.

26. Position the finished bow on the back of the calash, covering the tightly gathered portion. Take a few stitches all the way through to secure the bow in place.

27. To store your new calash, untie the necktie and truncate the bonnet flat.

You made it! You're done! You never have to make another calash bonnet again! . . . Unless, of course, you would like to explore the different shapes for later decades. Experiment with the width of the back edges and the overall size and length of the calash body to achieve smaller, rounder shapes.

CHAPTER 8

1776–1779

Coiffure Ski Alpin

When seeking a particularly revolutionary period of hairstyling, look no further than, well, the Revolutionary period. Fashionable hair in the second half of the 1770s took on mountainous proportions and silhouettes, ascending up the back of the head with cascades of buckles tumbling down the sides and crested with the almighty pouf. Hairstyles of the last half of the 1770s are feats of geometric and architectural genius.

The widening of the headdress was simply a progression from earlier forms. Once the hair gets as tall as it can in the early 1770s, something has to be done with it. The broad coiffures provided an excellent platform for the incredible millinery that came about during these years, like the pouf. An excellent example of this hairstyle is the *Portrait of Anne, Countess of Chesterfield* by Thomas Gainsborough, 1777–1778.

We bet you're wondering why we're not calling this hairstyle the "pouf." It's because poufs are not the hairstyle but the headgear that sat on top of the hair. [1] Poufs came into fashion in April of 1774 thanks to Marie Antoinette's hairdresser, Léonard, and provided a new and exciting way to decorate the hair, as opposed to a mere hat or cap. [2]

> *"[. . .] there came to me one of those grand ideas, which overthrow all pre-existing vogues, and to sit proudly on the ruins of all caprices . . . I invented the sentimental puff [pouf] . . . Great things are never boasted of; they are described. I find among my notes the description of the puff [pouf], worn in the month of April 1774, by Madame la Duchesse de Chartres."*

The pouf became exceedingly popular amongst the fashionable and their milliners alike. The thematic nature of the pouf meant that milliners could sell a huge and constant variety of them to their customers. [3]

The sloping hairstyle of the last part of the decade lends itself beautifully to showing off the pouf, and honestly, the look isn't complete without a gauzy, feathered and thematic confection resting on top of the mountainous coiffure. So hold on to your poufs, y'all—things are about to get wacky.

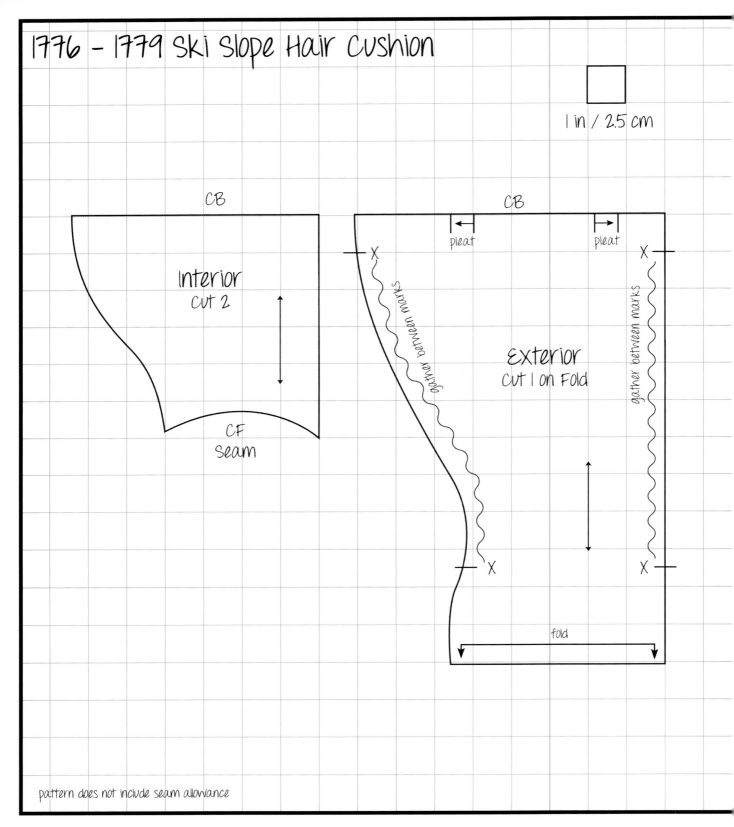

1776 - 1779 Ski Slope Hair Cushion

1 in / 2.5 cm

CB

Interior
Cut 2

CF
Seam

CB

pleat

pleat

gather between marks

Exterior
Cut 1 on Fold

gather between marks

X

X

X

X

fold

pattern does not include seam allowance

Ski Slope Hair Cushion

Just as with the donut cushion in the previous chapter, size and proportion really matter with the ski slope. If you choose to make this structure larger, make sure you've got the hair to cover it, particularly in the back. You may also wish to make this cushion smaller—more of a foothill than a mountain—which will also result in a fashionable and accurate coiffure. Play around with proportions—heights in front and back, depth and width—for a variety of different effects.

- ½ yard (0.5 m) wool knit matching hair color
- #30 thread
- Horsehair, granulated cork, wool roving or other stuffing material

H. J. The Village Barber. *1778. [England: Pubd. M Darly, 39 Strand, June 1] Photograph. Library of Congress. https://www.loc.gov/item/2006685336/*

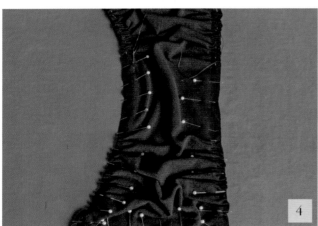

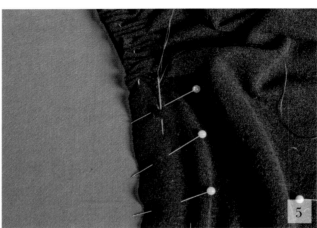

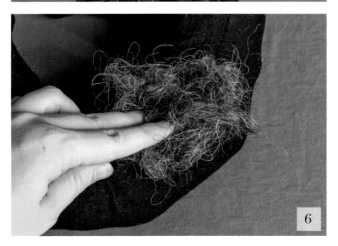

1. Choose a wool knit that is close in color to your hair when powdered. Cut out the pattern, and mark the match points on the outer piece.

2. Pleat the short ends of the outer piece, and pin to hold in place.

3. Stitch a running stitch between the Xs and draw up the thread to gather this section. Repeat for the opposite side.

4. Place the gathered outer piece atop the inner piece, matching the marks and arranging the gathers to ease the fullness between the match points. Pin.

5. Starting a few inches away from the center of one long edge, backstitch all the way around the pieces, stopping a few inches short of where you started.

6. Turn the pieces right side out, then stuff the cushion with horsehair. Be sure to get it into the front nub particularly and use enough stuffing to fully fill out the form but not so much as to stretch your knit too much.

7. Turn in the seam allowance on the opening, pin the edges together and whipstitch them closed from the outside.

8. Now bend the cushion around so the taller back "wings" meet. Stitch these edges together—this is a little tricky. It doesn't have to look nice, but it does have to be strong.

9. You may have some excess here and there that needs a little nip and tuck. We needed to pinch the base of the cushion near the front and whip it closed. Pinch and whipstitch as needed to manipulate the final shape of the cushion.

10. Whew! That was intense, but you did it! Now your late 1770s ski slope cushion is ready to adorn with hair and decorate with all manner of things. Read on to see the resulting hairstyle.

Coiffure
Ski Alpin Hairstyle

Because our model, Jenny, is Chinese, we've done some things differently to accommodate her hair type. While her hair is gorgeous and shiny, it also has a lot of breakage and flyaways. We researched the traditional tools and products used to create the similarly sculptural hair of the geiko and maiko in Japan, and used a comb made of tsuge wood (boxwood) because of how it helps keep the hair smooth. [4] While we did powder and pomade Jenny's hair, we opted for a light powder application, knowing that we were going to add more pomade later. This is a style best suited to long hair, particularly in the back. The ski slope cushion is quite large, so be sure to size it according to your hair length. Additionally, this is a great project with which to use a profusion of false buckles (page 45).

- *Mareschal Pomatum (page 24)*
- *Large powder brush*
- *White Hair Powder (page 28)*
- *Rattail comb*
- *Tsuge wood (boxwood) comb*
- *Alligator hair clips*
- *Ski Slope Hair Cushion (page 119)*
- *Hairpins (short & long)*
- *1 small hair elastic*
- *6–9 fake buckles (page 45)*
- *Bobby or roller pins (optional)*
- *Pouf (page 127)*
- *Feathers (page 132)*

DRESSING THE HAIR OVER THE MOUNTAIN

1. Pomade and powder the hair per page 36, until it is the desired texture. For Jenny's hair, we opted to use the Mareschal Pomatum (page 24) instead of the Common Pomatum (page 20) because of the additional beeswax in it. The extra beeswax helped "stick" her hair together and prevent even more flyaways.

IA   IB

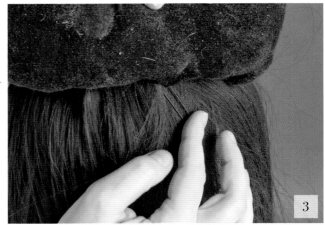

2. Find the apex of the scalp and comb your hair forward. You'll temporarily look like Cousin Itt. [5]

3. Pin the cushion onto the scalp as shown (see page 168 for more instructions) with small hairpins until the cushion is secured to the scalp. It doesn't have to be super tight, as pinning the hair to and around the cushion will help keep it in place.

4. Starting with the front, comb the hair smooth into your hands, keeping tension between your fingers. You might want to run hard pomatum over the hair and comb it through a few times to help keep the hair smooth and together. Keeping the hair taut between the fingers, bring the hair up and over the cushion, into the hole of the ski slope. Pin the hair into place inside the cushion. Don't worry if there is extra hair at the end, we're going to hide that with the pouf.

5. Continue combing, smoothing and pinning around the front half of the cushion. Pin the hair securely so the cushion does not wander around the head. You can pin into the cushion and underneath it, to make sure it is secure and comfortable.

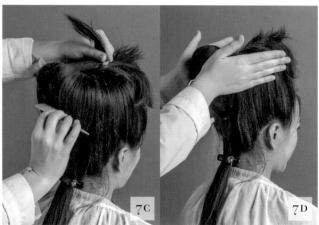

6.   Separate the back of the hair out into two sections: the part that goes into the ski slope and the chignon. Part the hair as shown, so you have enough to do both sections of the hairstyle, and clip the chignon out of the way using alligator hair clips. If you have very fine, thin hair, and are worried your chignon is going to look scrawny, this would be a good time to use your false chignon from page 40.

7.   Finish covering the ski slope per the previous steps, making sure that the hair covers the cushion evenly and that you have no gaps or holes.

8.   At the top of the cushion, coil up the excess hair and tuck it down into the hole, pinning to secure.

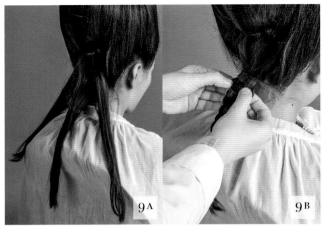

THE CHIGNON AND BUCKLES

9. For Jenny's hair we decided to do a simple braid, but you can do different options (for examples, see pages 79 and 169). Once braided, pull the chignon up to where you like it, and pin it into place. We pulled ours up fairly high, so we could hide the ends of the chignon under the pouf.

10. Buckles are next, and for this hairstyle, you definitely need fake ones (see page 45). This makes life so much easier, and you just can't achieve buckles in this configuration unless you're using fake ones. Pin the lowest buckles in first, using hairpins, roller pins or bobby pins—whatever works best for your hair. Next, arrange the other 2 to 3 buckles on the cushion in your desired arrangement. Pin the buckles directly into the cushion using a couple hairpins. See how easy that was? Hooray!

FINISHING YOUR STYLE

11. Alright, now it's time for the final smoothing. Warm up some mareschal pomatum between your hands and *very lightly* smooth the hair. This is just to get any flyaways to stick to the hair. If you have any particular unruly bits, do your best to carefully pin them in place to the cushion.

12. Now, let's powder the hair. With Jenny's hair type, brushing or fluffing the hair with powder caused her flyaways to break as free as from a Lynyrd Skynyrd song. [6] So, we took a salon-grade dry shampoo product with a jazzy pump applicator, dumped out the dry shampoo and filled it with our eighteenth-century hair powder. Then we used it as a modern bellows and lightly puffed powder all over Jenny's finished 'do. The result was powdered finish with minimal flyaways.

That wasn't so bad, was it? Now it's time to decorate the Coiffure Ski Alpin hair! The flat top of this style makes a perfect stage for the pouf (page 127). Also feel free to stack on your ostrich plumes (page 132). There is no limit to the creativity and fun to be had with this fantastical late 1770s hairstyle.

1770s Pouf

The perfect accessory for your mad, late 1770s hair is a pouf. Claimed by Léonard, hairdresser to Queen Marie Antoinette, as his invention, [7] these confections were thematic, whimsical, political, fun and beautiful. They could have all sorts of insane things on them, such as the stereotypical tall ship, but could also be adorned with figurines, food, birds or just elegant bits of ribbon and flowers. Have fun with decorating your pouf, and look for all the amazing references and variations out there. There's more to a pouf than just a tall ship.

- ¼ yard (25 cm) silk taffeta
- ¼ yard (25 cm) linen
- ¼ yard (25 cm) heavy-weight linen or millinery buckram
- #30 and #50 silk thread to match
- 1 yard (1 m) silk organza
- Ribbon
- Flowers
- Birds

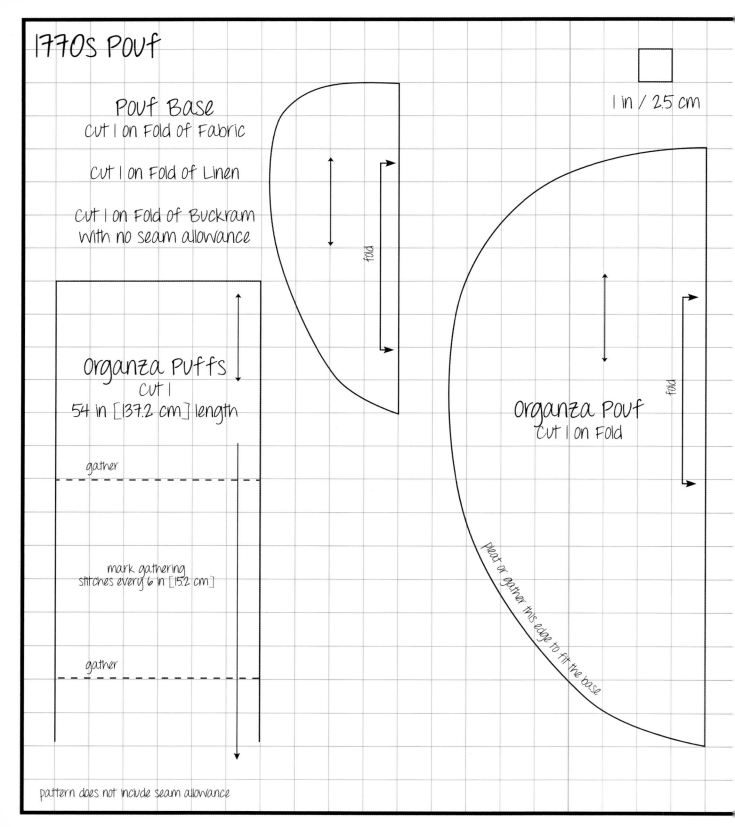

1770s Pouf

Pouf Base
Cut 1 on Fold of Fabric

Cut 1 on Fold of Linen

Cut 1 on Fold of Buckram
with no seam allowance

1 in / 2.5 cm

fold

Organza Puffs
Cut 1
54 in [137.2 cm] length

gather

mark gathering
stitches every 6 in [15.2 cm]

gather

Organza Pouf
Cut 1 on Fold

fold

Pleat or gather this edge to fit the base

pattern does not include seam allowance

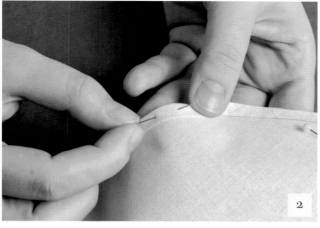

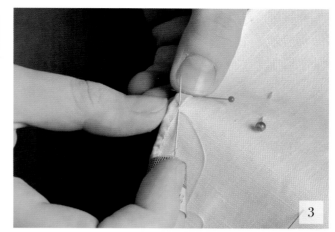

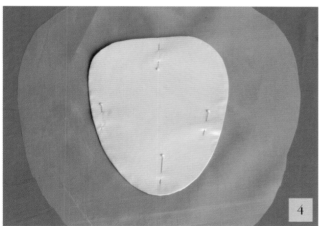

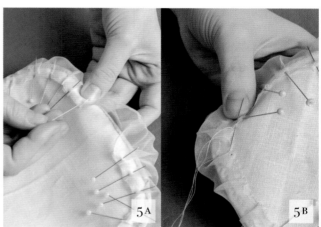

1. Cut out the silk taffeta and linen with ½-inch (1.2-cm) seam allowance and the buckram layer without seam allowance.

2. Pin the buckram to the linen layer, fold and running stitch the linen layer over top the buckram.

3. After the linen is stitched in place, lay the silk taffeta over top the buckram, and pin or baste into place. You will then baste and hem the silk on the underside of the pouf, to finish the pouf base.

4. Next, it's time to start decorating this thing. Take your pouf base pattern, line it up on the silk gauze, and give yourself 4 inches (10 cm) of seam allowance. Cut gauze and baste the raw edge up ¼ inch (6 mm).

5. On the underside of the pouf, pleat and pin the silk gauze to the base. Hem stitch the silk gauze to the linen layer only.

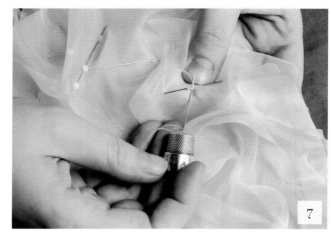

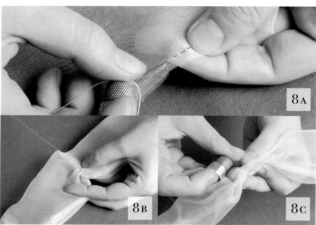

6. Flip back over to the top of the pouf and begin gathering, puffing and pinning the silk gauze to the base. There is no right or wrong way to do this, you just keep pinning it into place until you're satisfied with how it looks. This technique does require you to let those creative juices flow, so just sit back, relax and allow the pinning to take over.

7. Once you've pinned the organza, tack stitch down where all the pins are. You can travel around and tack them all at once, no one is going to see the underside of the pouf, so it's OK that it's a bit messy.

8. Now, we need to start trimming this thing, because no pouf can call itself a true pouf without it looking like a craft store exploded all over it. Starting with the edge puffs, follow the cutting instructions in the pattern, sew the long edges together, right sides together with a running stich. Turn right side out, then sew running stitches at 6-inch (15-cm) increments, gathering up the silk organza and tacking it together.

9. Once you have the row of puffs made, arrange them on the edge of the pouf, pin and tack stitch into place. If you have extra length at the end, just fold the puffs over to create an extra double puff or looped bow.

Decorating Your Pouf

10. Now that you have the base of your pouf, there is no limit of possibility for decoration. This is not a section that we can step-by-step, so our best advice is to open those boxes of ribbons, flowers, feathers, tassels, beads, birds, Lego mini-figs and bows, and go to town. Whatever you choose, opt for lightweight doodads and plenty of them.

11. Arrange and tack stitch your craft store hoard in a pleasing manner. You may choose to tell a story on your pouf, such as the tall ship HMS Acasta battling the Kraken upon the high seas, or splatter your pouf with an aviary of songbirds alighting in a fairy garden of fanciful foliage. Be creative and have fun!

Wearing Your Pouf

12. A fancy, frilly pouf is very easy to wear with the right hairstyle (page 123). Just lay the pouf on the top of your hair and pin it onto the cushion with a few straight pins. Et Voilà! You are now Pouf the Magic Fashion Dragon!

Ostri-rageous DIY Plumes

Ostrich plumes were all the rage in the 1770s. The impressive plumage added even more height to the already tall hairstyles and adorned a variety of hats as well. Of plumes Léonard writes, " . . . there resulted from this combination a curling which could hold three white plumes . . . The Dauphine at this moment has a head seventy-two inches [76.75 inches today] long, from the lower part of the chin to the top of her head-dress." [8]

- Ostrich feathers (plumes, drabs or spads)
- Scissors
- Utility knife
- Seam ripper
- #30 heavy thread in an inconspicuous color
- Dull knife or scissors
- Long hairpin (optional)

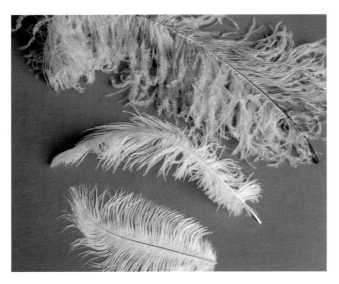

Ostrich feathers are not as straightforward as one would think. There are three different types of feathers you should know about.

PLUMES

We often use "plume" to describe any ostrich feather, but they are specifically the feathers that come from the wing of the bird. They are typically 20 to 30 inches (51 to 76 cm) long, very full and have lovely heavy ends that dip gracefully. They're also the most expensive and hard to find.

DRABS

Ostrich drabs are the most common ostrich feathers found in craft stores. Drabs come from the ostrich's shoulder and are about 10 to 22 inches (25 to 56 cm) long. Compared to plumes, the fibers are much shorter, but are typically full. Drabs make good, affordable hat decoration.

SPADS

Spads come from the tail of the ostrich, are about 18 to 22 inches (46 to 56 cm), and are somewhat thin and spindly. Spads are the least expensive, but are the least attractive—although several spads can be combined and shaped to create a fuller, more drab- or plume-like appearance.

In this tutorial, we will share a few techniques for combining feathers and curling the fronds and strategies for attaching feathers to hats and hair.

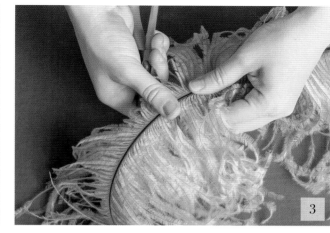

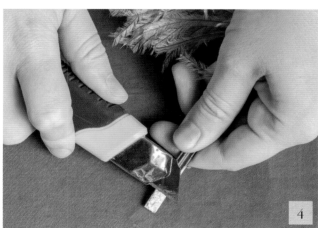

JOINING FEATHERS TOGETHER

1. In this example, we are using plumes, which are very full and floaty. They can be a little tricky to work with but give a splendid result. However, if plumes are not available, joined drabs and spads can also create beautiful plume-like appearance.

2. Prep your feathers by stripping away any fluff from the base of the quills about 3 inches (8 cm) up from the bottom. This will give you something to attach the hairpin to later.

3. The first thing to do is curve the quills. Open a pair of scissors and using one blade, gently crease the quill between your thumb and the blade of the scissors, all along the quill. You don't want to make big creases—just every ½ inch (1.2 cm) or so, press the quill to the blade, all the way down the quill, again and again, until the quill curves how you like. Do this to both feathers before stacking them.

4. Before sewing the feathers together, you may need to skiv the quills toward the base so they lay atop one another nicely. This technique works best with drabs or spads. With a small, sharp knife, carefully carve away the underside of the quill that will lay on top. The interior of quills are hollow, so a correctly skived quill should "nest" with the other nicely.

5. Now you're going to sew the quills together. Starting from the thickest end, very carefully punch a hole through the quill with a seam ripper. Try to avoid splitting the quill, but if this happens don't fret. You only need an anchor point to start the thread.

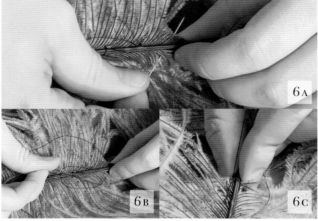

6. Work from the underside of the feathers. With an inconspicuous thread color, pass the needle through the first hole at the base of the stacked quills. Tie the thread securely and wrap it around the quills to bind them together. Make a little knot by passing the needle through the thread loop twice and carry on up the quill. Do not cut the thread, just continue up the quill. Every ½ to 1 inch (1.2 to 2.5 cm) or so, wrap the thread around the two quills and tie off in a little knot before continuing on. When you've reached a few inches from the end, tie off the thread securely and clip close to the knot.

7. Some of the feather fronds will be caught in the thread. Use a small pair of scissors to gently pull them out and back into the desired position.

8. Trim to shape your feather as desired.

CURLING FEATHERS

9. If you are using drabs or spads for your project, you may wish to curl the fibers to give the effect of a plume. Heat curling can give a good result, but is temporary. Instead we will carefully curl the fronds with a dull blade, such as a small pair of not-very-sharp scissors. This a careful operation and requires a delicate hand.

10. Separate each frond individually and place it between the dull edge of the knife and your thumb.

11. Gently and loosely pull your knife and thumb along the frond to curl it. This takes practice—you will break fronds—but you'll have the hang of it in no time.

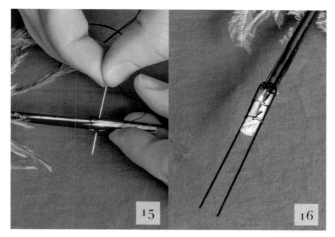

Preparing Feathers for Wearing

12. Plumes are one of those "assets" that can be put on and taken off of hats and hair whenever needed.

13. Secure your feathers to your hat with just a couple loose tacking stitches at the base and further up the quill.

14. Additionally, you can stitch a long hairpin to the bottom of the quill and wear the feathers in your hair. Carefully poke three holes through the bottom of the quill with a seam ripper. Try not to split the quill but don't freak out if you do—it will still hold.

15. Knot your thread and pass it through the top hole in the quill, then wrap around each side of the top of the hairpin in a figure-eight pattern, each time stitching through the hole.

16. Move down the quill to the next hole and repeat with the figure-eight pattern, taking at least two stitches on each side of the hairpin. Continue to the last and bottom-most hole, repeat the stitches, tie off and clip the thread.

17. To sport your new plumes, slide the hairpin into the back of the hair, so the plume is anchored into place. Next, slide hairpins into the hair cushion to secure the plume and keep it vertical. You don't want a droopy ostrich plume that looks like it's trying to take flight off the back of your head! Secure as needed.

CHAPTER 9

Early 1780s

Coiffure Chenille

John Singleton Copley, 1738–1815. Mrs. Robert Hyde. 1778. Yale Center for British Art, Paul Mellon Collection. B1981.25.162.

The first couple years in the 1780s were transitional for ladies' hairstyles. As with all things, there wasn't the immediate abandonment of the large styles of 1778–1779, but a gradual shift that results in some overlap. This is why we have two chapters that cover roughly the same years in the early 1780s. One style is formed over a cushion, and the other is created using crape'd and curled hair (page 159), with a much smaller cushion as support. Looking at the prints from the era, both techniques are contemporary, but the large cushions fall out of favor within the first three years of the decade, thanks to the ebb and flow of fashion and to Léonard Autié cutting Marie Antoinette's hair *à l'enfant*. [1]

However, before Marie Antoinette cut her hair, the tall hairstyles were already deflating and frizzed hair was already coming into fashion. The in-between style in this chapter illustrates the switch to width on the sides and shortening at the top of the hair. It's a great option for women with longer hair that wish to play in the 1780s, and there's even evidence of this hairstyle being worn through the end of the decade in America, as seen in Ralph Earl's portrait of Esther Boardman, 1789. [2]

To accent this early '80s style, we have patterns and instructions for a ruffle-less cap called a toque (page 145) and a very simple hood known as a therese (page 149). Both of these accessories are very easy to make, can be worn together and may be dressed up or down in material choice and trimmings.

As with all transitional styles, the Coiffure Chenille is a little of this and a little of that. There is scope here for self-expression, as seen in myriad fashion plates [3] and paintings from these years. Play around with height, width and texture to find what you love the most.

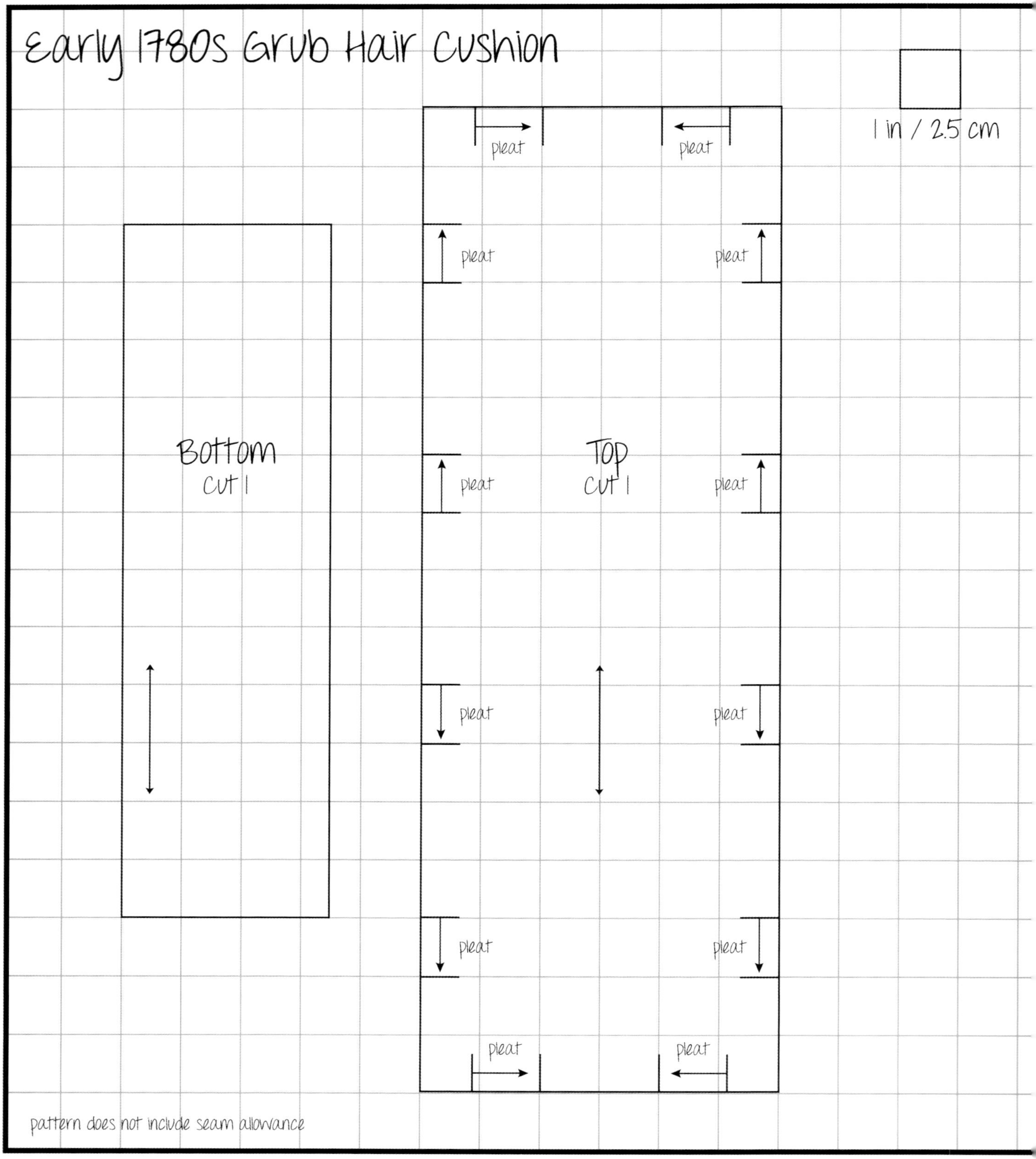

Early 1780s Grub Hair Cushion

1 in / 2.5 cm

Bottom
Cut 1

Top
Cut 1

pleat

pleat

pleat

pleat

pleat

pleat

pleat

pleat

pleat

pleat

pleat

pleat

pattern does not include seam allowance

"Grub" Hair Cushion

Abby's weird sense of humor has dubbed this cushion "The Grub" because of its resemblance to a bug. Even with its unfortunate name, this cushion was designed to give your hair the broader and rounder shape that was in fashion at the beginning of the 1780s without needing to frizz, crepe or curl your hair. As with most of our cushions, it's fairly simple in construction. We strongly suggest that you experiment to figure out what size cushion works best for your hair length and proportion. We stuffed this one with wool roving, and while it's a historic material that's easy to purchase nowadays, we found it to be springy and difficult to pin through. Horsehair or granulated cork are good alternatives.

- *¼ yard (25 cm) wool knit*
- *Matching thread of your choice*
- *Horsehair, wool roving, granulated cork or other filler*

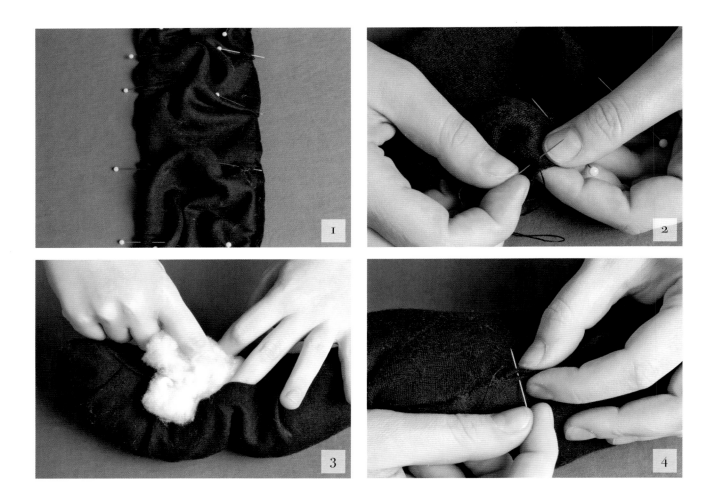

1. Cut out the pieces according to the pattern, and pin together, making small pleats to ease the larger piece onto the smaller.

2. Backstitch the pieces together, leaving a 2- to 3-inch (5- to 8-cm) gap on one side.

3. Turn the cushion right side out and stuff it. You will want it to be full enough to hold its shape, but not so overstuffed that it's rigid. It needs to be able to shape to the head.

4. Fold the raw edges in, and whipstitch the hole closed.

5. The Grub is now prepared for total head domination!

Coiffure Chenille Hairstyle

DIFFICULTY: EASY

HAIR LENGTH: BELOW THE EARS OR LONGER
SHORTER HAIR MAY REQUIRE A SMALLER CUSHION

This simple hairstyle is a great alternative for ladies who want to have the rounded shape of the 1780s, but do not have short enough hair in the front for the crape'd style (page 159). It can be done with straight or curly hair.

With Jasmine, we consulted Cheyney McKnight regarding the use of hair powder for women of color during the eighteenth century. There is evidence for both the use and omittance of powder for freed and enslaved women of African descent during this era (page 157). If you are of African descent, the use of powder is your choice. We also suggest you pay close attention to how we created the buckles and chignon for Jasmine, though, as it is a bit different. If you're not of African descent, please disregard the particular pomade and powder instructions in this chapter, and proceed to pomade/powder your hair as instructed on page 36.

- Common Pomatum (page 20)
- Rattail comb
- Alligator hair clips
- "Grub" Hair Cushion (page 139)
- U-shaped hairpins (short & long)
- Bobby pins
- White Hair Powder (page 28)
- Large powder brush
- Flat iron (optional)
- ½-inch (1.2-cm) curling iron
- Size 50 (25-mm) knitting needle
- Silk thread matching hair color
- Hair tie
- Hard Pomatum (optional, page 22)

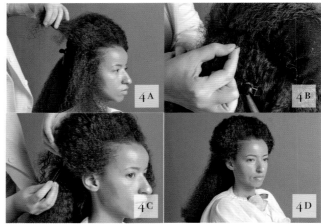

Dress the Front of the Hair

1. Pomade the hair carefully, using a wide-tooth comb to help protect the curls.

2. Part the hair from ear to ear. Clip the back hair out of the way and comb the front hair forward.

3. Place the cushion next to the part, above the ears, and pin into place using the U-shaped hairpins following the technique on page 190.

4. Once the cushion is pinned securely to the head, begin working the hair over the cushion, arranging and pinning into place so the cushion is completely covered.

5. Next, separate the chignon from the buckles. Divide the hair into three parts, the center portion greater in volume for the chignon, and the hanks behind each ear even with one another. Clip the sections out of the way, leaving one side section free for starting the buckles.

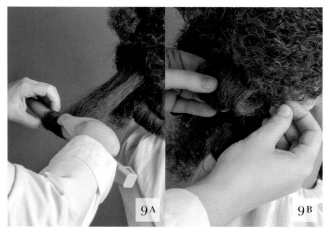

STACKS OF BUCKLES

The treatment of the buckles in this tutorial is specific to our model's hair type. If you have very curly 3C or 4C hair, follow these instructions. However, if you have straight or fine hair, such as 1A or 2A texture, see pages 77 or 100 for making buckles with your own hair.

6.   With Jasmine's hair we had enough to make three buckles on each side. We divided the side section into three 1-inch (2.5-cm)-wide chunks of hair. You can always do more or less depending on how much hair you have. If you're using clip-in buckles, go to town and skip the next part!

7.   Now, this is where things get a little different than what we've done before. We lightly powdered and straightened Jasmine's hair, but did not tease it, to get it to go easily into the buckles. Straighten the hair slightly with a hot flat iron. You do not want the hair stick-straight. This will smooth the curl out just enough to make it easier to curl with the iron, but will still maintain texture.

8.   After the powder and iron, use the ½-inch (1.2-cm)-wide curling iron and curl the end of the hair upwards a couple of inches/centimeters.

9.   Next, roll the hair upwards around the large knitting needle until the roll is at the height and angle that looks best. Slide the knitting needle out, keeping the roll pinched between your fingers. Using two large U-pins, pin the buckle into place, as shown on page 190.

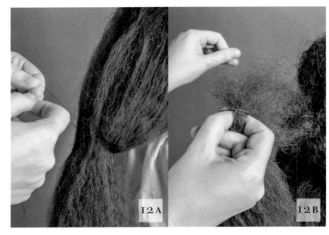

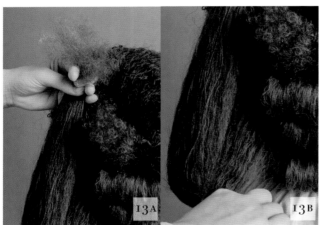

10. Repeat steps 8 and 9 for the next two buckles, but this time, curl them all the way to the head. It is helpful to pin the buckles together for extra security. Repeat on the other side.

THE LOOPED CHIGNON

11. Finally, it's time for the chignon. We repeated the light powdering and straightening in sections, then gently combed all the hair together.

12. Using a heavy silk thread in a color matching the hair, tie the chignon loosely at the base of the neck. Then secure the end of the chignon with a hair tie.

13. Grab the end of the hair and place a rattail comb where you want the fold of the chignon to be. Flip the hair up over the comb, keeping the tension at the fold with the comb.

14. Pin the hair into place with hairpins or bobby pins, making sure you hide the elastic. Arrange any leftover hair with the curls so it blends. We left Jasmine's natural curls in place, but if your hair is straight you can curl the ends under with a curling iron or create buckles (page 77) and arrange into place.

Voilà! You are now ready to throw on a chemise gown and strut your stuff!

Toque

For this project, we set out to find something that was just a little different but still appropriate for the early 1780s. We stumbled upon what the French called a toque, [4] a cross between a turban and a cap. This is a very easy addition to your 1780s headgear repertoire. Incredibly simple and elegant, the toque helps give off that exotic flair that was growing in popularity at the start of the decade.

- *1 yard (1 m) cotton voile or organdy, linen or silk organza*
- *#30 and #50 silk thread*
- *20 inches (51 cm) cording or candlewicking*
- *1 yard (1 m) 1- to 2-inch (2.5- to 5-cm)-wide silk ribbon*
- *Flowers or feathers*

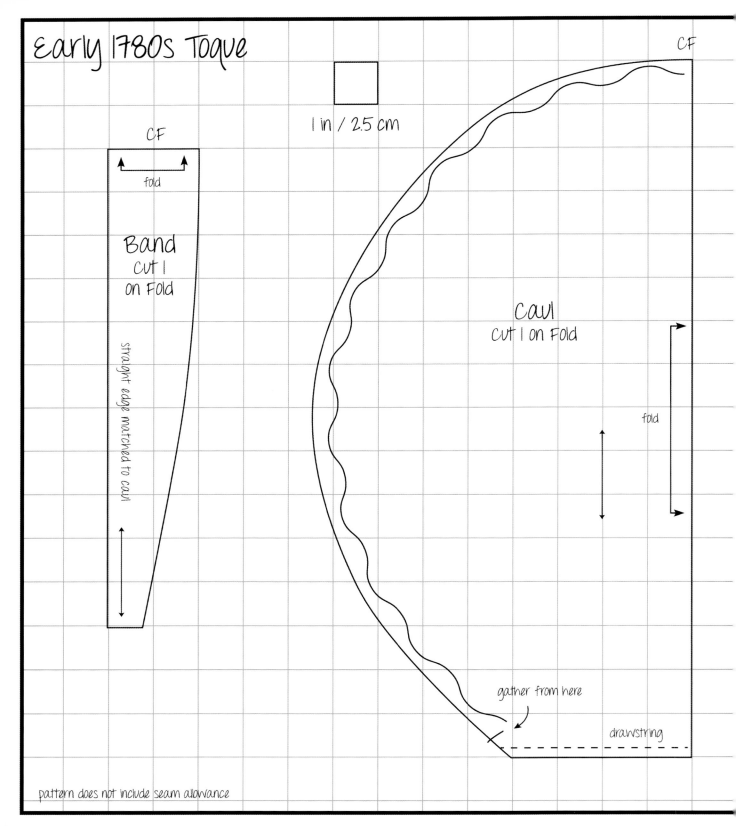

Early 1780s Toque

1 in / 2.5 cm

CF

Band
Cut 1
on Fold

fold

straight edge matched to caul

CF

Caul
Cut 1 on Fold

fold

gather from here

drawstring

pattern does not include seam allowance

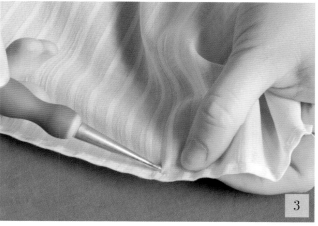

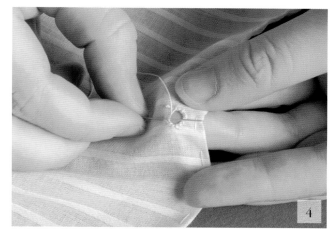

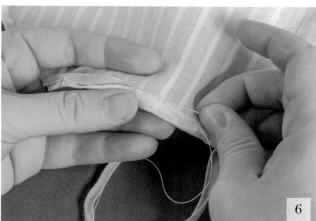

1. Baste the caul edges all the way around ⅛ to ¼ inch (3 to 6 mm), except for the bottom.

2. Baste up the bottom of the caul ¼ inch (6 mm).

3. Fold the caul in half, and using an awl poke a hole just above the bottom basted edge.

4. With heavy silk thread, whip the eyelet open and poke the hole with the awl again to open it back up.

5. Backstitch the cord or candlewicking to each side of the bottom edges of the caul, and pull the tails through the hole.

6. Turn up the bottom edge of the caul over the cord and hem (10 to 12 stitches per inch [2.5 cm]), making sure to not catch the cord.

7. Fold the remaining basted edges up again and hem (10 to 12 stitches per inch [2.5 cm]).

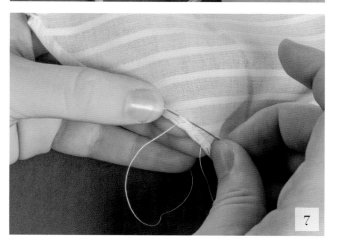

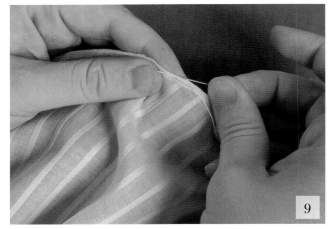

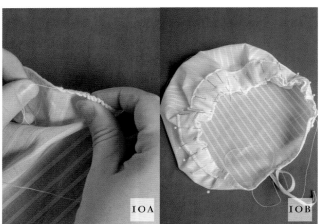

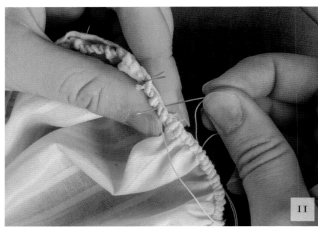

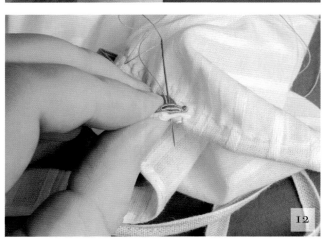

8. On the band piece, baste ⅛ to ¼ inch (3 to 6 mm) and hem (10 to 12 stitches per inch [2.5 cm]). Mark the straight sides of the caul just where the sides begin to curve into the top of the caul. Reference the pattern for these points. Fold the caul in half and pin to mark the halfway point at the top.

9. Whip gather over the hemmed edge of the caul from one mark up to the top center point. Repeat with a new thread on the other side.

10. Working one side at a time, pull the thread to tightly gather up the caul, then match the gathered edge to the straight edge of one half of the band. Arrange evenly and pin. Repeat for the other side.

11. Tightly whipstitch the gathered caul and edge of the band together, catching every little bump. This is tedious, but the result will be splendid. When done, open the two pieces out and gently tug to "pop" the stitches into place. Press it flat if needed.

12. Following fashion plates, we opted for a simple 1-inch (2.5-cm)-wide silk ribbon with some small ostrich feathers (page 132). Tuck the silk ribbon on both ends where the back attaches to the straight bottom of the caul and make a few tacking stitches. Tack stitch the feather to the side.

1780s Therese

Want a simple head covering that can protect you from the sun and add some serious sex appeal and is super simple to make? Meet the Therese, a popular hood worn in the late 1770s and throughout the 1780s. [5] Usually constructed of silk organza or black silk taffeta, these very large hoods are meant to cover some very large hair, a cap and maybe even another hat. When made in organza, the hood may also be pulled over the face to act as a veil. While our pattern is quite large, the proportions are easy to adjust for earlier or later decades.

- *1 yard (1 m) black silk taffeta or ivory/white silk organza*
- *#30 and #50 silk thread to match*
- *2 yards (2 m) ½- to 1-inch (1.2- to 2.5-cm)-wide silk ribbon*

1. Cut out the pattern accordingly, keeping in mind that you will want to make good use of your selvage. For our version, we used the selvage edge for the front of the hood. If you are not using a selvage for the front of your Therese, baste and hem the front edges using ¼-inch (6-mm) folds.

2. Offset the back seam by ¼ inch (6 mm) and pin the length of the seam according to the pattern. Mantua maker's seam the back seam of the hood (page 13).

1780s Therese

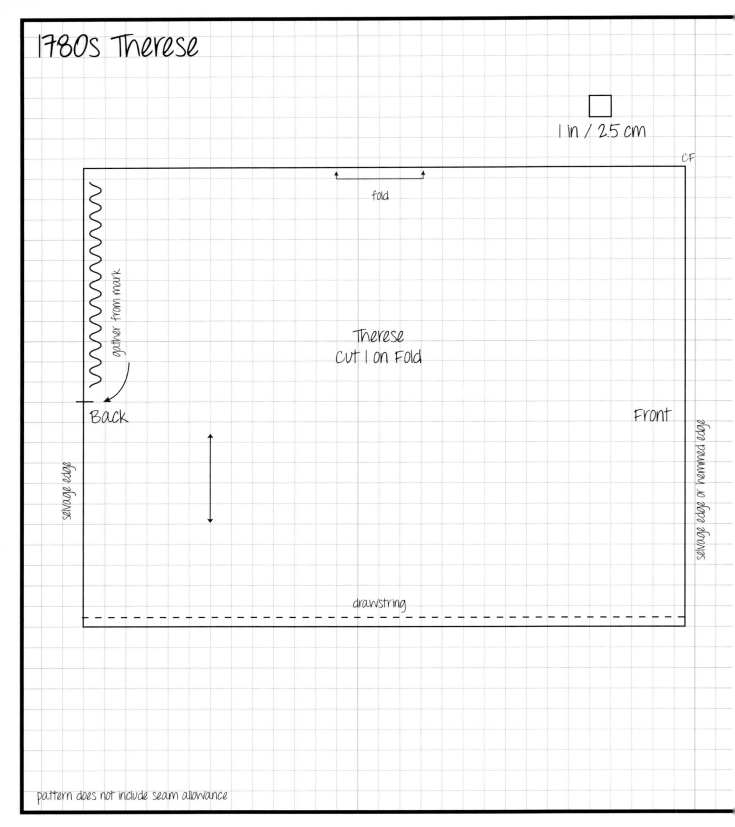

1 in / 2.5 cm

CF

fold

gather from mark

Therese
Cut 1 on Fold

Back

Front

salvage edge

salvage edge or hemmed edge

drawstring

pattern does not include seam allowance

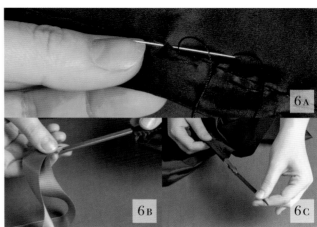

3. Fold, baste and hem the open top of the back of the hood.

4. Using the #30 thread, sew gathering stitches around the opening at the back of the hood.

5. Pull the gathers up to completely enclose the back of the hood. Using #30 thread, tack the opening closed.

6. Next, fold up and baste the bottom of the hood ½ inch (1.2 cm), then fold up another 1 inch (2.5 cm) and hem. Run your ribbon through the casing.

7. Yay! Your massive hood of glamour doom is ready! If it's particularly windy, we suggest securing it with a small hat pin to your hair. Trust us, this parachute-like hood is a choking hazard with a brisk walk.

PART 3

Let's Get Frizzical, Frizzical!

In the 1780s, headdress transitioned from very tall and sculptural to wide, fluffy and a little wild. The transition between these two quite different looks can be seen in the Coiffure Chenille (page 141), which coexisted with the crape'd style (page 159) in the early 1780s. Eventually the fluff wins out: long hair goes out and a new haircut comes in, lopping off the length at the crown but leaving the long locks in the back.

What we incorrectly call a "hedgehog" hairstyle [1] today was in the 1780s just called a frizzed hairstyle or, in French, a *coëffure a l'enfant*, or child's hairstyle. The *Gallerie des Modes* published multiple fashion plates illustrating and describing this style in 1780,[2] though Léonard, hairdresser to Marie Antoinette, claims he invented it in 1781 [3] after the birth of the Queen's second child. Though his claims may be simply self-aggrandizement, Léonard nevertheless further popularized the *à l'enfant* and its myriad creatively named offshoots, [4] all pomaded, powdered, curled, coiffed, frizzed, fluffed and decorated in the latest fashion.

Adélaïde Labille-Guiard. Madame Élisabeth de France (1764–1794), *c. 1787. The Metropolitan Museum of Art. 2007.441.*

So popular and easy-to-keep were the full and frizzy styles that they persisted in fashion for a good fifteen years, changing only subtly in shape of cushion or treatment of the chignon. However, by the mid-1790s, fashion took another course with hairstyles relaxing into more natural, loose and un-powdered looks. So marks the end of the eighteenth century and the reign of high and mighty coiffure.

The 1780s, much like the 1980s, was all about the frizzy curl. How these curls were achieved and the resulting shape and effect of the hairstyle varied. In this part, we show you four methods for curling your hair for creating any of the 1780s and early 1790s styles.

Crape-ing – This method of curling the hair relies on heat, patience and courage. Recommended for chin-length hair or shorter, the resulting curl is a tight spiral frizz that creates a 3 or 4C effect. This method is time-consuming but can be set once and worn over a period of time, [5] with minimal overnight maintenance. It is a good one to do the day before and filet [6] for a weekend-long event. To learn more about the fascinating history of crape-ing and how to do it, flip to page 159.

Pomade Wet-Set – Wet-set curling achieves long-lasting, tight curls overnight. Though this method is not historically accurate for the eighteenth century, it is a good one for event days where time is short in the morning. The effect achieved is the same as for heat-set papillote curls, but depending on your hair, the curls may hold tighter and for longer. The key is to use very small curlers, rags or other methods, even straws! [7] Pin curls are typically not tight enough. The downside is in having to put the work in the night before and then sleep on the curlers or rag rollers. To see the pomade wet-set in action, turn to page 188.

Papillote Heat-Set – The term *papillote* references curls folded in parchment and heat-set with a purpose-made iron. [8] The method is used for both crape-ing and curling and relies on the combination of pomade and heat to set the curls. This method is very effective and produces surprisingly long-lasting curl, but takes quite a long time to achieve. Learn about papillote curling on page 210.

Curling Iron Heat-Set – Pomaded hair may also be heat-set using a curling iron. We recommend a ½-inch (1.2-cm) barrel for nice tight curls, and clipping the curls into place to allow them to cool and the pomade to reset. The result will be the same as papillote curls but with a much shorter styling time, as this method combines the historical concept of heat-setting with the modern convenience of hair clips.

CHAPTER 10

1780–1783

Coiffure Friseur

In this chapter, we introduce you to "crape-ing," an original hair curling technique that will literally make your hair stand on end. Hold on to your combs; it's about to get wild.

Crape-ing the hair was done through at least the last half of the eighteenth century. It is described by Legros in *L'Art de la Coëffure des Dames Françoises* in 1768 and features heavily in the illustrations in this book. [1] Crape'd hair falls out of fashion in the 1770s but returns with a vengeance in the early 1780s when the large, frizzy hairstyles come into fashion. You know that infamous portrait of Marie Antoinette in the chemise gown? [2] Yeah, that's crape'd hair she's rockin'. Turn to page 159 for our step-by-step guide to achieving this technique.

Adélaïde Labille-Guiard. Self-Portrait with Two Pupils, Marie Gabrielle Capet (1761–1818) and Marie Marguerite Carreaux de Rosemond (died 1788). *1785. The Metropolitan Museum of Art. 53.225.5*

Also in this chapter, we demonstrate two pieces of large and impressive millinery to pair with your epically crape-d 'do. The Bonnet à la Jeannot cap is crisp and complex, featuring fashionable lappets in just one of many configurations popular during this period. Additionally, the black silk bonnet is both a statement piece and very useful hat to shield the eyes at outdoor events.

We hope you enjoy this fascinating period of eighteenth-century hair history. Experiment with the technique and patterns, and have fun!

A Word on African Hair in Eighteenth-Century Europe and the Colonies
by Cheyney Mcknight

Cheyney McKnight.
Photo by Lindsey Mulholland.

Eighteenth-century Europeans viewed hair as an indicator of a person's character. Smooth European tresses were considered to be ordered, modest and civilized. African hair was referred to as "wool," as some did not consider it to be hair, but wool like an animal. [3] The tightly coiled, kinky hair of Africans was looked upon as wild, disordered and uncivilized. [4]

Europeans did not—or did not want to—see that the styling of hair did indeed play an important role in communicating something about the self among and between the different groups living in West Africa. One's hair could indicate occasion, marital status, religion, familial affiliation, economic status, ethnic group, age, occupation or region. [5] West Africa had a complex system of customs and traditions that differ across hundreds of ethnic groups, and hairstyle was usually the first clue to identifying a people.

Like other bodily customs, hair varies throughout West Africa. [6] Shaved portions, cut designs, cornrows, twists, braids, dreadlocks, afros and threading are skilled techniques that were passed down through the generations. Time is dedicated daily, weekly or during ceremonies to communally tend to hair. Most transitions in life were marked by a ceremonial change in hair. Among the Wolof people a girl's haircut would be transitioned into the longer more elaborate style of a woman's when she attained womanhood. [7]

These varied traditions were brought over in the bellies of slave ships and trading vessels, through the memories of the human cargo to England and North America.

When the first Africans were forcibly brought to Europe and North America in the sixteenth and seventeenth centuries, they forged new traditions and rituals that connected diverse West African traditions with their new homes and status. Upon their arrival, they gradually learned how to adapt their grooming rituals to the plants, barks, roots and flowers present in these new worlds. For example, skin moisturizer and hair sealant made from shea butter processed from the shea tree throughout West Africa were replaced with animal fats. [8] The ornamental long wide-tooth picks that were used for combing springy, tightly coiled hair were remade in Europe and America using local woods and later replaced almost entirely with implements used for carding wool. [9]

However, there was no local resource that could be substituted for the time needed to create, maintain or change complex West African hairstyles. Without the time (and likely energy after long days of forced labor), enslaved Africans often wore their hair shorn, in less elaborate twists, threads, cornrows or braids, in European hairstyles, in caps and headwraps. Although in middling and gentry households the bodies of the enslaved represented a fashionable extension of the owner, the physical control over the enslaved African body seldom extended to the hair itself. [10] Control over the length of hair and head coverings seems to have been exerted more on the enslaved whose roles put them in more direct contact with guests in middling and gentry households.

Print made by Agostino Brunias, 1728–1796. A Negroes Dance in the Island of Dominica. *1779. Yale Center for British Art, Paul Mellon Collection. B1981.25.1958.*

Gradually Africans in Europe and Colonial America started appropriating European styles and grooming products. Some beauty aids used by Europeans to achieve height and volume, such as hair cushions or pomades, were not always used by those of African descent, who did not need them to achieve the elaborate high hair shapes popular during the third quarter of the eighteenth century. Rather ironically, these expensive hairstyles could be more easily and cheaply achieved by Africans because of the moldability and structure of tightly coiled hair. Records show that both free and enslaved Africans used hair powder, but often made pointed efforts to retain the natural texture of their hair as a form of passive resistance to white control over their bodies and beauty standards. [11]

The hairstyles from the 1780s through the 1790s involved achieving a frizzy, rounded look surrounding the face, not at all dissimilar from an afro. This fashion required white women to twist and heat-set their hair to achieve a kinky, voluminous hairstyle similar to African hair textures. While this texture on African women was seen as an indicator of low moral control, European white women appropriated it as early as the 1750s. Tobias Smollett in 1766 described French women as:

"[. . .] *covered with a vast load of false hair, which is Frizzled on the forehead, so as exactly to resemble the wooly heads of the Guinea negroes.*" [12]

By the 1780s, English and European white women wearing the fashionably crape'd and frizzed hairstyles did not appear to receive this same moral judgment for their artificially textured hair. Rather, being able to wear this style was seen as an indicator of wealth because of the amount of time and product that went into its creation. Despite the common verbal connection and moral connotation made between "wool" and African-textured hair, the popularity of this style makes it evident that it was not the texture of the hair, but the color of one's skin, that was important. Scholarship has yet to identify a recognition of this irony during the time, but this suggests how much more work there is to be done on this history of African hair and hairstyles in North America.

Folding Papillote Papers

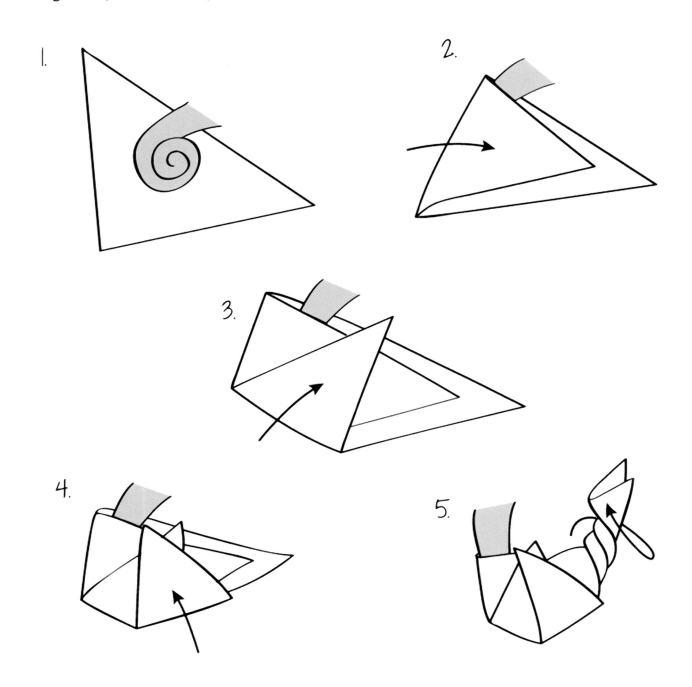

1.

2.

3.

4.

5.

Crape Expectations: How to Crape Your Hair

DIFFICULTY: DIFFICULT

RECOMMENDED HAIR LENGTH: CHIN-LENGTH OR SHORTER ONLY

The term "crape hair" comes from crape fabric, a textile made from yarn that has been twisted onto itself resulting in a kinky texture. [13] Crape-ing completely changes the texture of the hair, making it easy to achieve the voluminous hairstyles so popular in the early 1780s. This long-lasting frizz allowed the hair to be reset only periodically to keep the curl looking fresh and the scalp healthy. David Ritchie explains,

"[. . .] it may be dressed so firm as to stay in dress for some months; but all hair dress'd should be new pinned up once a week at least, to prevent a disagreeable dandriffe from contracting at the roots, occasioned by the want of air; but while it stays in dress it ought to have a little pomatum and powder every day, to give it a new gloss." [14]

James Stewart's *Plocacosmo: or the Whole Art of Hair Dressing &c.* from 1782 has been invaluable in cracking this unique eighteenth-century technique. [15]

You may also try this technique on your toupee hairpiece and never have to deal with it again, shortening your styling time significantly the morning of your event.

- *Common Pomatum (page 20) or Mareschal Pomatum (page 24)*
- *Large powder brush*
- *White Hair Powder (page 28)*
- *Rattail comb*
- *Alligator hair clips*
- *Papillote Papers (page 31)*
- *Flat iron*
- *Teasing comb and pick*

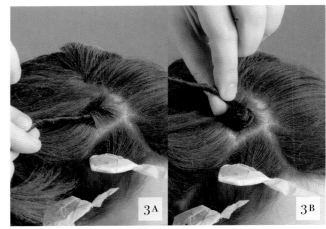

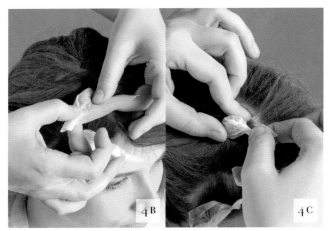

1.   Pomade and powder your hair as seen on page 36.

2.   Part the hair so it will be easy to work with. Most styles will call for the hair behind the ears forward. Work in ½- to 1-inch (1.2- to 2.5-cm) sections of hair, rubbing some common pomatum into the section you're working on.

3.   Begin twisting the hair around itself until it wants to coil on top of itself. You will be twisting the hair incredibly tight when you do this. Work the twisted hair into a little twisted nub on the head. Be careful while doing this that you don't create a massive knot of hair.

4.   Wrap the nub of hair into the tissue paper according to the diagram on page 158 so it's all held together.

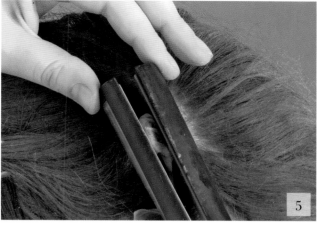

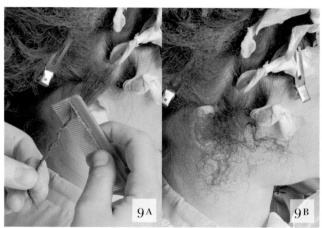

5. Apply the flat iron to the hair (on the hottest setting) for 20 to 45 seconds.

6. Continue steps 1 through 4 until all of the hair you're working with is crape'd. Then revisit all papers with the flat iron one more time.

7. Allow the hair to cool in the papers, and gird your loins for the next steps.

8. Working one paper at a time, remove the paper from the crape'd curl, and find the end of the hair. Carefully untwist the hair from its nub and continue to untwist it while holding on to the end of the hair. If you let go of the hair too soon it can twist and knot onto itself and obviously no one we know wants a Meg March [16] level bald spot. Also, our imaginary lawyers require us to remind you that any damaged hair from a bad crape is not the responsibility of the authors.

9. When you've untwisted the hair enough that a comb can be pulled through, go ahead and comb that crape'd piece out to see what it does (it goes POOF!). Repeat these steps for each papered section.

10. Now it's time to tease and comb the crape'd hair. If you have short hair, you might not need to tease at all, but if your hair is below the ears, you're going to have to tease the hair enough to make it sculpt-y and even.

11. This is the basic how-to of crape-ing hair. The final hairstyle will involve different techniques, but this section has, hopefully, explained the basics of this method.

1780 – 1783 Spearhead Hair Cushion

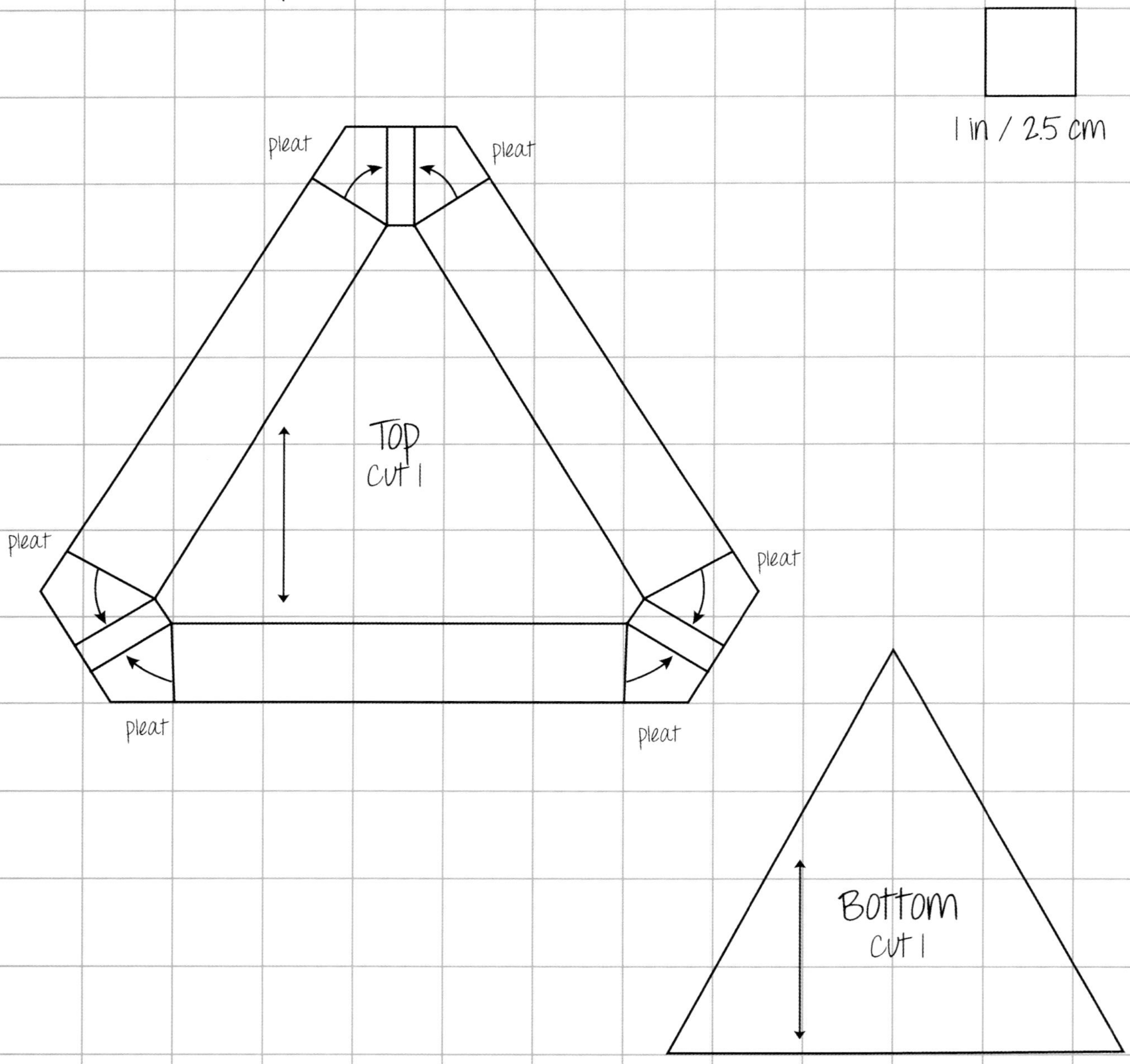

1 in / 2.5 cm

pleat   pleat

TOP
CUT 1

pleat   pleat

pleat   pleat

pleat   pleat

Bottom
CUT 1

pattern does not include seam allowance

Spearhead Hair Cushion

This shape of this hair cushion comes from the tutorials found in *Plocacosmos* [17] and the print found in *Encyclopédie Méthodique, ou par Ordre de Matières; par une Société de Gens de Lettres, de Savans et d'Artistes.* [18] It's not really meant to shape the hair too much, but help keep it up and also gives you something to pin your hats or caps on to.

- *1 foot (30 cm) square wool knit that matches the hair color*
- *#30 silk thread*
- *Cork, horsehair, wool roving or other stuffing material*

1. Cut out the pieces according to the pattern.

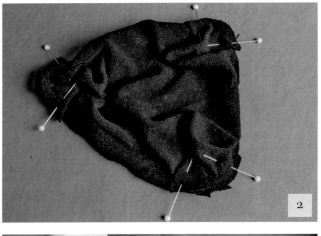

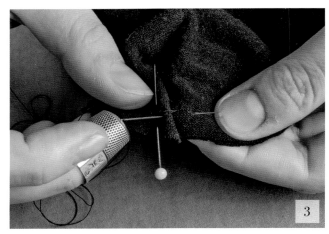

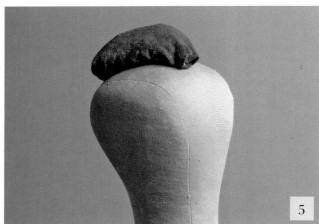

2.　Pin the small pleats of the top piece.

3.　With right sides together, pin and stitch the top triangle to the bottom triangle using a backstitch. Leave a 1-inch (2.5-cm) hole in the middle of one side.

4.　Turn the pieces right side out, then stuff the cushion with your filler of choice (we used cork), and whip the opening closed.

5.　It may not look like much, but this little triangle is enough to keep your hair fashionably full and prevent your hat or bonnet from crushing it flat. Turn to page 165 to see this cushion in use.

Coiffure Friseur Hairstyle

We're going to be really honest about this hairstyle: we did this so you don't have to. For those with straight hair, crape-ing is difficult to do and takes forever, but is a fascinating technique and makes for an engaging public interpretation or demonstration. This method also produces a very long-lasting style, a counterpoint to the time it takes to achieve.

For this hairstyle, we followed the basic instructions in one of our favorite hairdressing manuals, *Plocacosmos*, [19] combined with images from *Encyclopédie Méthodique* [20]. Ideally, you'll want a layered bob between ear-length and chin-length in the front. Bangs or layers in front are splendid, and extra length in back will help as well. What you lack in length can be made up with your hairpieces, particularly in the back. We recommend the use of your chignon hairpiece and false buckles to finish the back of this style, unless you have the mother of all rock-and-roll mullets. Pixie cuts with short sides will achieve excellent results with the toupee hairpiece in addition to the chignon and false buckles. [21] For other hair types: If you have hair type 4A, 4B or 4C (page 15), you are in luck! This hairstyle is perfect for you! Skip the crape-ing and curling sections in this tutorial and go right to fixing the hair around the cushion. You may not need to tease the hair, but as always, you know your hair texture best.

- Mareschal Pomatum (page 24) or Common Pomatum (page 20)
- Large powder brush
- White Hair Powder (page 28) or Mareschal Powder (page 30)
- Alligator hair clips
- Rattail comb
- ½-inch (1.2-cm) curling iron
- Tissue paper
- Flat iron

- Teasing comb with pick
- Hard Pomatum (page 22)
- Spearhead Hair Cushion (page 163)
- Assortment of hairpins and roller pins
- Size 15 (10-mm) knitting needle
- Clip-in chignon (if needed)
- Small hair elastics
- Clip-in buckles/curls (if needed)

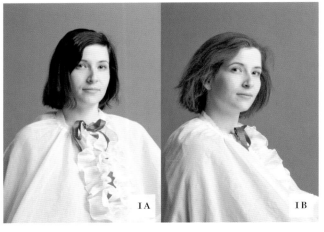

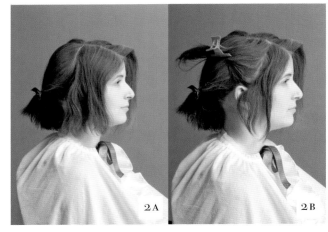

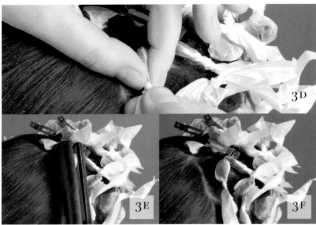

CRAPE-ING AND CURLING THE FRONT

1. Pomade and powder the hair as we've shown before (page 36). For this look we used our mareschal pomatum, but common pomatum works just as well.

2. Part the hair from ear to ear, and clip the back of the hair to keep it out of the way. Part the front of the hair into 3 to 4 rows from ear to ear.

3. The front 2 to 3 rows will be crape'd (see page 159). The final row of hair will be put into papillote curls. Refer to page 210 for that tutorial.

4. Once everything is papered up, hit it all again with your flat iron for good measure, and allow the hair to cool completely.

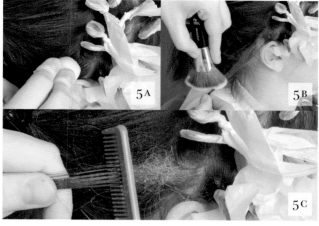

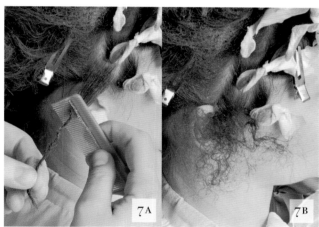

5.   Now it's time for the scary part. Starting from the back, take out your papillote curls one at a time, working each curl separately as you go. Rub some pomatum and powder onto the hair, and begin teasing the hair at the root. You're going to tease a lot of the hair so it stands up on its own. Rub hard pomade into the roots if the hair is having trouble standing up on its own.

6.   Blend the separate curls with your pick to hide any parting of the hair.

7.   Once the back row of curls is prepped, move on to the crape'd section. Work the rows together, two at a time, to blend the front more easily. Refer to page 161 for how to take the crape'd hair out of the papers.

8.   Continue taking the hair from the papers and teasing/working the hair together so the hair doesn't have any visible parting.

9. After you've teased, powdered, pomaded and teased the hair some more, add the triangular cushion. Part the frizzed hair to make room, then situate the cushion on the center of the head, with the front point about 1 inch (2.5 cm) back from the hairline. Secure the cushion into place with long hairpins at each point. A good way to do this is to stick the pin straight down through the cushion, twist it around to catch the hair and push the points back up into the cushion. This will keep the cushion secure and protect the scalp from naughty pin ends.

10. Arrange the hair around the cushion, and pin into place with hairpins. Pin the side sections first, then very gently pin the front to keep it up and back from the forehead.

11. Working the papillote-curled hair over a knitting needle will create the shell curls needed to cover the top of the cushion. Do a few here and there, or a whole long row if you're feeling sassy. If the hair is a bit too short to cover the back of the cushion, don't fret! We'll cover the gap later with the chignon, feathers, flowers or cap.

12. Continue to tease, fluff and pin the front of the hair into position.

The Chignon and Buckles

13. Divide the back of the hair into three sections, then pin curl the central section against the head. This will be covered by the chignon extensions in the next step.

14. Clip in your long extensions. If they are not already pom'd and pow'd, do this now.

15. Braid the hair and secure with a small elastic. "Pancake" the braid out to make it wider and fuller in appearance by pinching and separating out the hairs in the strands.

16. Depending on your preference, you can secure the chignon under or above the top of itself. We pinned ours under to hide the ends, and to make sure the loop hung low enough on the neck. Secure with hairpins or bobby pins.

17. Now, let's move on to the buckles. Part the hair behind the ear so you have a 3- to 4-inch (8- to 10-cm)-wide section to curl, but only about a ½ inch (1.2 cm) thick. Work pomatum and powder into the section and tease the hair from root to end until it can stand out away from the head. (Yes, this is hilarious, we still giggle every time!) [22]

18. With a ½-inch (1.2-cm) curling iron, curl the ends of the buckles upwards, hold until you can feel the heat through the hair, then release.

19. Next, roll the hair over the needle in the same direction, smoothing with a comb as you go, until you reach the head.

20. Carefully remove the knitting needle from the curl and pin inside the curl from each side using two large U-shaped hairpins, weaving in and out of the hair on the scalp-side of the curl. See page 190 for an illustration.

21. Repeat the above steps for the lower buckle. If you would like this to be a "hanging buckle," roll the hair up only part of the way, slide the knitting needle out, and pin inside the curl from both sides.

22. Repeat these steps on the other side of the head. Try your best to make both sides even!

23. Now for that final dusting of powder. We used Mareschal (page 30), but you can use just white powder if you'd like.

Add some ribbons, flowers and feathers as needed to cover up any unsavory bits. Or just put on your super cute cap or bonnet, and you're all set for a day at the market!

"Bonnet à la Jeannot" Cap

This cap is based on several illustrations in the *Gallerie des Modes* [23] between 1776 and 1785 as well as Adélaïde Labille-Guiard's 1785 self-portrait, [24] all depicting large, wide caps with various styles of ruffles topped with lappets, long rectangular pieces of lace or fabric matching the cap, applied in several creative ways. Our cap— called in French the *Bonnet à la Jeannot* in one 1783 fashion plate, [25] but whimsically re-named with every new publication—displays the lappets in a popular way, looped at the sides and pinned or stitched at the top. Placement, width and length of the lappets leaves room for personal preference, or you may omit them altogether.

For this project, we have used fine cotton organdy, a permanently-sized, lightweight, semi-sheer fabric with a stiff hand. Organdy is a wonderful, accurate material with which to make big caps, but feel free to use silk organza, well-starched cotton voile or handkerchief-weight linen for different effects.

- *1 yard (1 m) fine cotton organdy, silk organza, cotton voile or fine linen*
- *Silk or cotton thread (#30 for gathers & seams and #50 for hems)*
- *20 inch (51 cm) ¼-inch (6-mm)-wide fine cotton tape or candlewicking*

ALL THE RUFFLES

1. Turn up and narrow hem the band and the caul ruffle, with a fine ¼-inch (6-mm) hem. Hem stitch in place with a minimum of 12 stitches per inch (2.5 cm).

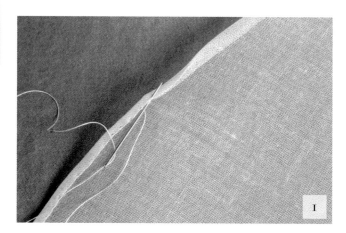

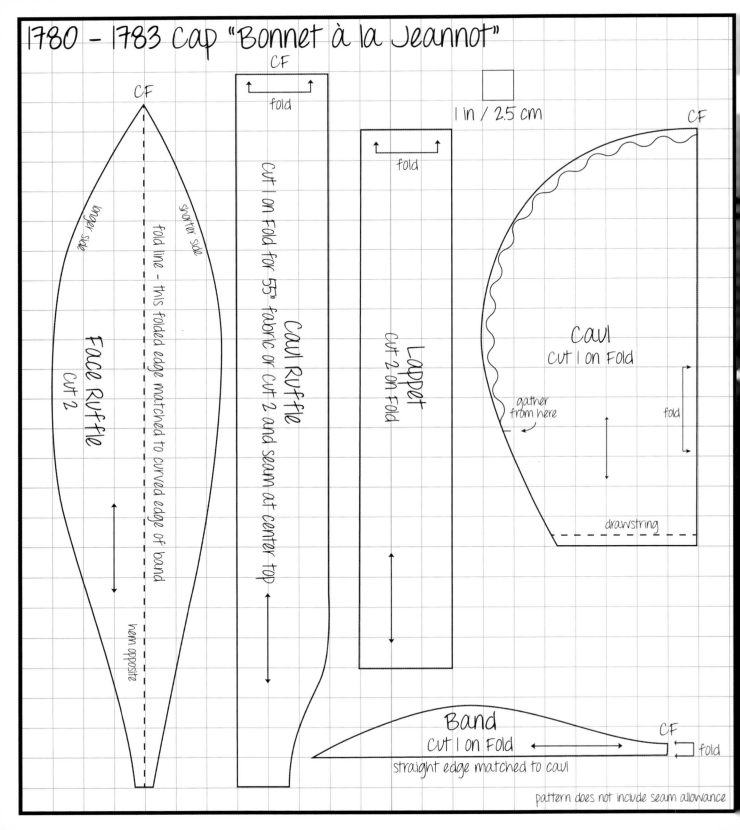

1780 – 1783 Cap "Bonnet à la Jeannot"

CF

fold

1 in / 2.5 cm

CF

Face Ruffle
Cut 2

longer side

shorter side

fold line – this folded edge matched to curved edge of band

hem opposite

Caul Ruffle
Cut 1 on Fold for 55" fabric or cut 2 and seam at center top

fold

Lappet
Cut 2 on Fold

Caul
Cut 1 on Fold

gather from here

fold

drawstring

Band
Cut 1 on Fold

CF

fold

straight edge matched to caul

pattern does not include seam allowance

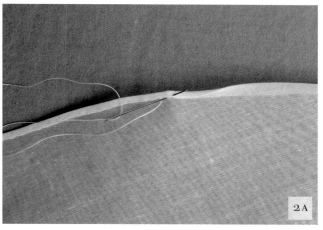

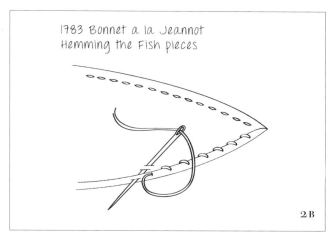

1783 Bonnet a la Jeannot
Hemming the Fish pieces

2 A

2 B

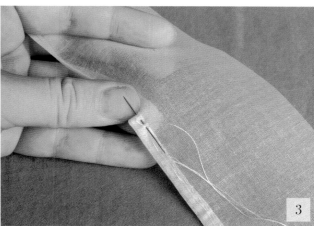

3

4

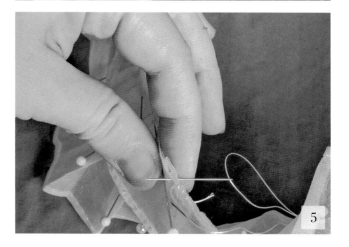

5

2.   On the face ruffle pieces, narrow hem each long side of the "fish" opposite of each other. Turn the shorter side under and the longer side up so that when the fish is folded in half along the fold line, the hems both turn under the same direction.

3.   Turn up, baste and hem all edges of the lappets, creating a ½-inch (1.2-cm)-wide hem. This is a decorative choice and looks nice on sheer and semi-sheer fabrics.

4.   Pleat up the caul ruffle to fit half of the band, and pin into place. Be sure you've matched the caul ruffle with the straight edge of the band.

5.   Right sides together, whipstitch the caul ruffle to the band, catching in all the layers of the pleats. Repeat this for the other side. Do not open out the pieces yet.

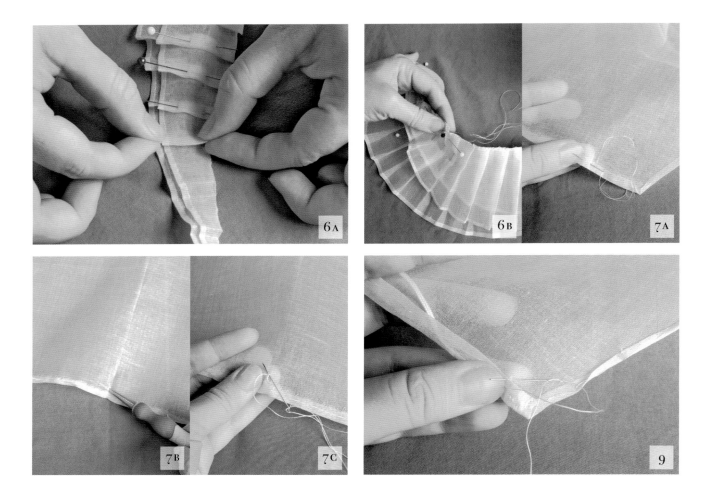

6. Fold the face ruffle pieces in half along the fold line, then pleat each "fish" to match the curved edges of the band. Working one side at a time, pin the pleated fish to the band right sides together. Whipstitch over the edges, then open the two pieces out flat, gently tugging them apart to "pop" the stitches into place.

The Caul

7. Turn up ¼ inch (6 mm) on all edges of the caul and baste. Fold the caul piece in half lengthwise to find the center and mark just above the basted seam at the bottom of the caul. Pierce the fabric with an awl at this mark, then stitch the eyelet open with heavy waxed thread (#30). When complete, poke with the awl again to further open and shape the eyelet.

8. Atop the turned and basted seam allowance on the bottom flat edge, secure the narrow tape to the base of the caul piece on each end using a few strong backstitches. Pull the excess tape through the eyelet, using an awl or pin to push it through.

9. Fold up the straight bottom edge of the caul piece over the tape. Finely hem, making sure not to catch the tape in the stitches.

10. Continue to hem the rest of the caul using the fine hem method shown on page 65.

11. Following the pattern, mark where the gathering should start on each side of the caul with a pin. Then fold the caul in half lengthwise to find the top center point and also mark it with a pin.

12. Loosely whip over the curved hemmed edge of the caul from one side to the center point, about 4 to 6 stitches per inch (2.5 cm). Pull up this thread to gather half of the caul to approximately half the length of the band. Repeat for the other side of the caul.

13. Pin the caul to the band and caul ruffle, right sides together, matching the center marks. Whipstitch the two pieces together, catching every "bump" of the gathers. When complete, open out the seam, gently tugging the pieces to "pop" the stitches into place.

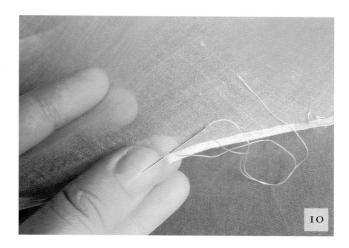

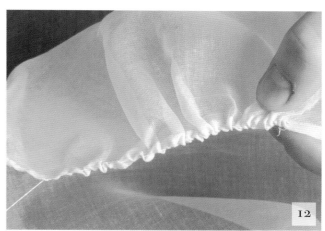

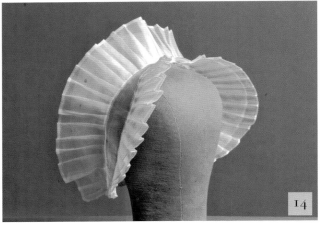

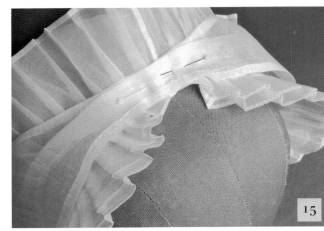

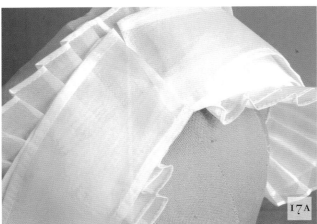

14. If needed, smooth the caul ruffle upwards over the caul, and loosely tack it down at every pleat to keep the ruffle from flopping forward. Iron the seams so everything lays smoothly and starch as needed.

FOR THE LOVE OF LAPPETS

15. Pleat one short end of each lappet at the center-front-top of the cap band, taking a tuck toward the back of the cap to fit the narrow part of the band. Stitch in place with a few tacking stitches.

16. Allow the lappets to loop down around the ears, pinning or tack stitching inside the loop to lightly hold this portion in place. Make sure both sides of the lappets are evenly placed for a symmetrical appearance when worn.

17. Loop each lappet back up to the center-front-top of the cap band, folding the lappet back on itself and allowing the loose ends to fly. Here you will pin or tack stitch the lappets at an angle to help them fly back rather than fall in your face constantly. This angle will be different for everyone, so experiment before making your final stitches. If you need more security with the tails of your lappets, you may wish to discreetly pin or tack stitch in other places on the cap to keep them in place.

1780s Black Silk Bonnet

Bonnets like these were worn for a large chunk of the last half of the eighteenth century, with variations on brim and caul shapes and sizes. Worn by working-class and fashionable women alike, these bonnets are a great option to have in your closet whenever you need a "goes with anything" piece to wear to all sorts of events. You'll notice that we've chosen to make this bonnet out of black silk taffeta. While other colors do appear in records and images, [26] the most common is black. [27] For fabrics, we recommend a heavy black silk taffeta, but a lighter weight interlined with cotton organdy, as we've done in this tutorial, will also work, as will worsted wool for a more working-class impression. [28]

- *1 yard (1 m) black silk taffeta*
- *¼ yard (25 cm) cotton organdy interlining (optional)*
- *Silk thread (#50 for hemming and #30 for construction)*
- *2 feet (61 cm) ½-inch (1.2-cm)-wide black silk ribbon*
- *1 piece heavy but flexible poster board*
- *Acrylic finishing spray*

THE CAUL

1. Because our taffeta had a light hand, we interlined the caul with cotton organdy to help it puff out fashionably. To do this, turn up and baste your seam allowance on the curved edges on both the taffeta and the organdy, leaving the straight bottom edges raw. Then place the two pieces wrong sides together, matching the edges, and prick stitch together from the taffeta side. You will now handle this piece as one.

2. Fold up the seam allowance on the bottom straight edge of the caul and baste.

3. Fold the caul in half and mark the center point along the straight bottom edge. Then poke an awl through at this point, and whip the edges with waxed silk thread to form the eyelet. Pass the awl through the finished eyelet to shape it.

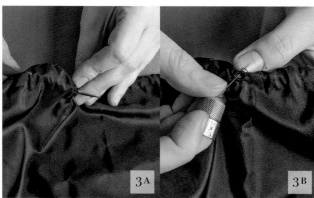

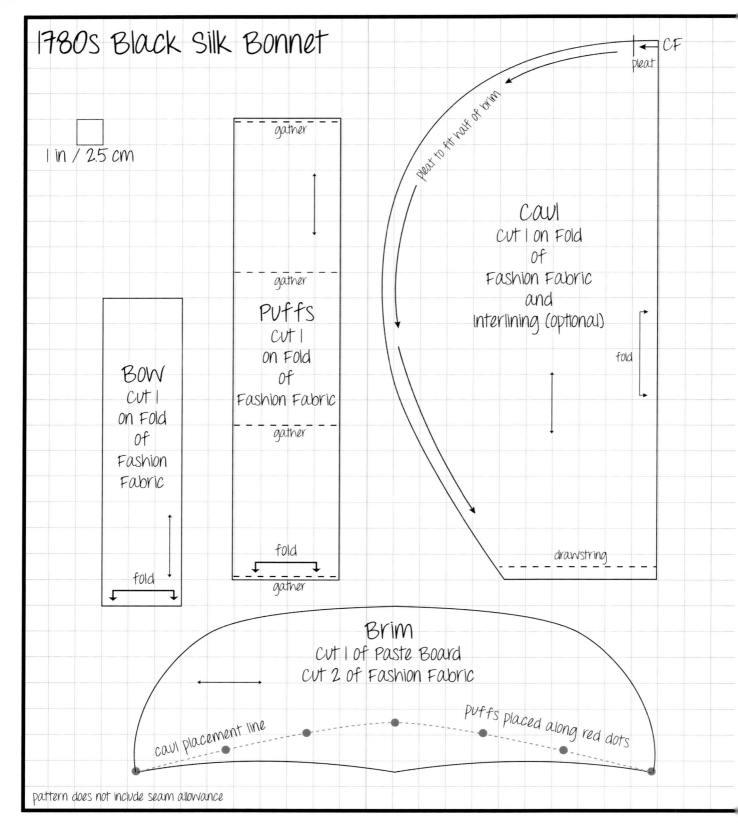

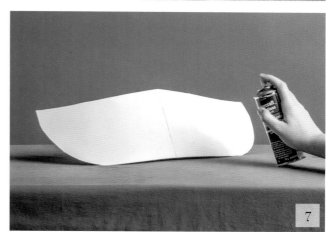

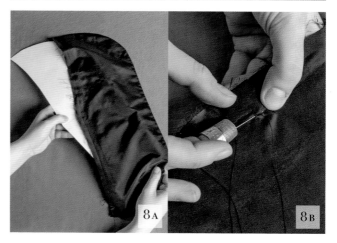

4. Atop the turned and basted seam allowance on the bottom flat edge, secure the narrow ribbon to the base of the caul piece on each end using a few strong backstitches. Pull the excess ribbon through the eyelet, using an awl or pin to push it through.

5. Fold up the straight bottom edge of the caul piece over the ribbon. Finely hem stitch, making sure not to catch the ribbon in the stitches.

6. With right sides together, backstitch the front of the taffeta brim pieces together at 6 to 8 stitches per inch (2.5 cm). Leave the back side of the fabric brim pieces open. Clip the curves seam allowance, then turn right sides out and press the seam.

7. Cut out the brim shape from the heavy poster board, then liberally spray both sides with the acrylic finishing spray. Allow to dry.

8. Insert the sprayed and dried poster board between the two layers of taffeta, pressing the board well into the seam and pinning the raw edges together at the back right along the edge of the board to hold it tightly in place. Backstitch along this pinned edge, right on the edge of the board, at 6 to 8 stitches per inch (2.5cm).

9. Fold the raw edges of the brim back up onto the top side of the brim, right along the edge of the poster board inside, and roughly hem stitch down. This part will not be seen once the caul is applied.

Joining the Caul and Brim

10. Fold the caul in half to find the center point at the top, then place this point on the center of the brim at the caul placement line. Form a large box pleat leaving about 2 inches (5 cm) visible as the pleat at the front. Continue to knife pleat and pin along the brim placement line, toward the back, with about 1-inch (2.5-cm) pleats visible, until you've reached the outer edge of the brim. There is no exact way to pleat this—futz and arrange until the caul fits and looks nice.

11. Once you've got the pleats arranged and pinned in place, bust out your thimble and stitch all these pleats down with 3 to 4 large stitches per pleat. This doesn't have to be nice—it will be covered by the puffs later on.

Puffs & Bows

12. Hem all four sides of the puff piece, turning up ¼ inch (6 mm) and basting, then turning up again and hemming at about 6 to 8 stitches per inch (2.5 cm).

13. Mark the gathering points for the puffs every 6 inches (15 cm) according to the pattern, then at each point run 8 to 10 small gathering stitches cross-wise, pulling up tightly and knotting to secure.

14. Marking the center point of the puffs, apply this point to the center-front of the bonnet and arrange the remaining puffs on each side, covering the join between the caul and brim. Stitch the puffs in place at each gathered point. This is a bit tedious—use a thimble!

15. Hem the two long edges of the bow piece, turning up ¼ inch (6 mm) and basting, then turning up again and hemming at about 6 to 8 stitches per inch (2.5 cm).

16. Cut the short ends in a zigzag pattern, then tie the ribbon into a bow. You may also construct a 4-Loop Bow (page 198) or 5-Loop Bow (page 206). Place this at the center front of the bonnet, and stitch it into place with a few strong tacking stitches. We flipped our bow so the tails were pointing upward to add an extra dose of pizzazz to the bonnet.

17. This bonnet is very large, designed to sit atop a full, round, 1780s hairstyle. If you intend to try this bonnet for lower hair or a lower-class impression, adjust the proportions to suit.

CHAPTER II

1785–1790

Coiffure Américaine Duchesse

Sir Joshua Reynolds RA, 1723–1792. Mrs. Robinson. 1784. Yale Center for British Art, Paul Mellon Collection. B1981.25.520.

The hairstyles of the late 1780s do not change drastically from the frizzled hairstyle that came earlier in the decade. The main difference seems to be the fluctuation in the size of the curls. Crape-ing, trendy in the early 1780s, appears to fall out of fashion by the end of this decade. [1] When comparing two hairdressing manuals from either end of the 1780s, the techniques are incredibly similar—it's just the type of curl that seems to really differentiate the styles.

In fashion and satirical prints from the late '80s, we also see a change in the chignon or "long hair." [2] Earlier, the chignon is braided or plainly looped up the back, but in the late 1780s, the long hair is sometimes tied simply with a ribbon or left curled and loose down the back, as seen in the print *Seated Woman, Seen from Behind* from the Metropolitan Museum. [3]

We cut Lauren's hair specifically for this style to explore what effect a specialized *à l'enfant* haircut might have on the ease of styling and final results of this coiffure. The haircuts could be what we might consider extreme today; *Plocacosmos* recommended that the front of the hair be shorn to a mere ½ inch (1.2 cm) with longer layers stacked onto the cushion in a cloud of curls. [4] Lauren's not that brave, so we cut her bangs at eyebrow level, which curled up and fluffed out nicely, if not still a little too long.

Headwear in the late '80s was large and playful. In this chapter, we show how to re-block a simple straw hat to a fashionable late 1780s shape (page 200). You'll also find quite a confection of a cap made in airy silk organza and bedecked with silk satin ribbons and bows (page 193). These both make wonderful toppers to your fashionable hairstyle.

1785 - 1790 Tootsie Roller Hair Cushion

1 in / 2.5 cm

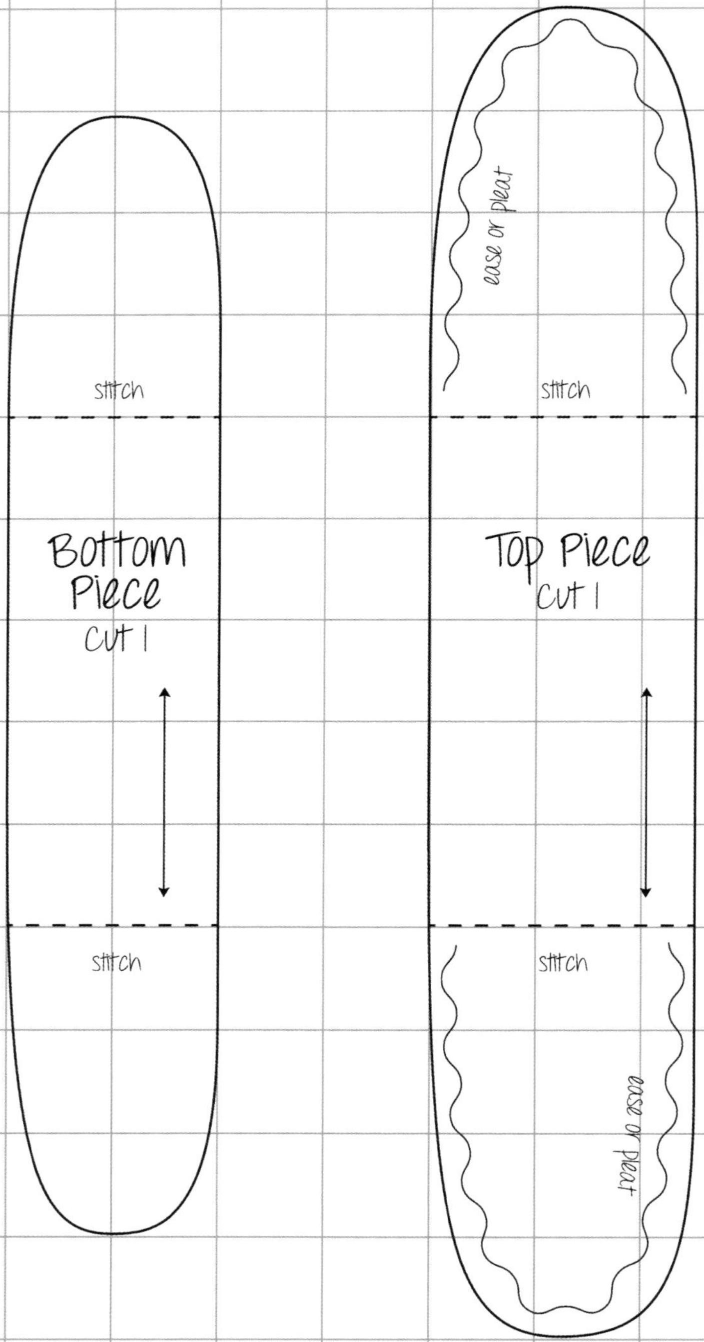

Bottom Piece
Cut 1

stitch

stitch

Top Piece
Cut 1

ease or pleat

stitch

stitch

ease or pleat

The finished length of the cushion should match your head measurement from top of ear to top of ear

pattern does not include seam allowance

Tootsie Roller Hair Cushion

Though the frizzed hairstyles of the 1780s look wild with abandon, and therefore easy, there are still structural elements underneath that keep the hair in the fashionable shape and form a solid foundation for headwear such as the large and fabulous "Gainsborough" hats. For Lauren's 1785 style we've created the "Tootsie Roller," a simple design that creates enough of a bump at the crown of the head for the frizzed hair at front to "rest" upon. The size of your cushion can vary—try scaling the pattern up for grander effects—but it's important to maintain silhouette of the hair being wider than it is tall.

- ¼ yard (25 cm) wool knit in matching color to your hair when powdered
- #30 silk thread in matching color
- Horsehair, ground cork or wool roving

1. Matching right sides together, pin, then stitch the cushion all the way around with a backstitch, leaving a small opening about 2½ inches (6 cm) long on one of the long edges.

2. Turn the piece right side out, then stuff with the horsehair, cork or wool roving.

3. Turn in the edges of the opening, pin, then whipstitch to close.

4. Make a few tacking backstitches through all layers and stuffing of the cushion along the marked dotted lines.

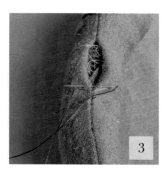

Coiffure Américaine Duchesse Hairstyle

DIFFICULTY: EASY TO INTERMEDIATE

RECOMMENDED HAIR LENGTH: THIS STYLE IS RECOMMENDED FOR HAIR LENGTH ANYWHERE FROM THE TOP OF THE BROW TO THE TOP OF THE SHOULDER. THIS STYLE IS NOT RECOMMENDED FOR VERY LONG HAIR PAST THE SHOULDERS.

In this tutorial, we explore the popular curled hairstyle as it evolves in the late 1780s. We've opted to use a modern wet-set to demonstrate a different method of curling, but this style is perfectly achievable with papillote curling (page 210) as well. We have also cut Lauren's hair *à l'enfant* to see what effect this would have on the ease of and finished look of the style. We understand this is a bit hardcore for most, so we are happy to report that this style is just as achievable with bangs, face-framing layers or by using your handy pre-curled toupee (page 41). Lastly, like its predecessors, this style makes use of yet another hair cushion. [5] Not only does a cushion provide an anchor to which the hair is pinned and secured, but it is also the support for the cap, bonnet or hat, preventing a perfectly coiffed style from getting squished under the weight of the millinery.

- Common Pomatum (page 20)
- Small foam rollers
- Hair dryer
- Handkerchief
- Rattail comb
- Large powder brush
- White Hair Powder (page 28)
- Alligator hair clips
- Bobby pins
- Teasing comb with wire pick

- Tootsie Roller Hair Cushion (page 185)
- Hairpins (short & long)
- Hard Pomatum (page 22)
- ½-inch (1.2-cm) curling iron
- Size 50 (10-mm) knitting needle
- Hair extensions (optional)
- Clip-in buckles and chignon (pages 45 and 41, optional)
- Small rubber hair ties
- Ribbon

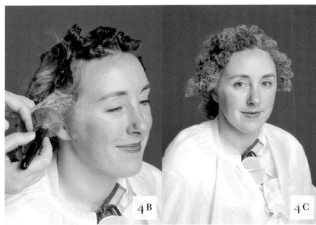

Overnight Pomade-Wet-Set

1. For this hairstyle, we are pomade-wet-setting the night before. While not a historical technique, this is a good way to shorten styling time in the morning before your event. Apply the pomade to very slightly damp hair, then roll 1-inch (2.5-cm) sections tightly onto small foam rollers. You need only roll the front and crown of the head, ear to ear. The back portion of your hair may be left straight.

2. Using a diffuser, blast each section of the rolled hair with a hair dryer on hot. You can also spend about 20 minutes under a hood dryer on the hot setting. (Don't burn yourself!) This both heats up the pomade and evaporates the remaining moisture and is essential in helping the curls to set. This pomade-wet-set technique takes the place of papillote heat-setting curls while using the same principles.

3. Tie a large handkerchief around your head to protect the curls overnight, then go to sleep. In the morning, carefully unroll one of the curls and feel for dryness. The curl should feel a bit oily from the pomade, but not cool or moist. If the curls are still damp, blast with the hair dryer or sit under a hood dryer again until they are dry.

Frizzing the Crown

4. Remove the rollers from the hair. With your fingers, pull and part the curls, then liberally apply powder to each one until the hair feels dry and fluffy.

5. Next, part the hair forward from ear to ear, clipping the front out of the way and leaving a goodly amount of volume toward the back. Also part the hair at the apex of the head (the toupee section), dividing the uncurled back portion from the center, curled portion.

6. Tease the toupee section to frizz it, laying it forward as you go. Place the Tootsie Roller hair cushion on the back-most parting, the ends just behind the ears, and securely pin into place with hairpins.

7. Pull the teased toupee portion of hair back over the cushion, fluffing and arranging the hair to cover the cushion completely. Pin the hair behind the cushion. This forms the "bump" that supports the rest of the hairstyle and any cap or hat you will wear.

8. Next, tease, pick and fluff the hair in front, applying more powder as needed to soak up any "wet"-looking pomade. Fluff and pick and work the hair away from the face, gently catching the hair to the cushion with hairpins. It is important to keep the hair back and off the forehead and face—the goal is Duchess of Devonshire, not Krusty the Clown.

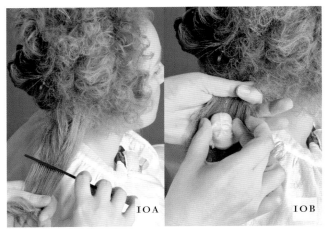

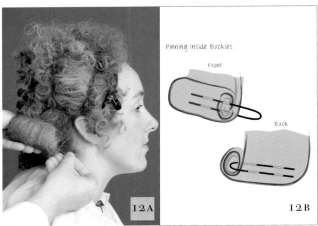

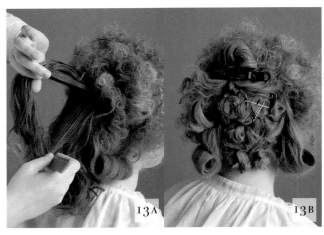

BUCKLES AND CHIGNON

9. Part the hair into three sections at the back, clipping the central section out of the way. The bulk of the remaining hair should be in the central section, with the side sections being considerably smaller. You don't want too much hair in your buckles.

10. With one of the small side sections, tease the hair from the top, working up to the root. Apply more pomade, hard pomade and powder as needed and work that hair into a tentacle that can stand away from the head on its own.

11. Curl the end of the buckle hair upwards with the curling iron, just a few inches, to help the curl start. Next, starting from the curled end, roll the hair upwards on the size 50 knitting needle. Be sure to angle the roll to achieve the position you want.

12. Carefully slide the hair off the knitting needle, then pinching the back of the buckle from inside the roll, work a large U-shaped hairpin first over the outer edge, then in and out of the hair on the back of the roll several times. Repeat on the other side of the buckle. Make sure the hairpins are relatively parallel to the rolled angle of the hair.

13. If you are using your own hair for the chignon, it needs to be about shoulder-blade length or longer. If you are using hair extensions for the chignon, section out a bit of your own hair at the top of the head and clip it up and out of the way for later. Then divide and pin curl the remainder of your hair against your head to keep it out of the way. This doesn't have to look nice; it just needs to be secure.

14. Attach your hair extensions at the part between the upper section and the pin-curled hair below. The extensions will cover the pin curls, and the hair at the top will be arranged in the next step to cover the extension tracks.

15. Divide the upper portion of hair into two or three sections. Tease each section, then roll under, using the knitting needle to aid the curl, and pin into place over the tracks of the hair extensions.

16. Moving on to the chignon extensions, pomade and powder the full length, then curl the ends with the curling iron.

17. Secure the hair with an elastic band about a third of the way up, then tie a pretty ribbon around this point. We've left the hair long down the back for this particular chignon, but feel free to use other styles such as the simple loop (page 101) or the braid (page 79).

18. Happy days! You created a lovely frizzed hairstyle for the last half of the 1780s! As always, feel free to experiment with different versions of this basic style, such as adding more buckles or leaving the chignon long and loose.

"Bonnet à la Méduse" Cap [6]

As hair in the late 1780s continues to be wide and very curly, fashionable caps broaden as well. These fanciful caps were designed to rest atop the amply coiffed head of the lady, an additional adornment to her hairstyle as opposed to a covering to obscure it. We have chosen a common style, simply constructed and heavily be-ribboned, giving it an impressive look similar to the caps worn by Madame Adélaïde and Madame Victoire in their portraits by Élisabeth Vigée Le Brun, 1791, [7] and a couple of portraits by Adélaïde Labille-Guiard. [8]

- ½ yard (0.5 m) silk organza
- #50 silk thread, white
- #30 silk thread, white
- 12 inches (30 cm) candlewicking or narrow cord
- 40 inches (1 m) 2-inch (5-cm)-wide silk ribbon
- #30 silk thread, matching ribbon color

THE CAUL AND BAND

1. Turn up ¼ inch (6 mm) on all edges of the caul and baste. Fold the caul piece in half lengthwise to find the center, and mark above the basted seam at the bottom of the caul. Pierce the fabric with an awl here, then stitch the eyelet open with waxed thread #30. When complete, poke with the awl again to shape the eyelet.

2. Atop the basted seam allowance on the bottom flat edge, secure the narrow tape to the base of the caul piece on each end using a few strong backstitches. Pull the excess tape through the eyelet, using an awl or pin to push it through.

1785 - 1790 Bonnet a la Méduse

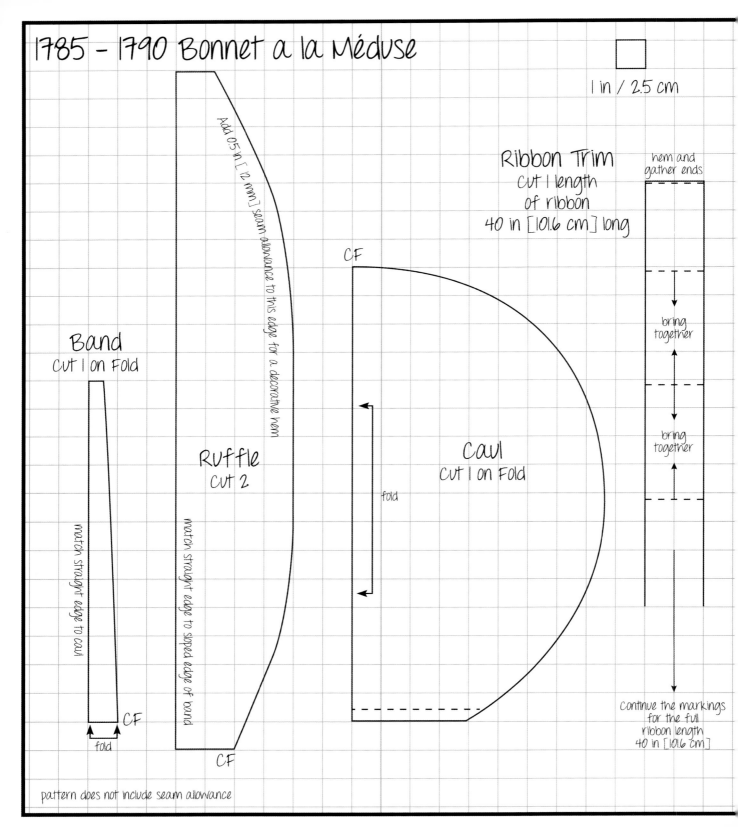

1 in / 2.5 cm

Add 0.5 in [12 mm] seam allowance to this edge for a decorative hem

Ribbon Trim
Cut 1 length
of ribbon
40 in [101.6 cm] long

hem and
gather ends

bring
together

bring
together

CF

Band
Cut 1 on Fold

Ruffle
Cut 2

Caul
Cut 1 on Fold

match straight edge to caul

match straight edge to sloped edge of band

fold

fold

CF

CF

CF

continue the markings
for the full
ribbon length
40 in [101.6 cm]

pattern does not include seam allowance

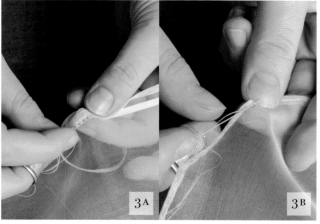

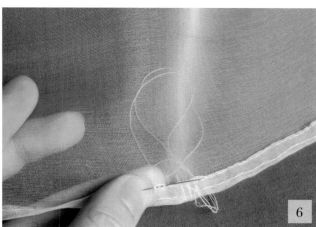

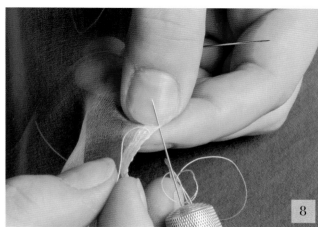

3. Fold up the straight bottom edge of the caul piece over the tape. Finely hem, making sure not to catch the tape in the stitches. Continue to hem the rest of the caul using the fine hem method shown on page 65.

4. Following the pattern, mark where the gathering should start on each side of the caul with a pin. Then fold the caul in half lengthwise to find the top-center point and also mark with a pin. Loosely whip over the curved hemmed edge of the caul from one side to the center point, about 4 to 6 stitches per inch (2.5 cm). Pull up this thread to gather half of the caul to approximately half the length of the band. Repeat for the other side of the caul.

5. Turn up and baste ¼ inch (6 mm) on all sides of the band piece, then turn up again ⅛ inch (3 mm) and finely hem all sides.

PREPPING THE RUFFLES

6. Turn up and baste ¼ inch (6 mm) on all sides of the ruffle pieces. On the curved edge, turn another ⅜ inch (1 cm) and finely hem stitch.

7. On the remaining three sides, turn up the seam allowance ⅛ inch (3 mm) again by folding the basted edge in half over itself. Finely hem stitch in place.

8. Loosely whip over the long straight edge of each ruffle piece.

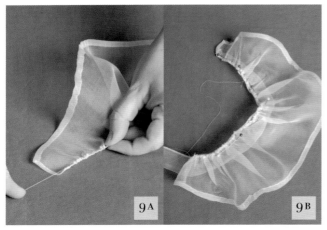

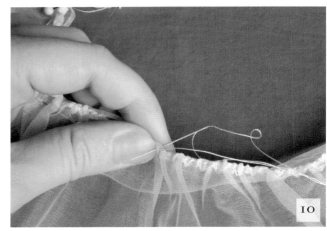

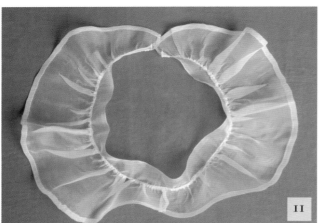

Joining the Ruffles to the Band

9. Pull up the thread to gather the ruffles. Then, working each side separately, pin the gathered edge of the ruffle to the curved edge of the band, right sides together, distributing the gathers evenly and pinning as you go.

10. Whipstitch the ruffle to the band, catching each bump of the gathers. This is a little tedious, but stick with it!

11. Open the ruffle and band out flat and gently tug the pieces apart to "pop" the stitches into place. Press the open pieces.

Attaching the Caul to the Band

12. Fold the caul in half and pin to mark the halfway point at the top.

13. Working one side of the caul at a time, pull the thread to gather the curved edge, then match the gathered edge to the straight edge of one half of the band. Arrange the gathers evenly and pin. Repeat for the other side of the caul and band.

14. Starting from one end, tightly whipstitch the gathered caul and straight edge of the band together, catching every tiny little bump. When done, open the two pieces out and gently tug to "pop" the stitches into place. Press it all flat if needed.

Looped Ribbon Decoration

15. Cut a piece of 2-inch (5-cm)-wide silk ribbon about 40 inches (1 m) long. Hem both short ends.

16. Mark the length of ribbon according to the pattern, going by the 4:1 markings with 3¼ inches (8 cm) left at both ends.

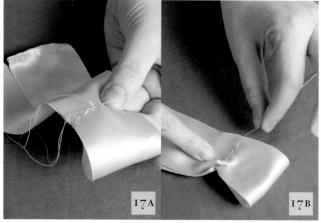

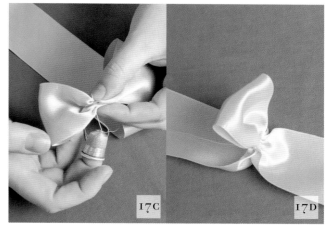

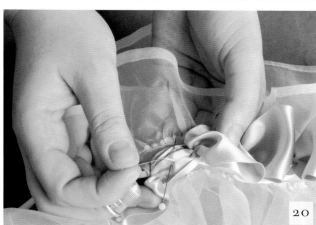

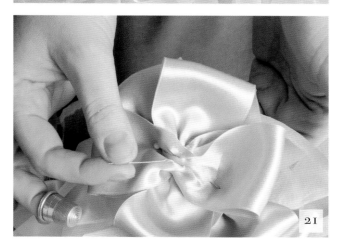

17. Starting at one end of the ribbon, match the first mark to the second, forming the first loop. Sew a running stitch across this point, gather up and then tack stitch in place.

18. Move to the next set of marks, bringing the two points together. Sew a gathering stitch, draw up the thread and tack stitch. Repeat these steps for the entire length of the ribbon and all of the marks.

19. On each short end of the ribbon, sew a running stitch, draw up the thread and tack stitch in place.

20. Arrange the ribbon floof on the band of your cap and pin in place. On the underside, stitch one end in place. Cut the thread, then start your stitches again at the first loop, moving from loop to loop and stitching each "in-between" portion with a backstitch.

21. At the center front, add a bow in matching ribbon. You can choose a 4-Loop Bow (page 198) or a 5-Loop Bow (page 206) with zigzag tails.

This beautiful bit of gauze and ribbonwork adds a fashionable dash of millinery, and it works well into the 1790s.

4-Loop Bows

Throughout this book we make many, many bows to decorate various caps and hats. Use this tutorial as your quick reference to making this ubiquitous bit of frippery.

- *20 inches (50 cm) 2-inch (5-cm)-wide silk ribbon or self-made hemmed fabric ribbon*
- *#50 silk thread*

1. Cut two short lengths of ribbon, approximately 6 inches (15 cm) long.

2. Match the raw ends right sides together, stitch, then press open. Then stitch across the width with a running stitch.

3. Without cutting the thread, make a running stitch across the width on the opposite side of the ribbon loop, then draw the thread up to gather each side of the loop and bring them together.

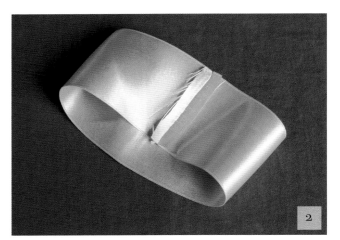

4. Still without cutting the thread, make a few strong stitches through all layers and knot.

5. Repeat for the second bow.

6. Place the two bows atop one another at right angles to form the rosette. Stitch through all layers to secure the bows together

7. To add tails, fold a length of ribbon about 8 inches (20 cm) long into a V roughly between 45 and 60 degrees. Take a few tacking stitches across the top.

8. Cut the ends of the ribbon at angles or in a zigzag pattern.

9. Place the rosette atop the tails and take a few tacking stitches on the back, making sure the stitches do not show through to the front of the bow.

10. Now your finished bow is ready to be pinned or sewn onto hats, caps or the front of your gown. If you would like to create these bows using narrower or wider ribbon, it's necessary to adjust the lengths needed for each piece. Use shorter lengths for narrower ribbon and longer lengths for wider.

A Refashioned 1780s Gainsborough Hat

With the popularity of pastoral dress [9] in the 1780s, very large straw hats came into fashion. These hats, now known as "Gainsborough Hats" after the prolific artist who depicted many a fine chapeau in his work, came in all shapes and sizes, some with huge brims and shallow crowns and others with tall crowns and turned-up brims. The hats could be simply decorated or elaborately fluffed and often featured black trim with a profusion of black or white ostrich feathers. [10] In this tutorial, we will re-block a standard straw hat to achieve a different crown shape, wire, mull and bind the edge of the brim and add a few more elements to create a fashionable country hat. You can use this tutorial as a reference point for re-shaping and refashioning just about any hat that will take steam, even lightweight felt hats.

- *15-inch (38-cm) diameter real straw hat*
- *6–7-inch (15–18-cm) diameter flower pot*
- *1 yard (1 m) narrow twill tape*
- *Spray bottle*
- *Steam iron*
- *1½ yards (1.5 m) 18-gauge millinery wire*
- *#30 silk thread, straw color*
- *¼ yard (25 cm) thin cotton muslin*
- *1½ yards (1.5 m) 1-inch (2.5-cm)-wide silk ribbon*
- *#50 silk thread, matching ribbon color*
- *¼ yard (25 cm) lightweight cotton fabric for lining*
- *20 inches (51 cm) ⅛-inch (3-mm)-wide twill tape*
- *20 inches (51 cm) 2–3-inch (5–8-cm)-wide silk ribbon or ¼ yard (25 cm) silk taffeta fabric to make your own ribbon*
- *2–3 white ostrich feathers*

RE-BLOCKING YOUR HAT

1. For this tutorial we are re-blocking an existing straw hat. It's very important to have a real straw hat for this project so that it responds to the steaming and shaping. Start by removing any decorations, interior hat bands, tags, wires and glue from your hat base.

2. Once your hat is naked, soak it in the sink or a bucket of water to "revert" the shape to a hood or capeline. [11] Remove the hat from the water and towel it off. The straw should be damp, not dripping wet, but moist all the way through.

3. For our fashionable crown shape we are using a 7-inch (18-cm) flower pot as a hat block. Because this hat sits atop the hair rather than down on the head, the inner circumference of the crown need not be the same as your head. Pull the damp, reverted straw hood down over the flowerpot, tugging downwards with some force until the straw starts to take the shape.

4. Tie the crown at the base very securely with tape or use a strong rubber band. Allow the straw to dry on the form overnight.

5. Once dry, remove the hat from the flower pot. You may need to iron the brim flat with a good application of steam to shrink and shape it if there are bubbles or uneven bits.

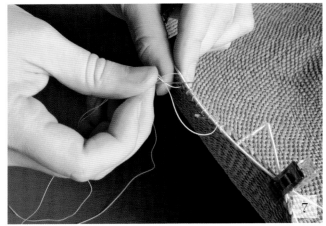

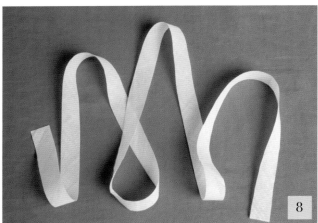

Wiring the Brim

6. Wiring the brim helps a floppy hat hold its shape while also allowing for curving the brim later on. Place the millinery wire around the brim and clip into place. Cut and overlap the ends by 2 inches (5 cm).

7. Using #30 silk thread, well-waxed, blanket stitch (see page 12) the wire to the hat brim 4 to 5 stitches per inch (2.5 cm). Make sure the wire is right on the edge.

8. Mulling is used to smooth, stabilize and pad edges while also providing something to sew coverings and decorative elements to. To create your mulling material, cut ¾-inch (2-cm) bias strips from cotton muslin and join together for about 1½ yards (1.5 m) in length.

9. Fold the cotton bias over the edge of the hat brim, stretching and clipping as you go. There is no need to turn in the raw edges at any point, including the overlap.

10. Stitch the mulling to the hat brim using a milliner's figure 8 stitch (page 11).

BINDING THE BRIM

11. Fold the 1-inch (2.5-cm)-wide satin ribbon over the edge of the brim, covering the mulling completely, and clip into place.

12. Stitch the brim binding into place using a milliner's figure 8 stitch (page 11). Turn under the raw edge at the end where the ribbon overlaps, and neatly hem stitch to finish.

LINING THE CROWN

13. Crown linings serve multiple purposes in eighteenth-century hats. They act as a stabilizing interior band, adjust the fit of the hat and also hide the sometimes messy interior of the crown. Measure the interior circumference and depth of your crown. This may differ from ours depending on your hat base and the block you use to re-shape it, so double check! Our hat lining is 19½ inches (49.5 cm) by 3 inches (8 cm), including the seam allowance.

14. Turn up ½ inch (1.2 cm) on one long edge and baste.

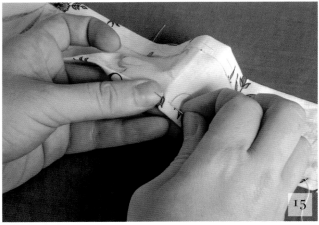

15. Turn in ¼ inch (6 mm) on the short edges and baste. Turn up another ¼ inch (6 mm) on the short edges and hem stitch.

16. Turn up ¼ inch (6 mm) on the remaining long edge, baste, then turn up another ¼ inch (6 mm) and hem stitch, leaving the ends open. Using a large, dull upholstery needle, thread the ⅛-inch (3-mm) twill tape through the channel.

17. Place the lining inside the crown of the hat, aligning the basted long edge with the base of the crown. Carefully sew the lining to the hat with applique stitches through all layers. It is OK for the stitches to show on the outside of the hat—these will be covered in the next steps.

18. Once you reach the short ends, abutt the edges and whipstitch together, leaving the drawstrings open and free.

The Hat Band

19. To create the exterior hat band you may use wide satin or grosgrain ribbon ready-made or make your own band. Ours is silk taffeta fabric cut and sewn into a band 20 inches (51 cm) long and 2 inches (5 cm) wide, but yours may differ depending on crown circumference and depth. We made ours sewn right sides together and turned right side out. One raw short end was turned and basted.

20. Apply your hat band to the outside of the crown, covering the lining stitches. Overlap the short end you turned under over the raw edge of the other short end and pin through the hat to hold in place.

21. Stitch the band to the hat through the straw layer, but avoiding the lining inside, using applique stitches at the base of the band. These stitches can be placed quite far apart and are there only to secure the band to the hat. This whole process is a little tedious, so be careful!

22. Take a few prick stitches across the short end to secure the band further. There is no need to stitch around the top of the hat band.

DECORATE!

23. We decorated our hat with a 5-loop bow in black taffeta and a large white ostrich feather. To learn how to make 5-loop bows, turn to page 206. To see our tips on working with ostrich feathers, see page 132.

Hooray! Your lovely new Gainsborough Hat is complete! Pull up the drawstrings of the hat lining to adjust the crown depth and wear your new hat at a jaunty angle, secured through your hair cushion with a hat pin.

5-Loop Bows

Beautiful 5-loop bows are a great decoration to add to hats, caps and other accessories. They add a bit more texture and interest than the standard 4-loop bow and are oh-so-eighteenth century. This style of bow can be used to decorate all kinds of things. We used one 5-loop bow on the front of the Gainsborough Hat on page 200. Feel free to pile them on for more floof!

- 1 yard (1 m) 2-inch (5-cm)-wide ribbon
- #30 silk thread

1. Cut two pieces of ribbon, the first 12½ inches (32 cm) long and the second 8 inches (20 cm) long. The length and width of your ribbon will determine the size of your bow. For smaller bows using a narrower ribbon, use shorter lengths; for larger bows using wider ribbon, use longer lengths.

2. With the longer length of ribbon, roll the first loop over, matching the raw end to about one-third of the way down the ribbon.

3. Sew a fine running stitch, draw up the thread and tack stitch in place. Do not cut the thread.

4. Find the length of the second loop by rolling it up toward what will be the center of your bow. Just mark this length with your fingers or a pin, then open flat again.

3

5A

 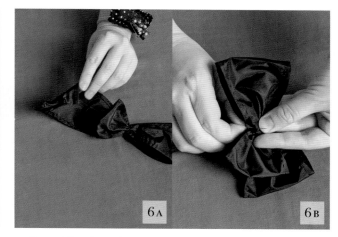

5. Sew a fine running stitch at this point, draw up the thread, roll the loop back up to the base of the first loop and tack stitch in place.

6. Now on the opposite end, run a fine gathering stitch, draw up the ribbon and roll the loop to the base of the other two bows. Once again, tack stitch in place.

7. For the remaining two loops, match the raw edges of the shorter length of ribbon right sides together and stitch. Press the seam flat.

8. Run a fine gathering stitch across this join, then without cutting the thread, gathering stitch on the opposite side, stitching in the opposite direction. Pull the thread to gather up both sides together, and tack stitch the center in place.

9. Place the two-loop bow behind the three-loop bow, and tack stitch the bows together from inside the loops.

CHAPTER 12

1790–1794

Coiffure Révolution

John Hoppner. Portrait of a Woman. *1790s. The Metropolitan Museum of Art. 06.1242.*

As with anything in fashion, there is a transition from one distinct style to the next. The early 1790s was one such transitional period wherein hair continues to be very curly and frizzed, but cushions slowly disappear and styles relax into a more "natural" design.

The use of hair powder begins to decline in the 1790s, but it would be incorrect to assume that hair powder just disappeared from one year to the next. Heideloff's *Gallery of Fashion* was still publishing fashion plates showing pomaded and powdered hair from 1794 to 1803. [1] In addition, careful examination of portraits from the mid-1790s show a matte finish to the hair, indicating at least a small amount of powder was still being used, [2] though public sentiment and taxation eventually brought it to an end. To find out more about the demise of hair powder in the 1790s, turn to page 221.

In this chapter, we demonstrate a casual, curly 'do using heat-set papillote curls, a popular and historically accurate curling method. You will notice that we powder Zyna's hair very little, in keeping with the changing laws and fashions of this period. For millinery, we've opted for a very simple head wrap, called a chiffonet, [3] made from silk organza, an easy and very period way to decorate your 1790s coiffure.

How to Papillote Curl Your Hair

Quintessentially Georgian, papillote curls are the go-to method for curling your hair in the eighteenth century. This interesting method uses folded and twisted papers (the "papillotes") to hold the curl in place [4] and protect it while it is heated through with the papillote iron, a special heat-setting tool made for the purpose. We've substituted an electric flat iron, which works a treat. While this curling method takes a long time, it is the most accurate means of curling the hair. This tutorial will show you how to easily achieve this curl.

- *Common Pomatum (page 20)*
- *Papillote Papers (page 31)*
- *Double-pronged curl clips (optional)*
- *Flat iron*

1. Work some common pomatum through a ½- to 1-inch (1.2- to 2.5-cm) section of hair. If your hair is fine or short, 1 inch (2.5 cm) should be fine, but if you have very long or thick hair, you will have to work in smaller sections.

2. Wrap the hair tightly around your finger to create what we would call a pin curl today. Carefully slide the hair off your finger and pinch the curl to hold it.

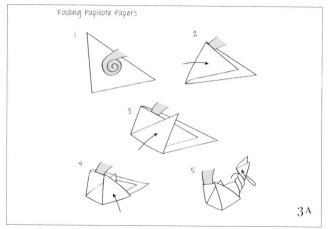

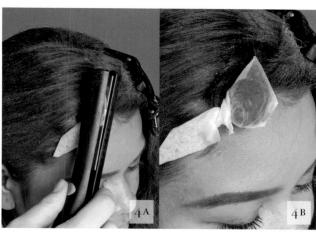

3. Place the long side of the triangular tissue paper beneath the curl, right up on the roots. Fold the left point of the triangle over to the right, covering the curl. Then fold the bottom edge of the paper up over the curl and lastly, fold the right bottom edge upwards, again over the curl. Twist the ends on the right side together to hold everything together. This takes practice! If you're having trouble getting the paper to stay, use a small double-pronged curl clip to hold it in place before the next step.

4. Pinch the papered curl between a small, very hot flat iron for 20 to 45 seconds. When you remove the flat iron, the paper will have an oily, smooshed appearance.

5. Once all the papillotes are complete, smoosh them again with the flat iron for good measure.

6. When the papillotes are completely cool, remove the paper from the hair and allow the curl to fall free, or gently pull and separate the hair. If the curl has not set, wrap it back up and heat it through with the flat iron again.

Hooray! You've just finished your first set! Don't worry if you thought it was difficult, it gets easier with practice!

Early 1790s Coiffure Révolution Hairstyle

Our model, Zyna, has lovely 3B hair that does extremely well with a heat-set. We used historically accurate papillote curls in the front of Zyna's hair and a curling iron to curl the toupee section. Both techniques are historically accurate, though we opted to use double-pronged curl clips to hold the un-papered curls in place while they cooled. This is a time-saving technique and yields the same results as papillote curling with papers. Feel free to try both methods.

DIFFICULTY: EASY

RECOMMENDED HAIR LENGTH: THIS STYLE IS RECOMMENDED FOR HAIR LENGTH ANYWHERE FROM THE TOP OF THE BROW TO THE TOP OF THE SHOULDER. THIS STYLE IS NOT RECOMMENDED FOR VERY LONG HAIR PAST THE SHOULDERS.

- *Common Pomatum (page 20)*
- *Large powder brush*
- *White Hair Powder (page 28)*
- *Wide-tooth or rattail comb*
- *Hair clips*
- *Papillote papers*
- *Double-pronged curl clips*
- *Flat iron*
- *¼-inch (6-mm) curling iron*
- *½-inch (1.2-cm) curling iron*
- *Teasing comb with wire pick*
- *Hard Pomatum (page 22)*
- *Hairpins (short or long)*
- *False hair for chignon*
- *Bobby pins*
- *Roller pins (optional)*

THE CURLS

1. After pomading and powdering the hair, part the hair from ear to ear and clip the back of the hair out of the way.

1 A   1 B

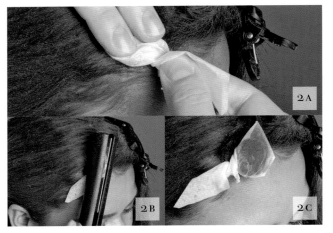

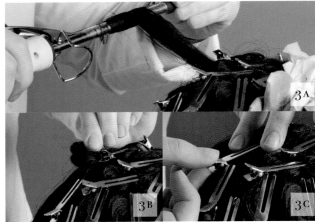

2. Starting at the very front of the head, papillote curl the hair in ½- to 1-inch (1.2- to 2.5-cm) sections, following the instructions on page 210. Make sure you have random parting, so there will be no awkward breaks in the hair once it's frizzed out.

3. For the back of the hair, we used ¼- and ½-inch (6-mm and 1.2-cm) curling irons, curling ½- to 1-inch (1.2- to 2.5-cm) sections of hair. Curl the entire section of hair in the curling iron, gently release from the iron, and immediately roll it back up into its pin-curl shape and pin to the scalp to cool.

4. Do this for the entire back of the head, using the smaller iron on top and the larger iron toward the bottom of the head.

5. Allow the hair to cool completely and set into its new curls. The longer you can allow your hair to set, the better the curls will hold. After the hair has cooled, take all the curls out, working from the front to the back.

6. Now it's time to have some fun! Shake out and work out all those curls with your fingers until you look like you stuck your finger in a light socket.

7. Unless your hair is pretty short in the front, you're going to have to do some teasing to get it to stand up and not flop forward into your eyes. Use as much hard pomatum, powder and common pomatum as you need. For Zyna, we didn't need to use much more than our comb, but that's simply because of her hair texture. You need to do what's best for your hair!

8. For the mid '90s, you want to have some defined curls standing up and out, not just a ball of frizz on your head like in chapter 10. You can shape larger, more defined curls over a knitting needle to hang below the ears and down the back, or tease and roll the hair up into buckles using the methods in previous chapters.

The Chignon

9. Part the hair horizontally across the scalp toward the top of the head.

10. Next, you're going to part down from your first part to the nape of the neck. Secure each side of hair with bobby pins to keep it out of the way of the chignon. This also helps add extra fullness to the lower sides of the hairstyle.

11. Clip your extensions in place and comb out to make sure there are no tangles or knots. Add any extra powder or pomatum you might need to make sure that the fake hair matches the real hair.

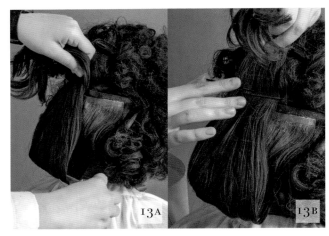

12. Using large roller pins, secure the extension at the nape of the neck, making sure to cover any visible bobby pins.

13. Rest the tail of your comb at that same part of the neck where the pins are, and holding the hair securely in your other hand, flip it up to where the chignon is attached. Pin the chignon into place.

14. Now curl the ends of the chignon with the curling iron. Allow them to cool.

15. Once cool, unclip the rest of the top of the hair, and blend the curls together so there is no visible hair break.

16. Continue to pin, tease, define and arrange until you are happy with your new 1790s 'do.

17. Tie your chiffonet (page 217) around your style, pulling a few curls through the wrap. Dang girl, now you're ready to start a revolution! (A fashion revolution, let's not get too ahead of ourselves!) [5]

1790s Chiffonet

The chiffonet is a mysterious bit of fabric heavily featured in *Gallery of Fashion* by N. Heideloff. [6] While examining all the different fashion plates that described a chiffonet, we've concluded that this simple rectangular piece of fabric could be worn tied around the head or in a more elaborate "traditional" turban style. [7] They seem to vary from about 1 to 3 yards (1 to 3 m) long and 4 to 10 inches (10 to 25 m) wide. We made ours a bit in the middle of those ranges, but you can alter the measurements to fit your preferences. Chiffonets could be wrapped elaborately around the head or just simply tied in a bow. They could be worn with bandeaus or feathers or on their own. Though this project is incredibly simple, there is much opportunity for styling your chiffonet.

- *1 yard (1 m) silk, cotton or linen material (We used silk organza.)*
- *#50 silk thread to match*
- *Hairpins (optional)*

1. Cut out your chiffonet according to the diagram. We cut ours to create horizontal stripes and used our selvage edges as the ends.

2. If you need to whip edges together to achieve the length, now is the time to do it.

3. Baste and hem the raw edges.

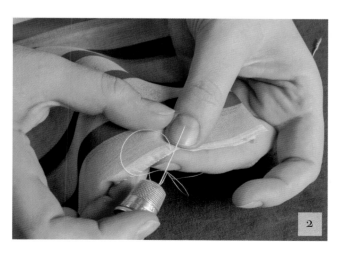

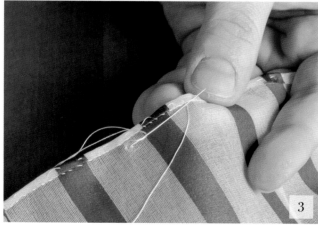

1790s Chiffonet

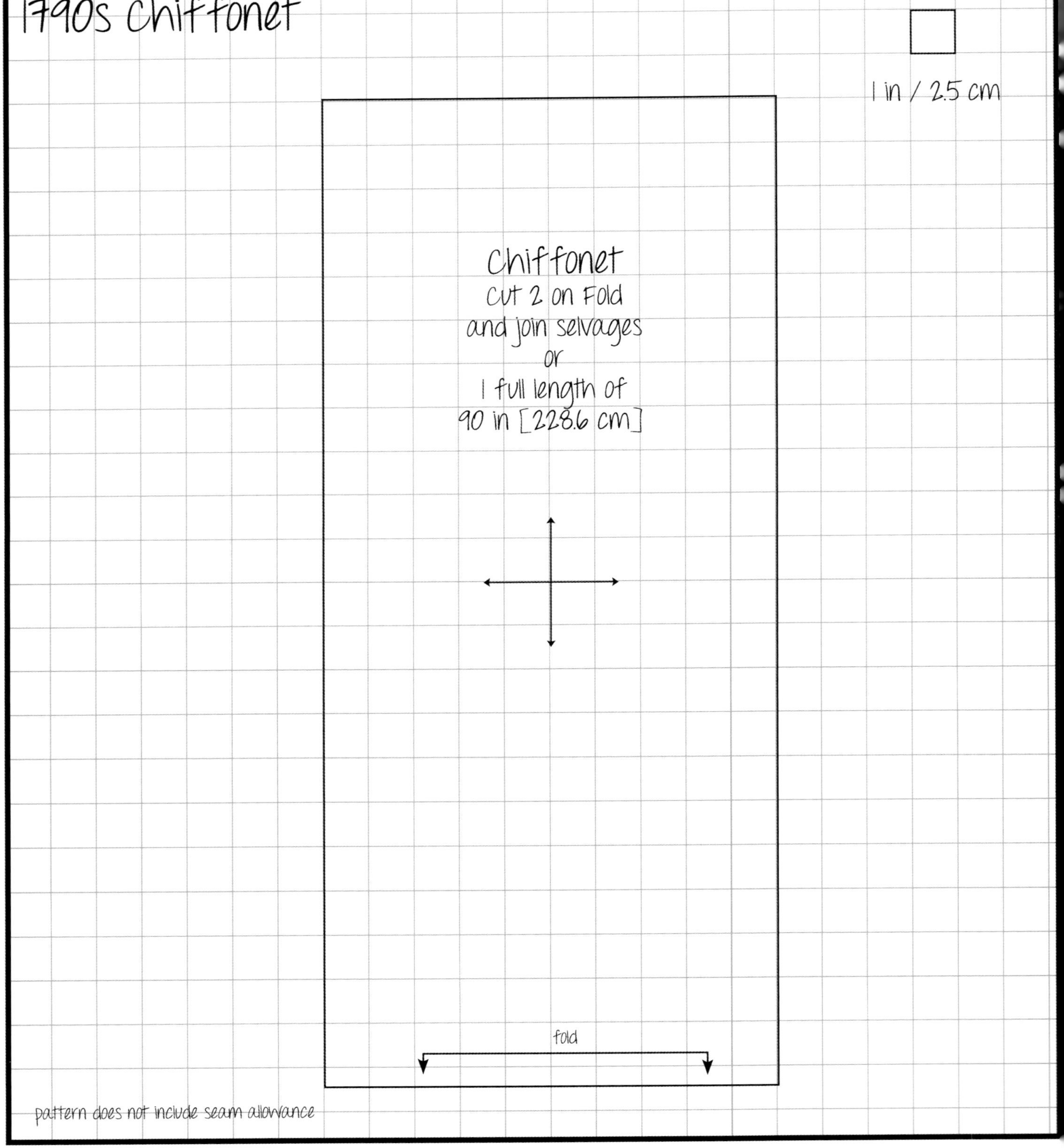

□

1 in / 2.5 cm

Chiffonet
Cut 2 on Fold
and join selvages
or
1 full length of
90 in [228.6 cm]

fold

pattern does not include seam allowance

Tying Your Chiffonet

There are a ton of different ways to do this! Here is just one example:

4. Fold or twist your chiffonet to add texture and interest, then align the middle of the chiffonet to the center of your head.

5. Wrap the twisted ends under your chignon, and bring them back up to the top of your head.

6. Tie a knot (or bow) slightly off to one side, for a jaunty look.

7. Arrange and fluff the chiffonet as needed to achieve your desired look, and pin it into place.

8. Voilà! You're the epitome of 1790s chic.

Epilogue

Post 1795 . . . The End of Hair Powder

In the late 1790s, fashion, especially in France, went completely bananas! By 1795, fashionable hairstyles began to shrink. The *à la Titus*, the *à la Victime* and other closely cropped hairstyles became extremely popular. [1] Hair this short doesn't even need pomatum, let alone powder!

The popularity of powder as a fashion statement dwindled even further when a new tax was levied by English Parliament in May of 1795. The purchase of hair powder now required the additional purchase of an annual certificate at the cost of one guinea. [2] The Royal Family, most military personnel and a few others were exempt. One guinea doesn't sound like much to us, but the new tax definitely made hair powder more cost-prohibitive for the working class. [3]

Hygiene practices were also changing. Washing the body and hair with water was being encouraged by doctors, which meant the use of powder as a hygienic practice was no longer popular. [4] That's not to say hair powder was *never to be heard from again!* It was still around. In fact, in 1812 there were over 46,000 hair powder certificates issued in the United Kingdom, and pharmaceutical books were still including recipes up through the mid-nineteenth century. [5,6]

Funnily enough, variations of pomatum and powder still exist and are used today! Pomatum recipes have remained the same up until the past 50 years, and hair powder has been reincarnated as dry shampoo. [7] While both products share shelf space, they will never be used together again. . . . or will they?

How to Get All This Stuff Out of Your Hair

OK everyone, we have now come to the most important part of the book.

How in the dang heck do I get this stuff out of my hair?!

Don't worry, it's not as difficult as you might think! We have a way to help speed up the cleaning process. It's a little trick Abby learned from her mother: Shampoo your hair when it is dry. That's right, after combing your hair out until it is tangle-free, fill your hand up with a heck of a lot of shampoo and massage it into your hair and scalp just like you would with wet hair. Make sure all of your hair has been shampooed, and then hop into the shower and rinse your hair as normal. Shampoo your hair and condition in the shower like you always do, and then your hair should be 95 to 100 percent pomade-free.

Extra bonus—your hair is going to feel amazing after the deep conditioning treatment you got from the pomatum!

Parisian Ladies in Their Winter Dress. *1799. [England: Pubd. 24th Novr. , by S.W. Fores, No. 50 Piccadilly. Folio's of Caracatures lent out for the Evening] Photograph. Library of Congress. https://www.loc.gov/item/2007677627/.*

Endnotes

Introduction

How to Use This Book

1. Please see our list of suppliers (page 234) for purchasing information.

2. We didn't use poly-fill because it's a modern stuffing, but you're welcome to experiment to see how you like it.

Hair Textures and Types

1. While there are other hair typing systems out there, this is the one that we have become the most familiar with and have chosen to use to give the widest breadth of description available. You can read more about the system here: https://en.wikipedia.org/wiki/Andre_Walker_Hair_Typing_System. We also referenced Nutrafol for additional information about this hair type system. https://www.nutrafol.com/blog/hair-texture-hair-types/

2. James Stewart. *Plocacosmos: or the Whole Art of Hair Dressing; Wherein Is Contained Ample Rules for the Young Artizan, More Particularly for Ladies Women, Valets, &c. &c.* Pages 246–269. 1782. London. Eighteenth Century Collections Online.

3. Please refer to Cheyney McKnight's essay on page 156 for more information.

Part 1: Preparing Your Toilette

1. According to Google, the average brown rat weighs around 8.1 ounces (230 g) and a black rat is 3.9 to 12 ounces (111 to 340 g), but there are articles citing New York City rats as big as 1½ pounds (680 g)!

2. Emma Markiewicz. *Hair, Wigs and Wig Wearing in Eighteenth-Century England.* Page 90. 2014. PhD thesis, University of Warwick.

3. While the products were available for everyone, there was an issue of "you get what you pay for." The cheaper products were often riddled with terrible additives such as lime dust, chalk, plaster, etc. Every hairdressing manual in our bibliography discusses this at length, as does Emily Markiewicz in her PhD thesis.

4. *The Toilet de Flora*, 1772, is filled with recipes on different ways to treat and dye the hair, and every hairdressing manual that we referenced discusses dyeing the hair. Additionally, lead combs were regularly sold in perfumer ads, and they are referred to as a great way to color light or grey hair black (see Bibliography).

5. "[. . .] the saltiness is of too great an astringent quality, and prevents the growth and nourishment of the hair." David Ritchie. *A Treatise on the Hair.* Pages 37 & 38. 1770. Eighteenth Century Collections Online.

Chapter 1: What the Heck Is Pomatum?

1. *Toilet de Flora* (1772) & *Plocacosmos* (1782) both discuss the different animal fats used in hair pomatums.

2. Emma Markiewicz. *Hair, Wigs and Wig Wearing in Eighteenth-Century England.* Page 90. 2014. PhD thesis, University of Warwick.

3. As an example, Natural Care Dog & Cat Flea & Tick Spray has peppermint oil (0.2%) and clove extract (0.48%) as a part of their active ingredients. (www.chewy.com)

4. LiceDoctors (www.licedoctors.com) & American Academy of Dermatology Association (https://www.aad.org/public/diseases/contagious-skin-diseases/head-lice#causes)

5. James Rennie. *A New Supplement to the Pharmacopoeias of London, Edinburgh, Dublin, and Paris [. . .].* Pages 339–340. 1833. London. Google Books.

6. James Rennie. *A New Supplement to the Pharmacopoeias of London, Edinburgh, Dublin, and Paris [. . .].* Page 340. 1833. London. Google Books. We also use this recipe.

7. "When properly incorporated take it off and keep stirring it with a spatula until it be about half cold or congealed, and then put it into small pots, as before directed, or make it up into rolls the size of the little finger." James Rennie. *A New Supplement to the Pharmacopoeias of London, Edinburgh, Dublin, and Paris [. . .].* Page 340. 1833. London. Google Books. Also, Raibaud and Lewis refer to "sticks of pomatum for the toupet." Raibaud et Louis (Perfumers : Paris, France). *A l'Etoile Orientale. Varia Aromata. London. Raibaud et Louis Marchands-Parfumeurs, ... à Paris, tiennent dans cette ville ... chez Mr. Bawen, Air-Street Piccadilly: savoir, ... = The Eastern Star. Varia aromata. London. Raibaud and Lewis perfumers, ... at Paris, have likewise a wholesale and retail perfumery warehouse, at Mr. Bawen's, Air-Street, Piccadilly: viz. ...* n.p. 1775 (?). London. Eighteenth Century Collections Online.

8. Raibaud et Louis (Perfumers: Paris, France). *A l'Etoile Orientale. Varia Aromata. London. Raibaud et Louis Marchands-Parfumeurs, ... à Paris, tiennent dans cette ville ... chez Mr. Bawen, Air-Street Piccadilly: savoir, ... = The Eastern Star. Varia aromata. London. Raibaud and Lewis perfumers, ... at Paris, have likewise a wholesale and retail perfumery warehouse, at Mr. Bawen's, Air-Street, Piccadilly: viz. ...* n.p. 1775 (?). London. Eighteenth Century Collections Online.

9. While the recipe is from an 1840s book, as we've stated before, pomatum recipes don't really change much throughout history. See Arnold James Cooley. *The Cyclopaedia of Practical Receipts in All the Useful and Domestic Arts: Being a Compendious Book of Reference for the Manufacturer, Tradesman, and Amateur.* 1841. London. Google Books.

Chapter 2: Hair Powder—The Original Dry Shampoo

1. Peter Gilchrist. *A Treatise on the Hair*. Page 6. 1770. London. Eighteenth Century Collections Online. In this case Gilchrist is himself a secondary source, reporting on the first use of hair powder 100 years before. While Madame de Montespan may or may not have been the first to pulverize wheat starch, there is a hair powder recipe found in *Polygraphice*, 1673, to support Gilchrist's statement regarding time period. Earlier portraiture may appear to show the use of pomade and powder, but further research and more primary evidence is needed here—another book for another time.

2. James Stewart. *Plocacosmos: or the Whole Art of Hair Dressing; Wherein Is Contained Ample Rules for the Young Artizan, More Particularly for Ladies Women, Valets, &c. &c.* Page 244. 1782. London. Eighteenth Century Collections Online.

3. We're referencing the use of wigs and powdered wigs/hair being worn by household servants, barristers and judges in the United Kingdom up through the nineteenth and twentieth centuries.

4. Kimberly Chrisman-Campbell. *Fashion Victims: Dress at the Court of Louis XVI and Marie-Antoinette*. Page 38. 2015. New Haven and London. Yale University Press.

5. John Hart. *An Address to the Public on the Subject of the Starch and Hair-Powder Manufactories [. . .]* 1795. London. Eighteenth Century Collections Online.

6. John Hart. *An Address to the Public on the Subject of the Starch and Hair-Powder Manufactories [. . .]*. Pages 14 & 15. 1795. London. Eighteenth Century Collections Online. According to Hart, this ill-formed propaganda also resulted in hairdressers, barbers and citizens wearing hair powder being verbally and physically assaulted in the streets.

7. Brian W Peckham. "Technological Change in the British and French Starch Industries, 1750–1850." *Technology and Culture* 27, no. 1 (1986): 18–39. doi:10.2307/3104943.

8. John Hart. *An Address to the Public on the Subject of the Starch and Hair-Powder Manufactories [. . .]*. Page 12. 1795. London. Eighteenth Century Collections Online.

9. James Stewart. *Plocacosmos: or the Whole Art of Hair Dressing; Wherein Is Contained Ample Rules for the Young Artizan, More Particularly for Ladies Women, Valets, &c. &c.* Pages 266–267. 1782. London. Eighteenth Century Collections Online.

10. William Moore. *The Art Of Hair-Dressing, and Making It Grow Fast, Together, with a Plain and Easy Method of Preserving It; with Several Useful Recipes, &C.* Pages 14–18. c. 1780. London. Eighteenth Century Collections Online. He also proceeds to explain how you can test your powder for lime, chalk or marble, and discusses the cost of decent powder. The best Common Powder should cost no less than 8 pence for a pound.

11. James Stewart. *Plocacosmos: or the Whole Art of Hair Dressing; Wherein Is Contained Ample Rules for the Young Artizan, More Particularly for Ladies Women, Valets, &c. &c.* Pages 321–322. 1782. London. Eighteenth Century Collections Online.

12. A Practical Chemist. *The Cyclopaedia of Practical Receipts in All the Useful and Domestic Arts*. 1841. London. Google Books.

13. Ingredients such as butane, isobutane, oryza sativa (rice) starch, propane, alcohol denat, parfume, limonene, linanool, geranol, benzyl benzoate, distearyldimonium and cetrimonium chloride can be found in dry shampoo bought at your favorite big-box store or drugstore.

14. However, modern developments in how the dry shampoo is applied are great options for eighteenth-century hair powder. You'll see on page 126 that we used a modern pump applicator for our powder application, like a modern bellows.

15. Pierre Joseph Buchoz, M.D. *Toilet de Flora*. Page 186. 1772. Google Books.

16. Many original hair powder recipes do not include the bone meal ingredients, such as one found in *Polygraphice*, 1673, calling for "iris roots in a fine powder one ounce and a half . . . some use white starch . . . "

17. James Stewart. *Plocacosmos: or the Whole Art of Hair Dressing; Wherein Is Contained Ample Rules for the Young Artizan, More Particularly for Ladies Women, &c. &c.* Pages 266–267. 1782. London. Eighteenth Century Collections Online.

18. A Practical Chemist. *The Cyclopaedia of Practical Receipts in All the Useful and Domestic Arts*. Page 153. 1841. London. Google Books; Anonymous. *The American Family Receipt Book: Consisting of Several Thousand Most Valuable Receipts, Experiments, &c. &c. Collected from Various Parts of Europe, America, and Other Portions of the Globe*. Page 248. 1854. London. Google Books.

19. James Stewart. *Plocacosmos: or the Whole Art of Hair Dressing; Wherein Is Contained Ample Rules for the Young Artizan, More Particularly for Ladies Women, Valets, &c. &c.* Page 321. 1782. London. Eighteenth Century Collections Online.

20. Pierre-Thomas LeClerc. *Gallerie des Modes et Costumes Français. 10e. Cahier des Costumes Français. 4e Suite d'Habillemens à la mode. K.57 Femme galante à sa toilette ployant un billet*. 1778. Museum of Fine Arts, Boston. 44.1321; Alexander Roslin. *Portrait of Marie-Françoise Julie Constance Filleul, Marquise de Marigny with a book*. 1754. Private Collection. https://www.gettyimages.com/detail/news-photo/portrait-of-marie-fran%C3%A7oise-julie-constance-filleul-news-photo/600054461#/portrait-of-mariefranoise-julie-constance-filleul-marquise-de-marigny-picture-id600054461; Joseph Siffred Duplessis. *Madame de Saint-Maurice*. 1776. The Metropolitan Museum of Art, New York. 69.161.

Chapter 3: Wigs, Hairpieces and Women

1. Emma Markiewicz. *Hair, Wigs and Wig Wearing in Eighteenth-Century England*. Page 24. 2014. PhD thesis, University of Warwick.

2. We have yet to find a portrait of a woman depicted wearing a hard-front wig. When a tête (wig) is worn, multiple hairdressing manuals stress that the hairline should be blended with the wearer's natural hairline, short though her natural hair may be. See James Stewart, Peter Gilchrist and David Ritchie.

3. Markiewicz, Emma. *Hair, Wigs and Wig Wearing in Eighteenth-Century England*. Pages 70 & 71. 2014. PhD thesis, University of Warwick.

4. Some excellent examples are: Thomas Rowlandson. *Six Stages of Mending a Face*. 1792. British Museum. 1876,1014.10; James Gillray. *Female Curiosity*. 1778. National Portrait Gallery, London. NPG D12976; Matthew Darly. *Lady Drudger Going to Ranelagh*. 1772. Yale University Library, Lewis Walpole Digital Collection. 772.04.25.01.1.

5. Amanda Vickery. "Mutton Dressed as Lamb? Fashioning Age in Georgian England." *Journal Of British Studies* 52:4 (2013). Pages 858–886.

6. David Ritchie. *A Treatise on Hair*. 1770. Eighteenth Century Collections Online; Peter Gilchrist. *A Treatise on the Hair*. 1770. London. Eighteenth Century Collections Online; William Moore. *The Art of Hair-Dressing, and Making It Grow Fast, Together with a Plain and Easy Method of Preserving It; with Several Useful Recipes, &c.* c. 1780. London. Eighteenth Century Collections Online; Diderot and d'Alembert. *Encyclopédie Méthodique, ou par Ordre de Matières; par une Société de Gens de Lettres, de Savans et d'Artistes*. 1789. Paris. Google Books; and Legros de Rumigny. *L'Art de la Coëffure des Dames Françoises*. 1768. Paris. Gallica Bibliothèque Numérique. Just to name a few.

7. William Moore. *The Art of Hair-Dressing, and Making It Grow Fast, Together with a Plain and Easy Method of Preserving It; with Several Useful Recipes, &c.* c. 1780. London. Eighteenth Century Collections Online.

8. Trust us, we failed with fake hair so you could avoid the suffering.

9. False chignons or long hair were extremely common in the eighteenth century, and most of our hairdressing manuals discuss their use (See Bibliography). James Stewart writes, "Now to put on: and first the false chignon; I have before said where this is to be placed; but if it is not made very flat and strong with a good small comb, it will make the head appear bumpy and aukward behind." *Plocacosmos*. Page 299.

10. David Ritchie. *A Treatise on the Hair*. Pages 64–72. 1770. London. Eighteenth Century Collections Online; James Stewart. *Plocacosmos: or the Whole Art of Hair Dressing; Wherein Is Contained Ample Rules for the Young Artizan, More Particularly for Ladies Women, Valets, &c. &c.* Pages 298–300. 1782. London. Eighteenth Century Collections Online.

11. Many cartoons and depictions of the hair being dressed show false buckles in use, such as "The Village Barber," 1778. The British Museum. J,5.121. Additionally, Gilchrist and Ritchie both offer false buckles for sale in their books, both aptly named *A Treatise on the Hair*, 1770, and there are many more references.

CHAPTER 4: DE-CLOWNING EIGHTEENTH-CENTURY MAKEUP

1. Anonymous. "Caution against using White Lead as a Cosmetic." *The Bristol and Bath magazine, or, Weekly miscellany.* Containing selected beauties from all the new publications, together with a variety of Pages 106 & 107. 1782–1783. Eighteenth Century Collections Online.

2. Le Camus. A. *Abdeker; or, the Art of Preserving Beauty. Translated from an Arabic manuscript or rather from the French of A. Le Camus*. Page 63. 1756. Google Books.

3. Pierre Joseph Buchoz, M.D. *Toilet de Flora*. 1772. London. Google Books.

4. Anonymous. "Caution against using White Lead as a Cosmetic." *The Bristol and Bath magazine, or, Weekly miscellany.* Containing selected beauties from all the new publications, together with a variety of. Page 107. 1782–1783. Eighteenth Century Collections Online.

5. Markiewicz, Emma. *Hair, Wigs and Wig Wearing in Eighteenth-Century England*. Pages 69, 70, 79 & 82. 2014. PhD thesis, University of Warwick.

6. We did not include an eyebrow "pencil," or burnt clove, in our book. If you are interested in trying this method, see *Toilet de Flora*. 1772. Pages 86 & 207. Google Books.

7. Pierre Joseph Buchoz, M.D. *Toilet de Flora*. Page 194. 1772. London. Google Books.

8. Every model in this book wore the rouge, and, in our opinion, they all looked amazing.

9. OutKast. "Hey Ya!" Speakerboxxx/The Love Below. 2003. LaFace & Arista Records.

10. Pierre Joseph Buchoz, M.D. *Toilet de Flora*. Page 162. 1772. London. Google Books.

11. This substitution was provided in *Toilet de Flora*. Page 172. 1772. London. Google Books.

Part 2: Up, Up and Away

1. Legros de Rumigny. *L'Art de la Coëffure des Dames Françoises*. 1768. Paris. Gallica Bibliothèque Numérique.

2. Legros followed up with supplemental publications in 1768 and 1770 with even more plates and descriptions.

3. *Recollections of Léonard*, page 21.

4. *Recollections of Léonard*, page 193. "...high head-dresses are becoming very common; it is long since the bourgeoisie has taken possession of it, and now it is the turn of the common people."

5. *Recollections of Léonard*, page 154. The *Journal des Dames* was resurrected in January 1774.

6. In *A Treatise on the Hair*, 1770, the description Ritchie gives aligns perfectly with Legros's hairstyles: "[Of a crape Toupee] Of a regular one-row of curls, and a crape before them." Page 50.

7. Take your pick between Gilchrist, Ritchie, Stewart and Moore, as they all discuss how the English were slow to adopt hair powder.

8. This personal preference amongst English (and American) women is visible through existing portraiture.

9. James Stewart. *Plocacosmos: or the Whole Art of Hair Dressing; Wherein Is Contained Ample Rules for the Young Artizan, More Particularly for Ladies Women, Valets, &c. &c.* Page 243. 1782. London. Eighteenth Century Collections Online.

Chapter 5: 1750–1770 Coiffure Française

1. Peter Gilchrist. *A Treatise on the Hair*. Pages 6–10. 1770. London. Eighteenth Century Collections Online.

2. See *Portrait of the Madame de Pompadour* by François Boucher, 1756; *The Marquise de Pompadour* by Maurice Quentin de La Tour, 1748–1755; and the marble bust of Madame de Pompadour by Jean-Baptiste Pigalle, 1748–1751.

3. James Stewart. *Plocacosmos.* Pages 242–243. 1782. London. Eighteenth Century Collections Online.

4. Jean-Étienne Liotard. *Portrait of Archduchess Maria Antonia of Austria (Marie Antoinette).* 1762. Musée d'Art et d'Histoire, Geneva. 1947-0042.

5. *Encyclopédie, ou Dictionnaire Raisonné des Sciences, des Arts et des Métiers, par une Société de Gens de Lettres*, 1773, and *The Lady's Magazine vol 16*, Robinson, 1785, both describe the tête or tête de mouton in relation to the front of the head only, but David Ritchie and Peter Gilchrist in their respective *A Treatise on the Hair*, 1770, and James Stewart in *Plocacosmos* also describe the tête de mouton by name as covering the back of the head in curls.

6. In *L'Art de la Coëffure des Dames Françoises*, 1768, Legros includes instructions and diagrams for cutting the hair to achieve these styles.

7. *Cap Back.* c. 1740. Victoria and Albert Museum. August 2018. http://collections.vam.ac.uk/item/O134732/cap-back-unknown.

8. Please read the chapter introduction for more information on what is, isn't, maybe is and maybe isn't a tête de mouton.

9. David Ritchie. *A Treatise on Hair.* Pages 64–72. 1770. London. Eighteenth Century Collections Online.

10. Legros de Rumigny. *L'Art de la Coëffure des Dames Françoises.* 1768. Paris. Gallica Bibliothèque Numérique. In the plates showing the back of the head, Legros illustrates tiny, closely-cut hairs at the nape of the neck. See pages 38 and 51 and their accompanying plates.

11. A description and illustration labeled "coëffure de dentelles" (or "lace head" in English) appears in *Diderot's L'Encyclopédie, Arts de l'habillement*, Chapter "Lingerie," plate 1.

12. *Cap.* 18th Century. MFA, Boston. 38.1206; Accessory Set. c. 1750. The Metropolitan Museum of Art, New York. 2009.300.2195a-d; Cap Back. c. 1740. Victoria and Albert Museum. T.27-1947.

Chapter 6: 1765–1772 Coiffure Banane

1. David Ritchie. *A Treatise on the Hair.* Page 59. 1770. London. Eighteenth Century Collections Online.

2. This is just our name for this piece, not the historical term. We have not found a proper name for this headgear, but if you have please let us know!

3. Anonymous. "Patterns for the Newest and Most Elegant Head Dresses." *The Lady's Magazine.* May 1771. Yale University Library. Lewis Walpole Digital Collections. 771.05.00.03.

4. Three American portraits by John Singleton Copley, between 1772 and 1773, depict this type of headgear: *Dorothy Quincy* (1975.13), *Mrs. Isaac Winslow* (39.250) and *Mrs. Richard Skinner* (06.2428). All Museum of Fine Arts, Boston.

5. Hat. c. 1760. The Metropolitan Museum of Art, New York. 1984.140.

Chapter 7: 1772–1775 Coiffure Beignet

1. Pierre-Thomas LeClerc, Nicolas Dupin, Esnauts et Rapilly. Galerie des Modes et Costumes Français, 6e Suite d'Habillemens à la mode en 1778. M.67. "Jeune Dame se faisant cöeffer à neuf . . .". 1778. Museum of Fine Arts, Boston. 44.1333.

2. Joseph Siffred Duplessis. *Madame de Saint-Maurice.* 1776. The Metropolitan Museum of Art, New York. 69.161. This painting was exhibited at the Salon in Paris in 1777 and is apparently dated 1776 according to the Metropolitan Museum of Art's webpage. However, the height and shape of her hair is more in keeping with the style of the previous years of 1774 and 1775. Madame was a bit out of fashion, but as with all modes in dress, fashions do not suddenly cease from December of one year to January of the next.

3. Every manual we've studied uses the term "cushion." Please see bibliography if you don't believe us.

4. Sarah Woodyard. "Martha's Mob Cap? A Milliner's Hand-Sewn Inquiry into Eighteenth-Century Caps ca. 1770–1800." Page 38. University of Alberta. Accessed June 2018. https://era.library.ualberta.ca/items/d08025c6-d1b7-4221-81f4-fc1601b57258.

5. If your hair is thinner and finer, you might not need/want to do this step, but instead just pin the hair to the inside of the donut. See the Ski Slope chapter (page 117) for an example of this technique.

6. Several examples are "Woman Wearing a Flowered Dress and Hat." 1770–1780. Lewis Walpole Library. 778.00.00.02; "Portrait of an Unknown Woman in a White Cap." Grigoriy Serdiukov. 1772; and "Lady Nightcap at Breakfast." 1772. Carington Bowles. British Museum. 2010,7081.1223.

7. A wonderful description of the calash bonnet from *Annals of Philadelphia* by John Fanning Watson reads, "'A Calash Bonnet' was always formed of green silk; it was worn abroad, covering the head, but when in rooms it could fall back in folds like the springs of a calash or gig top; to keep it up over the head it was drawn up by a cord always held in the hand of the wearer." John Fanning Watson. *Annals of Philadelphia.* Page 176. 1830. New York. Google Books.

8. *Woman's calash bonnet, green and rose silk.* 1777–1785. The Colonial Williamsburg Foundation. Acc. No. 1960-723.

9. See Art Works Cited (page 229) for a list of original calash bonnets held in various museum collections.

Chapter 8: 1776–1779 Coiffure Ski Alpin

1. Kimberly Chrisman-Campbell. *Fashion Victims: Dress at the Court of Louis XVI and Marie-Antoinette.* Pages 54–55. 2015. New Haven and London. Yale University Press.

2. Léonard Autié. *Recollections of Léonard, Hairdresser to Queen Marie-Antoinette.* Translated from French by E. Jules Meras. Page 156. Originally published 1838. Translated 1912. London. Archive.org.

3. Kimberly Chrisman-Campbell. *Fashion Victims: Dress at the Court of Louis XVI and Marie-Antoinette.* Page 23. 2015. New Haven and London. Yale University Press.

4. We did a lot of YouTube and Google searches here, and one of our favorite videos on the subject can be found here: https://www.youtube.com/watch?v=q_61hv7tPU4.

5. "Cousin Itt is a fictional character in *The Addams Family* television and film series. He was developed specifically for the 1964 television series *The Addams Family*, and is a regular supporting character in subsequent motion picture, television, and stage adaptations." Wikipedia.org.

6. Freebird, y'all.

7. Léonard Autié. *Recollections of Léonard, Hairdresser to Queen Marie-Antoinette.* Translated from French by E. Jules Meras. Page 156. Originally published 1838. Translated 1912. London. Archive.org.

8. Léonard Autié. *Recollections of Léonard, Hairdresser to Queen Marie-Antoinette.* Translated from French by E. Jules Meras. Pages 98–99. Originally published 1838. Translated 1912. London. Archive.org.

Chapter 9: Early 1780s Coiffure Chenille

1. Léonard Autié. *Recollections of Léonard, Hairdresser to Queen Marie-Antoinette.* Translated from French by E. Jules Meras. Pages 194–196. Originally published 1838. Translated 1912. London. Archive.org.

2. Ralph Earl. *Portrait of Esther Boardman.* 1789. The Metropolitan Museum of Art, New York. 1991.338.

3. A treasure trove of hairstyle fashion plates can be found in the *Gallerie des Modes et Costumes Français*, Claude-Louis Desrais, in the collection of the Museum of Fine Arts, Boston (www.mfa.org).

4. Just to confuse us, *Gallerie des Modes* labels all sorts of headgear, hairstyles and parts of the hair as toque and also sans toque. For the sake of differentiating this project, and in reference to the many examples in *Gallerie des Modes*, we choose to call it a toque, but cap (bonnet in French) and even pouf are also correct. *Gallerie des Modes.* Museum of Fine Arts, Boston. www.mfa.org.

5. *Gallerie des Modes et Costumes Français* shows a black Therese from 1776 (mfa.org, 44.1265). More plates appear depicting both black and white Thereses from 1779 (mfa.org, 44.1403) and 1785 (mfa.org, 44.1633 and 44.1613).

Part 3: Let's Get Frizzical, Frizzical!

1. The hérrison (or "hedgehog") hairstyle first appears in *Gallerie des Modes* in 1776, showing the hair dressed over a tall cushion and corralled at the top by a ribbon or band, the ends left sticking straight up and uncurled creating the "spiky" effect the name eludes to. The term persisted through the early and mid-1780s craped and frizzed hairstyles. The common link is the ribbon and spiky top, not the frizzed or curled crown. *Gallerie des Modes et Costumes Français*, plates from 1776–1785 show many variations of the hérisson hairstyle. Museum of Fine Arts, Boston. www.mfa.org (Accession Nos. 44.1243, 44.1249, and 44.1527, for example).

2. Pierre-Thomas LeClerc and Pélissier. *Gallerie des Modes et Costumes Français.* Plates 200 (44.1498), 201 (44.1500) and 204 (44.1505). 1780. Museum of Fine Arts, Boston. www.mfa.org.

3. *Recollections of Léonard.* Pages 194–196.

4. The fashion magazines named these styles all manner of things, such as *Coëffure dite à la Princesse, Coëffure à la nouvelle Créole* or *Coëffure aux Colimaçous d'amour*, just to name a few from the *Gallerie des Modes et Costumes Français.*

5. David Ritchie. *A Treatise on Hair.* Pages 49–50. 1770. Eighteenth Century Collections Online. Ritchie describes the hair being crape'd and staying in dress for "some months." See page 157 for more on crape-ing.

6. James Stewart in *Plocacosmos* explains, "[. . .] after that take a very large net fillet, which must be big enough to cover the head and hair, and put it on, and drawing the strings to a proper tightness behind, till it closes all round the face and neck like a purse, bring the strings round the front and back again to the neck, where they must be tied; this, with the finest lawn handkerchief, is night covering sufficient for the head." Page 294.

7. Abby was actually crazy enough to do this with straws, and it totally worked!

8. A description and illustrations of papillote curls, paper and irons can be seen in *L'Encyclopédie, Arts de l'habillement* by Diderot, chapter "Perruquier, Barbier, Baigneur-etuviste," plate 2.

Chapter 10: 1780–1783 Coiffure Friseur

1. Legros de Rumigny. *L'Art de la Coëffure des Dames Françoises.* 1768. Paris. Gallica Bibliothèque Numérique.

2. Élisabeth Louise Vigée Le Brun. *Marie Antoinette in a Chemise Dress.* 1783. Hessische Hausstiftung, Kronberg.

3. Charles V. Linneaus. *A General System of Nature Through the Grand Kingdoms or Animals, Vegetables, and Minerals [. . .].* 1766/1802. London. Archive.org.

4. Charles V. Linneaus. *A General System of Nature Through the Grand Kingdoms or Animals, Vegetables, and Minerals [. . .].* 1766/1802. London. Archive.org.

5. S. White & G.J. White. *Stylin' African American Expressive Culture from Its Beginnings to the Zoot Suit*. Page 41. 1999. Ithaca. Cornell University Press.

6. S. White & G.J. White. *Stylin' African American Expressive Culture from Its Beginnings to the Zoot Suit*. Page 42. 1999. Ithaca. Cornell University Press.

7. L.L. Tharps. & A.D. Byrd. *Hair Story: Untangling the Roots of Black Hair*. Page 2. 2002. New York. St. Martins.

8. L.L. Tharps. & A.D. Byrd. *Hair Story: Untangling the Roots of Black Hair*. Page 17. 2002. New York. St. Martins.

9. L.L. Tharps. & A.D. Byrd. *Hair Story: Untangling the Roots of Black Hair*. Page 6. 2002. New York. St. Martins.

10. S. White & G.J. White. *Stylin' African American Expressive Culture from Its Beginnings to the Zoot Suit*. Page 41. 1999. Ithaca. Cornell University Press.

11. S. White & G.J. White. S*tylin' African American Expressive Culture from Its Beginnings to the Zoot Suit*. Page 38. 1999. Ithaca. Cornell University Press.

12. Aileen Ribeiro. *Dress in Eighteenth-Century Europe*. Page 155. 2002. New Haven and London. Yale University Press. Another example is a letter written by Elizabeth Montagu in 1764, "[I?] never saw such a set of people as appear in the publick rooms . . . [t]heir dress is most elaborately ugly. A friseur [to curl the hair] is employ'd three hours in a morning to make a young Lady look like a virgin Hottentot or Squaw, all art ends in giving them the ferocious air of uncomb'd savages." From Angela Rosenthal. "Raising Hair." *Eighteenth-Century Studies* 38, no. 1 (2004): 1–16. Page 5. https://muse.jhu.edu/.

13. Florence Montgomery. *Textiles in America 1650–1870*. Pages 207–209. 2007. New York & London. W.W. Norton & Company.

14. David Ritchie. *A Treatise on Hair*. Pages 49–50. 1770. London. Eighteenth Century Collections Online.

15. For this tutorial, we follow James Stewart's instructions in *Plocacosmos* as closely as we can. Pages 258–260.

16. Yes, we're referencing that classic scene in *Little Women*. It's Abby's favorite movie, by the way.

17. James Stewart. *Plocacosmos: or the Whole Art of Hair Dressing; Wherein Is Contained Ample Rules for the Young Artizan, More Particularly for Ladies Women, Valets, &c. &c.* Page 278. 1782. London. Eighteenth Century Collections Online.

18. Diderot and d'Alembert. *Encyclopédie Méthodique, ou par Ordre de Matières; par une Société de Gens de Lettres, de Savans et d'Artistes*. 1789. Paris. Google Books.

19. James Stewart. *Plocacosmos: or the Whole Art of Hair Dressing; Wherein Is Contained Ample Rules for the Young Artizan, More Particularly for Ladies Women, Valets, &c. &c.* Pages 257–280. 1782. London. Eighteenth Century Collections Online.

20. Diderot and d'Alembert. *Encyclopédie Méthodique, ou par Ordre de Matières; par une Société de Gens de Lettres, de Savans et d'artistes*. 1789. Paris. Google Books.

21. Before Stewart goes into the details of crape-ing and setting the hair, he explains the cut, which was as short as a half-inch (1.2 cm) in the front! *Plocacosmos*, pages 250–254.

22. That is, if we're not ugly crying because buckles are mean.

23. Designed by Pierre-Thomas LeClerc, Engraved by Nicolas Dupin. Much of the *Gallerie des Modes et Costumes Français* can be searched on the Museum of Fine Arts, Boston website (www.mfa.org). Caps very similar to this one appear in many fashion plates, both French and English, across a broad range of years.

24. Adélaïde Labille-Guiard. *Self-Portrait with Two Pupils, Marie Gabrielle Capet and Marie Marguerite Carreaux de Rosemond*. 1785. The Metropolitan Museum of Art, New York. Accession No. 53.225.5.

25. Claude-Louis Desrais and Nicolas Dupin. *Gallerie des Modes et Costumes Français. 41e Cahier des Costumes Français, 11e Suitte de coeffures à la mode en 1783. tt.250.* Museum of Fine Arts, Boston. Accession No. 44.1555.

26. Here are some examples of bonnets that are not black: Carrington Bowles. *A Decoy for the Old as well as the Young*. 1773. Yale University Library Digital Collections, Lewis Walpole Library. Call No. 773.01.19.02+; William Redmore Bigg. *A Lady and Her Children Relieving a Cottager*. 1781. Philadelphia Museum of Art. Accession No. 1947-64-1; William Redmore Bigg. *A Girl Gathering Filberts*. 1782. Plymouth City Council: The Box. Accession No. PLYMG.CO.3; Carington Bowles after Robert Dighton. *Youth and Age*. 1780–1790. The British Museum. 1935,0522.1.78.

27. There's more evidence of black bonnets existing than colored versions. In *Instructions for Cutting Out Apparel for the Poor*, black durant is presented as the fabric and color option. In *Annals of Philadelphia* the author comments on eighteenth-century bonnets, "As a universal fact, it may be remarked that no other colour than black was ever made for ladies bonnets when formed of silk or satin" (page 177). While this is not entirely true, based on observation of portraiture from the last quarter of the eighteenth century, it furthers the understanding that black was the dominant color for bonnets.

28. J. Walter. *Instructions for Cutting Out Apparel for the Poor [. . .]*. Pages 8 & 9. 1789. London. Google Books.

Chapter 11: 1785–1790 Coiffure Américaine Duchesse

1. *Plocacosmos* (1782) explains the process of both curling and crape-ing for the hair, with the crape-ing being at the front. *The Art of Hair Dressing* by Alexander Stewart (1788) only curls the hair. These differences can also be seen in the hair texture in portraiture as the 1780s progresses.

2. Alexander Stewart. *The Art of Hair Dressing*. Pages 12–16. 1788. London. Eighteenth Century Collections Online.

3. Anonymous. *Seated Woman, Seen from Behind*. c. 1790–1795. The Metropolitan Museum of Art, New York. Accession No. 2000.131.

4.   James Stewart. *Plocacosmos: or the Whole Art of Hair Dressing; Wherein Is Contained Ample Rules for the Young Artizan, More Particularly for Ladies Women, Valets, &c. &c.* Page 254. 1782. London. Eighteenth Century Collections Online.

5.   Alexander Stewart. *The Art of Hair Dressing.* Page 13. 1788. London. Eighteenth Century Collections Online.

6.   We've made up this name for the cap, because we think it looks like a jellyfish.

7.   Élisabeth Louise Vigée Le Brun. *Madame Victoire de France.* 1791. Phoenix Art Museum. Accession No. 1974.36; Élisabeth Louise Vigée Le Brun. *Madame Adélaïde de France.* 1791. Musée Jeanne-d'Aboville, La Fère, Aisne. Accession No. MJA 124.

8.   Adélaïde Labille-Guiard. *Portrait of a Woman (formerly thought to be Madame Roland).* 1787. Musée des Beaux-Arts de Quimper. Accession No. 873-1-787; Adélaïde Labille-Guiard. *Marie Adélaïde de France, Known as Madame Adélaïde.* 1786–1787. Palace of Versailles. Accession No. MV 5940.

9.   We're talking about Marie Antoinette and her chemise gown again.

10.   There are lots of lovely examples, such as *Mrs. Thomas Hibbert* by Thomas Gainsborough, 1786 (Die Pinakotheken, Munich. FV 4) and the *Comtesse de la Châtre* by Élisabeth Louise Vigée Le Brun, 1789 (The Metropolitan Museum of Art, New York. 54.182).

11.   In hat-making, hoods and capelines are the basic, roughly-shaped, un-blocked hat forms in straw or wool. Hoods produce more narrow-brimmed hats while capelines make for wider-brimmed hats.

Chapter 12: 1790–1794 Coiffure Révolution

1.   N. Heideloff. *Gallery of Fashion* Vol. 1 (April 1794) – Vol. 9 (March 1803). London. Bunka Gakuen Library, Digital Archive of Rare Materials. http://digital.bunka.ac.jp/kichosho_e/search_list2.php.

2.   If you have our first book, you know that our 1790s chapter was heavily influenced by the art of Élisabeth Louise Vigée Le Brun. Her Russian portraits in the 1790s have that slightly matte appearance to the hair, nothing like the glossy shine that appears in her 1800s portraits. This contrast, plus our experimentation, has brought us to this conclusion. Joseph Baillio, Katharine Baetjer, Paul Lang. *Vigée Le Brun.* 2016. New Haven and London. Yale University Press.

3.   The term chiffonet is used throughout Gallery of Fashion. Here is just one example: Heideloff. *Gallery of Fashion* Vol. 1 (April 1794) – Vol. 9 (March 1803). Vol. 1 (1794) Fig. VII. London. Bunka Gakuen Library, Digital Archive of Rare Materials. http://digital.bunka.ac.jp/kichosho_e/search_list2.php.

4.   For an extensive description of applying papillote papers, see Alexander Stewart's *The Art of Hair Dressing or, The Ladies Director,* 1788. London. Eighteenth Century Collections Online.

5.   Yeah, we just made a French Revolution joke . . . too soon?

6.   Heideloff. *Gallery of Fashion* Vol. 1 (April 1794) – Vol. 9 (March 1803). Vol. 1 (1794) Fig. VII. London. Bunka Gakuen Library, Digital Archive of Rare Materials. http://digital.bunka.ac.jp/kichosho/index.php.

7.   All of the figures in *Gallery of Fashion* for the first volume have a variety of turbans, caps, wraps, etc.

Epilogue

1.   Kimberly Chrisman-Campbell. *Fashion Victims: Dress at the Court of Louis XVI and Marie-Antoinette.* Page 278. 2015. New Haven and London. Yale University Press.

2.   While we're not going to go into much detail about how the British government almost stopped the use of hair powder in its tracks, you can read more about what was happening in John Hart's *An Address to the Public on the Subject of the Starch and Hair-Powder Manufactories [. . .].* 1795. London. Eighteenth Century Collections Online. It wasn't good. People were being attacked in the streets, and this tax was causing a great deal of damage to the starch manufacturing industry.

3.   Stephen Dowell. *A History of Taxation and Taxes in England from the Earliest Times to the Year 1885.* Volume III. Direct Taxes and Stamp Duties. Pages 255–59. 1888. London. Longmans, Green & Co.

4.   Emma Markiewicz. *Hair, Wigs and Wig Wearing in Eighteenth-Century England.* Page 95. 2014. PhD thesis, University of Warwick.

5.   Stephen Dowell. *A History of Taxation and Taxes in England from the Earliest Times to the Year 1885.* Volume III. Direct Taxes and Stamp Duties. Pages 255–59. 1888. London: Longmans, Green & Co.

6.   James Rennie. *A New Supplement to the Pharmacopoeias of London, Edinburgh, Dublin, and Paris [. . .].* Pages 353–54. 1833. London. Google Books.

7.   Recipes found in eighteenth-century manuals and nineteenth-century manuals are often identical in their composition, or incredibly similar. There are too many to list, but comparing *Toilet de Flora (1779)* to *A New Supplement to the Pharacopeoias of London, Edinburgh, Dublin, and Paris (1833)* comes to mind.

Art Works Cited

1. *Accessory Set.* c. 1750. The Metropolitan Museum of Art, New York. 2009.300.2195a-d.

2. Adélaïde Labille-Guiard. *Self-Portrait with Two Pupils, Marie Gabrielle Capet and Marie Marguerite Carreaux de Rosemond.* 1785. The Metropolitan Museum of Art, New York. Accession No. 53.225.5.

3. Adélaïde Labille-Guiard. *Madame Adélaïde de France.* 1787. Musée National des Châteaux de Versailles et de Trianon.

4. Adélaïde Labille-Guiard. *Madame Élisabeth de France.* c. 1787. The Metropolitan Museum of Art, New York. 2007.441.

5. Adélaïde Labille-Guiard. *Marie Adélaïde de France, Known as Madame Adélaïde.* 1786–1787. Palace of Versailles. Accession No. MV 5940.

6. Adélaïde Labille-Guiard. *Portrait of a Woman (formerly thought to be Madame Roland).* 1787. Musée des Beaux-Arts de Quimper. Accession No. 873-1-787.

7. Adélaïde Labille-Guiard. *Self-Portrait with Two Pupils.* 1785. The Metropolitan Museum of Art, New York. 53.225.5.

8. Alexander Roslin. *Portrait of Marie-Françoise Julie Constance Filleul, Marquise de Marigny with a Book.* 1754. Private Collection. https://www.gettyimages.com/detail/news-photo/portrait-of-marie-fran%C3%A7oise-julie-constance-filleul-news-photo/600054461#/portrait-of-mariefranoise-julie-constance-filleul-marquise-de-marigny-picture-id600054461.

9. Allan Ramsay. *Portrait of Horace Walpole's Nieces: The Honorable Laura Keppel and Charlotte, Lady Huntingtower.* 1765. Museum of Fine Arts, Boston. 2009.2783.

10. Ann Perrin. "Ann Perrin, French Milliner." *Public Advertiser* (London, England), Tuesday, April 22, 1755; Issue 3681.

11. Anonymous. *A collection of ladies' dresses taken from almanacs, magazines and pocket books bequeathed by the late Miss Banks, arranged in one portfolio.* 1760–1818. British Museum. C,4. 1-468.

12. Anonymous. *Marie-Joséphine-Louise de Savoie, comtesse de Provence.* 1760–70s. Versailles, châteaux de Versailles et de Trianon. MV2125.

13. Anonymous. *Patterns for the Newest and Most Elegant Head Dresses. The Lady's Magazine.* May 1771. Yale University Library. Lewis Walpole Digital Collections. 771.05.00.03.

14. Anonymous. *Portrait of a Lady.* c. 1730–1750. National Gallery of Art, Washington, D.C. 1947.17.31

15. *Art and Picture Collection.* The New York Public Library. Native of Benguela; Native of Angola. 1855. The New York Public Library Digital Collections. http://digitalcollections.nypl.org/items/510d47e1-082f-a3d9-e040-e00a18064a99.

16. Augustin Pajou. *Madame du Barry.* 1772. The Metropolitan Museum of Art, New York. 43.163.3a, b.

17. Bernard Lepicié after François Boucher. *Le Déjeune "The Luncheon."* c. 1750. The Metropolitan Museum of Art, New York. 50.567.34.

18. Boizot Simon Louis. *Marie-Antoinette, reine de France.* 1774–75. Versailles, châteaux de Versailles et de Trianon. MV2213.

19. Edmé Bouchardon. *Marie-Thérèse Gosset.* 1732. Musée du Louvre, Paris. RF4642.

20. *Cap.* 18th Century. Musuem of Fine Arts, Boston. 38.1206.

21. *Cap Back.* c. 1740. Victoria and Albert Museum. http://collections.vam.ac.uk/item/O134732/cap-back-unknown/.

22. Carington Bowles after Robert Dighton. *Youth and Age.* 1780–1790. The British Museum. 1935,0522.1.78.

23. Carrington Bowles. *A Decoy for the old as well as the young.* 1773. Yale University Library Digital Collections, Lewis Walpole Library. Call No. 773.01.19.02+.

24. Claude-Louis Desrais and Etienne Claude Voysard. *Gallerie des Modes et Costumes Français, 21e. Cahier des Costumes Français, 15e Suite d'Habillemens à la mode en 1779. V.125.* 1779. Museum of Fine Arts, Boston. Accession No. 44.1403.

25. Claude-Louis Desrais and Nicolas Dupin. *Gallerie des Modes et Costumes Français. 41e Cahier des Costumes Français, 11e Suite de coeffures à la mode en 1783. tt.250.* Museum of Fine Arts, Boston. Accession No. 44.1555

26. E. Evans. "For the Ladies." *Morning Herald and Daily Advertiser* (London, England), Friday, February 22, 1782; Issue 411.

27. Élisabeth Louise Vigée Le Brun. *Comtesse de la Châtre.* 1789. The Metropolitan Museum, New York. Accession No. 54.182.

28. Élisabeth Louise Vigée Le Brun. *Madame Victoire de France.* 1791. Phoenix Art Museum. Accession No. 1974.36.

29. Élisabeth Louise Vigée Le Brun. *Comtesse de la Châtre.* 1789. The Metropolitan Museum of Art, New York. 54.182.

30. Élisabeth Louise Vigée Le Brun. *Madame Adélaïde de France.* 1791. Musée Jeanne d'Aboville, La Fère, Aisne. Accession No. MJA 124.

31. Élisabeth Louise Vigée Le Brun. *Madame Victoire de France.* 1791. Phoenix Art Museum. 1974.36.

32. Élisabeth Louise Vigée Le Brun. *Marie Antoinette in a Chemise Dress.* 1783. Hessische Hausstiftung, Kronberg.

33. Esnauts et Rapilly. *Gallerie des Modes et Costumes Français.* 1776–1787. Museum of Fine Arts, Boston.

34. Esnauts et Rapilly. *Gallerie des Modes et Costumes Français.* 13e Suite de Coeffures à la mode en 1785. 6(282ter). 1785. The Museum of Fine Arts, Boston. Accession No. 44.1613.

35. Francis Milner Newton. *Portrait of Johanna Warner, half-length, in a yellow dress and bonnet.* 1753. Bonhams. https://www.bonhams.com/auctions/21834/lot/258/.

36. François Hubert Drouais. *Marie Rinteau, called Mademoiselle de Verrières.* 1761 (Updated c. 1775). The Metropolitan Museum of Art, New York. 49.7.47.

37. François Louis Joseph Watteau and Nicolas Dupin. *Gallerie des Modes et Costumes Français. 47e Cahier de Costumes Français, 42e Suite d'Habillemens à la mode en 1785. Ccc.299.* 1785. The Museum of Fine Arts, Boston. 44.1633.

38. Gilles Edme Petit after François Boucher. *Le Matin, La Dame a sa Toilete.* c. 1750. The Metropolitan Museum of Art, New York. 53.600.1042.

39. *Hat.* c. 1760. The Metropolitan Museum of Art, New York. 1984.140.

40. Houdon Jean Antoine. *La Comtesse de Jaucourt.* 1777. Musée du Louvre, Paris. RF2470.

41. Jean-Baptiste Pigalle. *Madame de Pompadour.* 1748–51. The Metropolitan Museum of Art, New York. 49.7.70.

42. Jeanne Étienne Liotard. *Breakfast.* Around 1752. Die Pinakotheken, Munich. HUW 30. https://www.sammlung.pinakothek.de/en/artist/jean-etienne-liotard/das-fruehstueck.

43. Jean-Étienne Liotard. *Portrait of Archduchess Maria Antonia of Austria (Marie Antoinette).* 1762. Musée d'Art et d'Histoire, Geneva. 1947-0042.

44. Jean-Michel Moreau le Jeune. *Have No Fear, My Good Friend.* 1775. The J. Paul Getty Museum, Los Angeles. 85.GG.416.

45. Johann Eleazar Zeissig, called Schenau. *A Woman at her Toilet with a Maid, a Boy, a Dog, and a Young Soldier; verso: A Sketch for a Similar Composition.* 1770. The Metropolitan Museum of Art, New York. 2008.506.

46. Johann Nikolaus Grooth. *Portrait of a Woman.* c.1740–1760. The Metropolitan Museum of Art, New York. 22.174.

47. John Collet, Bowles and Carver. *Tight Lacing, or Fashion Before Ease.* c. 1770. The Colonial Williamsburg Foundation. 1969.111.

48. John Singleton Copley. *Dorothy Quincy (Mrs. John Hancock).* c. 1772. Museum of Fine Arts, Boston. 1975.13.

49. John Singleton Copley. *Mr. and Mrs. Isaac Winslow (Jemina Debuke).* 1773. Museum of Fine Arts, Boston. 39.250.

50. John Singleton Copley. *Mrs. Richard Skinner.* 1772. Museum of Fine Arts, Boston. 06.2428.

51. John Smart. *Mrs. Caroline Deas.* c. 1760. The Metropolitan Museum of Art, New York. 59.23.79.

52. Joseph Siffred Duplessis. *Madame de Saint-Maurice.* 1776. The Metropolitan Museum of Art, New York. 69.161.

53. Benjamin Henry Latrobe. *Preparation for the Enjoyment of a Fine Sunday Among the Blacks Norfolk VA.* March 4, 1797. Maryland Historical Society, Baltimore.

54. Lewis Hendrie. "Bear Grease, Lewis Hendrie." *Morning Herald and Daily Advertiser* (London, England), Friday, February 15, 1782; Issue 405.

55. Matthew Darly. *The City Rout.* May 20, 1776. The Metropolitan Museum of Art, New York. 17.3.888-261.

56. Pierre-Thomas LeClerc, Nicolas Dupin, Esnauts et Rapilly. *Galerie des Modes et Costumes Français, 6e Suite d'Habillemens à la mode en 1778. M.67 "Jeune Dame se faisant cöeffer à neuf...".* 1778. Museum of Fine Arts, Boston. 44.1333.

57. Pierre-Thomas LeClerc, Nicolas Dupin. Esnauts et Rapilly, *Gallerie des Modes et Costumes Français. 4e Suite d'Habillemens à la mode. K.57 "Femme galante à sa toilette ployant un billet."* 1778. Museum of Fine Arts, Boston. 44.1321

58. Pierre-Thomas LeClerc and Pélissier. *Gallerie des Modes et Costumes Français, 1ere Suite des Costumes François pour les Coiffures depuis 1776. A.6.* 1778. Museum of Fine Arts, Boston. Accession No. 44.1243.

59. Pierre-Thomas LeClerc and Pélissier. *Gallerie des Modes et Costumes Français, 2e. Cahier des Nouveaux Costumes Français pour les Coeffures. B.9.* 1778. Museum of Fine Arts, Boston. Accession No. 44.1249.

60. Pierre-Thomas LeClerc and Pélissier. *Gallerie des Modes et Costumes Français, 34e Cahier de Costumes Français, 8e Suite de Coeffures à la mode en 1780. 204.* 1780. Museum of Fine Arts, Boston. Accession No. 44.1505.

61. Pierre-Thomas LeClerc and Pélissier. *Gallerie des Modes et Costumes Français, 34e Cahier de Costumes Français, 8e Suite de Coeffures à la mode en 1780. 201.* 1780. Museum of Fine Arts, Boston. Accession No. 44.1500.

62. Pierre-Thomas LeClerc and Pélissier. *Gallerie des Modes et Costumes Français, 3e. Cahier des Modes Françaises pour les Coeffures depuis 1776. C.17.* 1778. Museum of Fine Arts, Boston. Accession No. 44.1265.

63. Pierre-Thomas LeClerc and Pélissier. *Gallerie des Modes et Costumes Français. 34e, Cahier de Costumes Français, 8e Suite de Coeffures à la mode en 1780.* 200. 1780. Museum of Fine Arts, Boston. Accession No. 44.1498.

64. René Gaillard after François Boucher. *La Marchande De Modes.* 1746–55. The Metropolitan Museum of Art, New York. 53.600.1107.

65. Sayer & Bennett. *The Boarding-School Hair-Dresser.* 1774. British Museum, London. 2010,7081.1658.

66. *The village barber / H. J.* 1778. [England: Pubd. M Darly, 39 Strand, June 1] Photograph. https://www.loc.gov/item/2006685336/.

67. Thomas Gainsborough. *Mrs. Thomas Hibbert.* 1786. Die Pinakotheken, Munich. Accession No. FV 4.

68. Thomas Gainsborough. *Mrs. Thomas Hibbert.* 1786. Die Pinakotheken, Munich. FV 4. https://www.sammlung.pinakothek.de/en/bookmark/artwork/8MLvMjwjxz.

69. Johann Friedrich August Tischbein. *Portrait de Madame Schmidt-Capelle.* 1786. Allemagne, Cassel, Museumslandschaft Hessen Kassel, Neue Galerie

70. William Berczy. *Portrait of Marie du Muralt.* 1782. National Gallery of Canada. Accession No. 41972.

71. William Redmore Bigg. *A Girl Gathering Filberts.* 1782. Plymouth City Council: The Box. Accession No. PLYMG.CO.3.

72. William Redmore Bigg. *A Lady and Her Children Relieving a Cottager.* 1781. Philadelphia Museum of Art. Accession No. 1947-64-1.

Henry Walton, 1746–1813. Portrait of a Young Woman, Possibly Miss Nettlethorpe. *1770. Yale Center for British Art, Paul Mellon Collection. B1981.25.652.*

Bibliography

1. A Practical Chemist. *The Cyclopaedia of Practical Receipts in All the Useful and Domestic Arts*. 1841. London. Google Books.

2. Andrews, John. *Remarks on the French and English Ladies, in a Series of Letters; interspersed with Various Anecdotes [. . .]*. 1783. London. Eighteenth Century Collections Online.

3. Anon. *A Dissertation Upon Headdress; Together with a Brief Vindication of High Coloured Hair, And of the those Ladies on whom it grows*. 1767. London. Eighteenth Century Collections Online.

4. Anon. *Fashion: or, a trip to a foreign c-t. A poem*. 1777. London. Eighteenth Century Collections Online.

5. Anon. *The Lady's Magazine or Entertaining Companion for the Fair Sex, Appropriated Solely to Their Use and Amusement*. Vol. 10. 1779. London. Google Books.

6. Anon. *The Lady's Magazine or Entertaining Companion for the Fair Sex, Appropriated Solely to Their Use and Amusement*. Vol. 16. 1785. London. Google Books.

7. Anon. *The Statutes at Large, From the First Year of the Reign of King George the First to the Third Year of the Reign of King George the Second*. Vol. 5. 1763. London. Google Books.

8. Anon. "Caution against using White Lead as a Cosmetic." *The Bristol and Bath magazine, or, Weekly miscellany. Containing selected beauties from all the new publications, together with a variety of 1782—1783*. Pages 106 and 107. Eighteenth Century Collections Online.

9. Anon. *The American Family Receipt Book: Consisting of Several Thousand Most Valuable Receipts, Experiments, &c. &c. Collected from Various Parts of Europe, America, and Other Portions of the Globe*. 1854. London. Google Books.

10. Autié, Léonard. *Recollections of Léonard, Hairdresser to Queen Marie-Antoinette*. Translated from French by E. Jules Meras. Originally published 1838. Translated 1912. London. Archive.org.

11. Baillio, Joseph, Katharine Baetjer, Paul Lang. *Vigée Le Brun*. 2016. New Haven and London. Yale University Press.

12. Bennett, John. *Letters to a Young Lady, On a Variety of Useful and Interesting Subjects, Calculated to Improve the Heart, to Form the Manners, and Enlighten the Understanding: In Two Volumes*. 1795. London. Eighteenth Century Collections Online.

13. Buchoz, Pierre Joseph. *Toilet de Flora*. 1772. London. Google Books.

14. Chrisman-Campbell, Kimberly. *Fashion Victims: Dress at the Court of Louis XVI and Marie-Antoinette*. 2015. New Haven and London. Yale University Press.

15. Cooley, Arnold James. *The Cyclopaedia of Practical Receipts in All the Useful and Domestic Arts: Being a Compendious Book of Reference for the Manufacturer, Tradesman, and Amateur*. 1841. London. Google Books.

16. Diderot and d'Alembert. *Encyclopédie Méthodique, ou par Ordre de Matières; par une Société de Gens de Lettres, de Savans et d'artistes*. 1789. Paris. Google Books.

17. Diderot, Denis. *L'Encyclopédie, Arts de l'habillement, recueil de planches, sur les sciences, les arts libéraux, et les arts méchaniques, avec leur explication*. 1751–1780. Paris. gallica.bnf. fr / Bibliothèque nationale de France.

18. Dowell, Stephen. "*A History of Taxation and Taxes in England from the Earliest Times to the Year 1885. Volume III. Direct Taxes and Stamp Duties.*" 1888. London: Longmans, Green & Co. Pages 255–59.

19. Eminent English physician at the Russian Court. *The Art of Beauty, or, a Companion for the Toilet [. . .]*. 1760. London. Eighteenth Century Collections Online.

20. Equiano, O. *The Interesting Narrative of the Life of Olaudah Equiano, or Gustavus Vassa, the African [. . .]*. Second Edition. 1789. London.

21. Gilchrist, Peter. *A Treatise on the Hair*. 1770. London. Eighteenth Century Collections Online.

22. Grose, Francis. *A Guide to Health, Beauty, Riches, and Honour*. 2nd ed. 1796. London. Eighteenth Century Collections Online.

23. Hart, John. *An Address to the Public on the Subject of the Starch and Hair-Powder Manufactories [. . .]*. 1795. London. Eighteenth Century Collections Online.

24. Heideloff, N. *Gallery of Fashion*. Vol. 1 (April 1794) – Vol. 9 (March 1803). London. Bunka Gakuen Library, Digital Archive of Rare Materials. http://digital.bunka.ac.jp/kichosho_e/search_list2.php.

25. Hendrie, Lewis. *Lewis Hendrie, at His Perfumery Shop and Wholesale Warehouse, Shug-Lane, near the top of the Hay-Market, St. James's, London, Sells the Following and All Other Articles in the Perfumery Way, on Remarkably Low Terms, and Warrants Them as Good in Quality as Any Shop or Warehouse in Great Britain ...* [London]: n.p., [1778]. Eighteenth Century Collections Online.

26. Herzog, Donald J. "The Trouble with Hairdressers." *Representations* 53 (1996): 21–43.

27. Le Camus, A. *Abdekar, or, the Art of Preserving Beauty*. 1756. London. Google Books.

28. Leca, Benedict. *Thomas Gainsborough and the Modern Woman*. 2010. Giles Ltd. London.

29. Linneaus, Charles V. *A General System of Nature through the Grand Kingdoms or Animals, Vegetables, and Minerals [. . .]*. 1766/1802. London. Via openlibrary.org.

30. Markiewicz, Emma. *Hair, Wigs and Wig Wearing in Eighteenth-Century England*. 2014. PhD thesis, University of Warwick.

31. Mather, J. *A Treatise on the Nature and Preservation of the Hair, in which the Causes of Its Different Colours and Diseases are Explained [...]*. 1795. London. Eighteenth Century Collections Online.

32. Montgomery, Florence, *Textiles in America 1650–1870*. 2007. W.W. Norton & Company. New York & London.

33. Moore, William. *The Art of Hair-Dressing, and Making It Grow Fast, Together, with a Plain and Easy Method of Preserving It; with Several Useful Recipes, &c.* c.1780. London. Eighteenth Century Collections Online.

34. Peckham, Brian W. "Technological Change in the British and French Starch Industries, 1750–1850." *Technology and Culture* 27, no. 1 (1986): 18–39.

35. Physician. *Letters to the Ladies, on the Preservation of Health and Beauty*. 1770. London. Eighteenth Century Collections Online.

36. Physician. *The Art of Preserving Beauty: Containing Instructions to Adorn and Embellish the Ladies; Remove Deformities, and Preserve Health*. 1789. London. Eighteenth Century Collections Online.

37. Postle, Martin. *Johan Zoffany RA Society Observed*. 2011. New Haven and London. Yale University Press.

38. Pratt, Ellis. *The Art of Dressing the Hair. A Poem*. 1770. London. Eighteenth Century Collections Online.

39. Raibaud et Louis (Perfumers: Paris, France). *A l'Etoile orientale. Varia aromata. London. Raibaud et Louis marchands-parfumeurs, ... à Paris, tiennent dans cette ville ... chez Mr. Bawen, Air-Street Piccadilly: savoir, ... = The Eastern Star. Varia aromata. London. Raibaud and Lewis perfumers, ... at Paris, have likewise a wholesale and retail perfumery warehouse, at Mr. Bawen's, Air-Street, Piccadilly: viz. ...* n.p.1775 (?).London. Eighteenth Century Collections Online.

40. Rebora, Carrie, Paul Staiti, Erica E. Hirshler, Theodore E Stebbins Jr. and Carol Troyen. *John Singleton Copley in America*. 1995. New York. The Metropolitan Museum of Art.

41. Rennie, James. *A New Supplement to the Pharmacopoeias of London, Edinburgh, Dublin, and Paris [...]*. 1833. London. Google Books.

42. Ribeiro, Aileen. *Dress in Eighteenth-Century Europe 1715–1789*. 2002. New Haven & London. Yale University Press.

43. Warren, Richard. (Perfumers: London, England). *Richard Warren and Co. perfumers, at the Golden Fleece, in Marylebone-Street,[…]*. 1780. London. Eighteenth Century Collections Online.

44. Ritchie, David. *A Treatise on Hair*. 1770. Eighteenth Century Collections Online.

45. Rosenthal, Angela. "Raising Hair." *Eighteenth-Century Studies* 38, no. 1 (2004): 1–16. https://muse.jhu.edu/.

46. Rumigny, Legros de. *Supplément de L'Art de la Coëffure des Dames Françoises*. 1768. Paris. Gallica Bibliothèque Numérique.

47. Rumigny, Legros de. *L'Art de la Coëffure des Dames Françoises*. 1768. Paris. Gallica Bibliothèque Numérique.

48. Salmon, William. *Polygraphice or The Arts of Drawing, Engraving, Etching, Limning, Painting, Washing, Varnishing, Gilding, Colouring, Dying, Beautifying, and Perfuming in Four Books*. 1673. Google Books.

49. Steele, Richard. *The Ladies' Library: or, Encyclopedia of Female Knowledge, in Every Branch of Domestic Economy: Comprehending in Alphabetical Arrangement, Distinct Treatises on Every Practical Subject....* 1790. London. Eighteenth Century Collections Online.

50. Stevens, George Alexander. *A Lecture on Heads, Written by George Alexander Stevens, with Additions by Mr. Pilon; as Delivered by Mr. Charles Lee Lewes, at the Theatre Royal in Covent Garden, and in Various Parts of The Kingdom. To Which is Added an Essay on Satire*. 1785. London. Eighteenth Century Collections Online.

51. Stewart, Alexander. *The Art of Hair Dressing, or The Ladies Director; Being a Concise Set of Rules for Dressing Ladies Hair [...]*. 1788. London. Eighteenth Century Collections Online.

52. Stewart, Alexander. *The Art of Hair Dressing, or, The Gentleman's Director; Being a Concise Set of Rules for Dressing Gentlemen's Hair [...]*. 1788. London. Eighteenth Century Collections Online.

53. Stewart, Alexander. *The Natural Production of Hair, or its Growth and Decay, Being a Great and Correct Assistance to its Duration [...]*. 1795. London. Eighteenth Century Collections Online.

54. Stewart, James. *Plocacosmos: or the Whole Art of Hair Dressing; Wherein Is Contained Ample Rules for the Young Artizan, More Particularly for Ladies Women, Valets, &c. &c.* 1782. London. Eighteenth Century Collections Online.

55. Stowell, Lauren, and Abby Cox. *The American Duchess Guide to 18th Century Dressmaking*. 2017. Salem, Massachusetts. Page Street Publishing.

56. Tharps, L.L. & A.D. Byrd. *Hair Story: Untangling the Roots of Black Hair*. 2002. New York. St. Martins.

57. Van Cleave, Kendra. *18th Century Hair & Wig Styling: History & Step-by-Step Techniques*. 2014.

58. Vickery, Amanda. "Mutton Dressed as Lamb? Fashioning Age in Georgian England." *Journal Of British Studies*. 52:4 (2013).

59. Walter, J. *Instructions for Cutting Out Apparel for the Poor [...]*. 1789. London. Google Books.

60. Watson, John Fanning. *Annals of Philadelphia, Being a Collection of Memoirs, Anecdotes, and Incidents of the City and Its Inhabitants, from the Days of the Pilgrim Founders*. 1830. E.L. Carey & A. Hart, New York. Google Books.

61. White, Shane and Graham White. *Stylin' African American Expressive Culture from Its Beginnings to the Zoot Suit*. 1999. Ithaca. Cornell University Press.

62. Woodyard, Sarah. *Martha's Mob Cap? A Milliner's Hand-Sewn Inquiry into Eighteenth-Century Caps ca. 1770–1800*. University of Alberta. https://era.library.ualberta.ca/items/d08025c6-d1b7-4221-81f4-fc1601b57258.

Supplier List

Models in Order of Appearance

Fabric, Thread, Ribbon and Notions

1. Renaissance Fabrics: www.renaissancefabrics.net

2. Burnley and Trowbridge: www.burnleyandtrowbridge.com

3. Britex Fabrics: www.britexfabrics.com

4. Lacis Museum of Lace and Textiles: www.lacis.com/retail.html

5. Mill End Fabrics, Reno, Nevada. While they don't have a website, if you're ever in the Biggest Little City, this treasure trove needs to be on your "to do" list! (Hi Connie!)

Lard and Tallow

1. Fatworks: www.fatworks.com

Spices, Herbs and Ingredients for Cosmetics

1. Mountain Rose Herbs: www.mountainroseherbs.com

2. Raven Moon Emporium: www.etsy.com/shop/RavenMoonEmporium

3. CupidFalls: www.etsy.com/shop/CupidFalls

All That Other Stuff

1. The Great and Powerful Amazon: www.amazon.com

2. Horsehair came from eBay: www.ebay.com

3. Granulated Cork: www.corkstore.com

Sparkles & Jewels

1. Dames à la Mode Jewelry: www.damesalamode.com

1. Abby Cox

2. Cynthia Settje

3. Laurie Tavan

4. Jenny Zhang

5. Jasmine Smith

6. Nicole Rudolph

7. Lauren Stowell

8. Zyna Navarte

Biographies

Lauren Stowell

Lauren Stowell is an entrepreneur and author. She started sewing and costuming in 2003 and became particularly interested in the eighteenth century. By 2009, Lauren started the blog American Duchess to chronicle her historical costuming adventures—the good, the bad and the ugly. In 2011, Lauren launched her first eighteenth-century shoe design, which quickly snowballed into a broad collection of Georgian, Victorian and Edwardian shoes and accessories under the "American Duchess" label and a range of 1920s, 1930s and 1940s shoes under the "Royal Vintage" label. Along with a range of Simplicity historical costume patterns, Lauren co-authored and published her first book, *The American Duchess Guide to 18th Century Dressmaking*, in 2017. Lauren lives in Reno, Nevada, with her husband Chris and a lot of dogs. She loves historical dress, watercolor painting, travel, the stock market and racing cars.

Abby Cox

Abby's passion for historic costume flourished while studying art history, history and theatre & drama at Indiana University–Bloomington. From there, she went on to achieve a postgraduate degree in Decorative Arts and Design History from the University of Glasgow, Scotland (MLitt 2009). After graduating and a fun jaunt around Europe, she began putting her knowledge and skills to use at The Colonial Williamsburg Foundation, where she served as an Apprentice Milliner/Mantua maker. There she learned and studied eighteenth-century dressmaking techniques and began her deep rabbit hole dive into historic hair care. In 2016, she left the museum world to work at American Duchess Inc. and Royal Vintage Shoes, where she serves as Vice President. A book, podcast, some dress patterns and several shoe collections later, she's happily settled in Reno, Nevada, with her dog and partner.

Cheyney McKnight

Cheyney, founder of *Not Your Momma's History*, graduated from Simmons College with a Bachelor's degree in Political Science in 2011 and has since dedicated herself to the research and education of American slavery. She has interpreted eighteenth, early nineteenth- and mid-nineteenth-century slavery as a Living Historian in 26 states, and worked with over 45 historic sites. She is trained to the standards of the National Association of Interpretation (NAI) and is an experienced historical interpreter with more than 4,500 hours of interpretive experience. Cheyney has also crafted and written more than eighteen tours for sites in Virginia and has written thirteen specialized museum programs throughout America. In 2015, Cheyney took her passion for education and interpretation and created *Not Your Momma's History*, as a way to help further outreach and understanding of the life of an enslaved person in the eighteenth and nineteenth centuries. You can find Cheyney at www.notyourmommashistory.com.

Acknowledgments

LAUREN STOWELL

I would like to thank Page Street Publishing for offering us the opportunity to write a second book. This was the perfect time and format to bring Abby Cox's amazing experience and research with eighteenth-century hair to the world and deeply dive into this fascinating subject. I have to thank Abby for being patient with me while I played "catch up" with the research, and for then debating minutiae endlessly as we worked through this second book.

I would also like to thank all of our models for being so patient with us, Nicole Rudolph and Cynthia Settje for making the trek out to Reno and helping us sew as well as being our guinea pigs, and Marni, my hairdresser, for fixing the horror that was my hair after we cut it for the *à l'enfant* hair experiment. Additionally, thank you to my mother for editing the heck out of our essays. Lastly, thank you eternally to Chris for his patience and help in setting up the photo studio (again and again and again) and listening to me go on ad nauseum about archaic hair stuff.

ABBY COX

It truly takes a village to birth a book-baby, doesn't it? This time is no different. However, before I begin my long list of thank yous, I want to give a special shout-out to every single person who bought our first book and has expressed excitement over this one. Without you, this book would not have happened. Thank you, from the bottom of my heart.

My passion and obsession for eighteenth-century hair was first encouraged by my former colleagues at The Colonial Williamsburg Foundation: Janea Whitacre, Mark Hutter, Sarah Woodyard, Mike McCarty, Rebecca Starkins, Brooke Welborn, Neal Hurst and Angela Burnley. Thank you to all of my friends and former coworkers (too many to name) who were willing guinea pigs for me back then, and to Tim Logue for planting the seed for the idea of the knitting needle hair roller! I also would like thank Anne Bissonette Ph.D. for her earth shattering lecture on eighteenth-century hairstyles that inspired me so many years ago, and her encouragement with my research.

To Cheyney McKnight, thank you for sharing your knowledge and wisdom with us, and contributing to this book. You were invaluable to this project, and, frankly, I think you're a goddess, in my humble opinion.

A huge thank you to Nicole Rudolph not only for your sewing and modeling in this book, but for also being my sounding board, test model and second pair of hands when I was first deep into this subject many years ago. I also have to thank Cynthia Settje, Jenny Zhang, Laurie Tavan, Jasmine Smith and Zyna Navarte for being the most patient and beautiful models.

I want to thank Lauren, for jumping down this research rabbit hole with me, head first, and always being the best co-author I could ask for. I'm sorry about your hair, but I did the best I could. Thanks for being a willing mullet victim, and thank you for translated Legros and Léonard because I really don't care about anything pre-1765 when it comes to hair.

Thanks to Chris for the photo studio and photography assistance, to Dana Reeser for looking over our scribbles, to Amanda for the behind-the-scenes footage and to Nastassia Parker-Gross and Jenny-Rose White for your advice and input.

I feel so blessed to have such a supportive partner and family to support me in this second go around. Thank you, Jimmy, for your love and support, to my father, Mark, and his wife, Leigh, for being the best cheerleaders, and finally, to my amazing mother, Susan, I have no words to express how important you were to this process, and not just because you sent amazing care packages.

Finally, a huge thank you to our editor, Lauren Knowles, and the incredible team at Page Street Publishing for their encouragement and support with our slightly wacky idea for our second publication. Thank you for helping make my dreams come true.

Index